Making Friends as an Adult

Making Friends as an Adult

by Rebecca Greene, MSW, LMSW

A Wiley Brand

Making Friends as an Adult For Dummies®

Published by: **John Wiley & Sons, Inc.**, 111 River Street, Hoboken, NJ 07030-5774, www.wiley.com

For general information on our other products and services, please contact our Customer Care Department within the U.S. at 877-762-2974, outside the U.S. at 317-572-3993, or fax 317-572-4002. For technical support, please visit https://hub.wiley.com/community/support/dummies.

Wiley publishes in a variety of print and electronic formats and by print-on-demand. Some material included with standard print versions of this book may not be included in e-books or in print-on-demand. If this book refers to media that is not included in the version you purchased, you may download this material at http://booksupport.wiley.com. For more information about Wiley products, visit www.wiley.com.

Library of Congress Control Number: 2024949633

ISBN 978-1-394-28845-8 (pbk); ISBN 978-1-394-28847-2 (ebk); ISBN 978-1-394-28846-5 (ebk)

SKY10091799_112224

Contents at a Glance

Table of Contents

Introduction

There's a little secret about making new friends as an adult that no one talks about: It's hard. In fact, sometimes it can seem downright impossible. When you're out of high school or college, you're on your own, and the opportunities to meet new people that were once so plentiful become few and far between. When you're an adult, it can feel like a friend-making desert out there.

Sure, some people manage to make friends at work, but if you work from home and don't see your coworkers in person (or if you work in an office and just don't really like your coworkers enough to hang out after work), you aren't as lucky. Maybe you've tried joining a group or two and putting yourself out there over and over, hoping that someone will eventually bite and accept your invitation to coffee. But soon you find that everyone is too busy and no one responds to your texts or emails. After months or years of floundering in this friendship no-man's land, you may start to anxiously wonder, "What's wrong with me? I used to be well liked. I used to have friends. What the heck happened?"

The truth is, you're the same likable person as you always were — it's just that it's harder to make friends as an adult, for everyone. The reasons are many: Finding the time to meet new people is a challenge, everyone's crazy-busy and overcommitted, putting yourself out there is stressful, making small talk over and over isn't fun. . . . You may think you're the only one having difficulty, and it may seem like friend-making comes easily to everyone else, but that's just an illusion. *Everyone* is thinking the same thing: "Why am I having so much difficulty making new friends?"

I know this is the case because I've been a mental health therapist for many years and I've heard clients describe their confusion about why they can't make friends and lament their friendship-making mishaps in my therapy office. I also know this is the case because I've interviewed adults of all ages about their friendship-making journeys for this book. It can be heartbreaking to hear people describe the depths of their loneliness and despair and worry that they'll always feel so alone.

One thing that I believe could really help many adults is a friendship-skills refresher course, which is one of the goals of this book. Friendship skills are not explicitly taught in school (though I think they should be!). By the time most people reach adulthood, they have rusty friendship-making skills from years of disuse. Just as your biceps and triceps will atrophy if you're not using them, you have to regularly use your friendship muscles to keep them strong and healthy.

Every chapter of this book addresses a specific aspect of the friend-making process. I walk you through why making new friends as an adult is challenging and why some groups have a harder time making friends than others. I also help you do a deep dive into your specific friendship preferences and do a friendship audit of your current friends, to weed out the friendships that are no longer fulfilling and allow room for new relationships to flourish. You'll discover how to approach new people, which groups to join for maximum friend-making success, and how to make small talk less of an annoying chore. You'll learn how to be a good friend, with specific actions to take, and you'll learn what to do when a friendship goes south.

This book is your road map to better friendships. It will open the door to more satisfying relationships with friends from all walks of life. With the tips and recommendations in this book, you'll be able to improve your friendship skills and be the best friend you can be so that you can enhance your life and be a happier and healthier person.

About This Book

In this book, I explain how to assess your friendship needs and how to determine the kind of friends who would be your best match. I help you manifest your ideal friend and learn about the benefits of having different friends for different parts of your life. I also talk about how to improve your communication with your friends to reduce conflicts and misunderstandings and help you cope with rejection more easily. I show you how to work on positive self-talk so you can reframe your negative, self-defeating thoughts and turn them into uplifting, confidence-building statements.

The purpose of this book is for you to gain confidence in your friend-making skills and learn the most effective ways to make new friends, so you can make a new friend and improve your overall quality of life. Each chapter is packed with tips and recommendations, as well as helpful examples and self-reflection activities, to help you build the skills you'll need as you move forward in your friendship quest.

Within this book, you may note that some web addresses break across two lines of text. If you're reading this book in print and want to visit one of these web pages, simply key in the web address exactly as it's noted in the text, pretending as though the line break doesn't exist. If you're reading this as an e-book, you've got it easy — just click the web address to be taken directly to the web page.

Foolish Assumptions

As I wrote this book, I assumed the following:

» You're struggling to make new friends, and you want to improve your chances of making a new friend.

» Your social skills are a tiny bit rusty, and you could use a refresher on certain topics pertinent to making new friends.

» You're willing to do some self-reflection to gain further insight.

» You want to enhance your life with improved friendships.

Icons Used in This Book

To draw your attention to specific tips and resources, I use the following icons throughout the book:

The Tip icon marks practical recommendations that you can put into practice right away to help improve your friend-making skills.

The Remember icon points to important information you'll want to file away in your memory bank.

The Warning icon lets you know that you should proceed with caution.

The Technical Stuff icon marks information of a highly technical nature that you can skip over if you're short on time.

The Example icon highlights anecdotes that support the main point of the chapter.

The Explore icon prompts you to ask yourself questions and explore your own thoughts and feelings.

Beyond the Book

In addition to what you're reading right now, this book also comes with a free access-anywhere Cheat Sheet that covers ways to be a good friend, how to know when you've made a new friend, ways to be more friendly, and small talk do's and don'ts. To get this Cheat Sheet, simply go to www.dummies.com and enter **Making Friends as an Adult For Dummies Cheat Sheet** in the Search box.

Where to Go from Here

Although all the information in this book is pertinent to making new friends as an adult, some parts may be more relevant to your situation. Use the Table of Contents to find the chapters that resonate with you and start there. You don't have to read the book from beginning to end — each chapter stands alone as a complete unit, so you can bounce around letting your curiosity be your guide.

If you're looking to start with some self-reflection on the topic of making new friends, start with Part 1. If you're ready to jump in and find out about the best places to make new friends, head to Chapter 5. If you'd like to improve your communication skills with your friends, go directly to Chapter 15.

Now, it's time to jump right in! Turn to whichever page or section resonates with you the most to get started. I hope that this book provides you with eye-opening insights, a toolbox brimming with new skills, and a renewed hope that a vibrant social life is well within your reach.

1

Uncovering the Challenges of Making New Friends as an Adult

You've always wondered why it's so hard to make new friends, and this part has the answers. Here, you find out why some groups have a harder time making new friends. You also assess your current friendships and determine which ones are working and which ones aren't. You determine whether you're an introvert or an extrovert and how that impacts friendships. Finally, you explore how to manifest your ideal friend and describe the qualities that your ideal friend will have.

Chapter **1**

Understanding the Challenges of Making Friends

Given that you've picked up this book, chances are you've been finding it challenging to make new friends as an adult. If so, you're in good company, because lots of people feel exactly the same way.

As a mental health therapist, I've found that loneliness, having no one to talk to, feeling left out, not fitting in, and lacking a support system are all emotionally painful and difficult issues that are often on people's minds. If you've been finding it hard to make new friends for a long time — even years — don't despair. Making friends does get more challenging the older you get, but making a new friend as an adult is still very realistic and doable. Making new friends is one of life's joys, and friendship makes life fun and exciting. This book can be your road map to creating the connections you've always hoped for.

Many people feel that making new friends is a lot like dating. You have to put yourself out there repeatedly, make small talk with lots of people, go on lots of friend dates, initiate get-togethers, and suffer through some rejection before you find your person. You'll find that you vibe with some people and you don't with others. Making new friends as an adult is ultimately a numbers game, and the more you put yourself out there, the more likely it is that you'll meet your ideal friend.

Before this book delves into all the steps (and skills) you'll need to master in order to make new friends, this chapter explores all the reasons why making new friends as an adult can be so challenging. Sometimes it's helpful to identify the reasons why something has been so hard in order to understand the journey better. It's also comforting to know you're not alone in your struggles. Understanding more about why making friends has been so difficult will give you new insight and help you feel less alone in your friend-making journey.

In this chapter, I explore the main reasons why making new friends is challenging as an adult. Then I discuss how difficulty making friends contributes to loneliness and social isolation. Next, I introduce several key turning points when making new friends is easier. And I wrap up the chapter with several reasons why adulthood is the ideal time to make new friends.

Exploring the Reasons Why Making New Friends Is Challenging

You've probably noticed that making new friends as an adult can be challenging, but you may be wondering exactly why that is. Understanding why it's so challenging for many people to make new friends can help you feel less alone in the journey and help you understand why it can sometimes feel so daunting. When you understand the challenges, you can gain new insight into your struggles and figure out what your best action plan is to make new friends.

Making new friends as an adult is challenging for many different reasons, including lack of free time and lack of opportunity to meet lots of new people the way you could back in your school days. It was easier to make new friends when you were younger because you had an abundance of free time to hang out with people and you saw lots of people at school. But when you're an adult, everyone is so busy — it's harder to justify making the time to meet and get to know new people when so many other things are demanding your time and attention. Plus, it takes a lot of time to make a new friend. A 2018 study by Professor Jeffrey Hall, published in the *Journal of Social and Personal Relationships*, found that it takes around 40 to 60 hours of spending time together to turn an acquaintance into a casual friend, 80 to 100 hours to turn a casual friend into a friend, and more than 200 hours to make a best friend. That's a lot of hours that many busy adults aren't willing or able to devote to friend-making.

Here are some of the things people complain about when it comes to making new friends as an adult:

>> Everyone already has their friends, and they aren't looking for new ones.

>> Everyone is too busy to make new friends.

>> People don't prioritize friendships.

>> No one has time for me.

>> I put myself out there and invite people to do things, but no one reciprocates.

>> All my friendships feel one-sided.

>> I reach out to others all the time, but no one bothers to reach out to me.

>> I moved just a little farther away, and now none of my friends will make time to see me.

Do any of these concerns resonate with you?

As you do some self-reflection about why it seems so hard to make new friends as an adult, it can also be helpful to contrast why it seemed so much easier to make new friends in high school and/or college. According to a 2019 report by Snapchat called "The Friendship Report," the average age to make a best friend is the age of 21. During your college years, you're surrounded by similar-age people for many hours a day, all in the trenches together, and all having new experiences together, so there's lots of time to get to know each other. That's especially true in college for those who live on-campus in dorms. All those late-night study sessions, parties, and hangout time with roommates often leads to lifelong friendships.

REMEMBER

There's no other time period, unless you live with roommates as an adult or live in a retirement community as an older adult, that can compare to the intensity of the social interaction in college and the young adult years.

Contrast this to adult life, where you're working full-time, and fitting in social time with friends in bits and pieces wherever you can. You no longer have leisurely time to spend hours getting to know people in a close-knit setting. For working adults, the workplace, which is one of the main places where adults make friends, isn't as conducive to making friends as college was. Sure, you're working in the same building (if you're even working in the office at all), but you're all at different ages and stages, and you may live far apart from each other, so it's not as ideal a situation as making friends when you were younger.

In the following sections, I explain all the key reasons why it's harder for adults to make new friends, including lack of time, prioritizing other aspects of their lives over friendships, and having rusty social skills, among others.

Believing they don't have time

One of the main reasons why it's so hard for adults to make new friends is that they don't have much free time to socialize. With many adults working full-time and taking care of all their other responsibilities (for example, raising children, doing household chores, running errands, exercising, wrangling pets, taking care of elderly parents or other family members, dealing with car repairs, and going to medical appointments, not to mention sleeping), it's no wonder so many of them feel that they have very little free time left over to socialize.

When they do socialize, many adults turn to the tried-and-true friendships they've had for decades (usually from high school or college) instead of putting in the time and effort to make a new friend from scratch. It makes sense — many adults are stretched thin and pulled in many different directions, leaving little remaining energy to make new friends.

REMEMBER

Proximity is very important for new friendships (see Chapter 5). The closer a potential new friend lives, the more likely you'll actually become friends because coordinating get-togethers with people who live close to you is easier than it is with people who live farther away.

One of the variables that makes it harder to make new friends as an adult is living far from your potential new friend. The "30-minute rule" from a 2007 study in the journal *Social Networks* says that people are less willing to visit a friend who lives more than 30 minutes away. If you live within a few minutes from a new friend, it's much more convenient and easier to fit a quick get-together into your busy schedules.

TIP

When looking to make new friends, focus on finding friends who live close by, which you can do by meeting neighbors, going to your local community center, and finding other local community places to make new friends.

REMEMBER

The difficulty of coordinating schedules makes it challenging for adults to make new friends, especially if they have kids. Juggling work, kids' activities and transportation, plus all the other household tasks really uses up a lot of time. Finding time to meet up can be challenging when people's schedules are so different. It really helps to join a hobby or interest group that has regular meetings, so you have that dedicated time on your calendar to socialize with others who share your interests (see Chapter 5 for more on joining groups).

Prioritizing work, family, and romantic relationships over friendships

Another reason why it's harder for adults to make new friends is that people tend to prioritize work, family, and romantic relationships over friendships. The relationships we have with our spouses or partners are often seen as the core relationships in our lives, and they're often thought of as essential to a happy and fulfilled life — friendships are usually viewed as secondary or nonessential.

Spending time and energy finding a romantic partner usually takes priority to spending time and energy finding friends, which tends to get shifted to the back burner, especially from the late 20s through the 40s.

Moving away and starting over

Another reason why it's hard to make friends as an adult is that people move a lot. You put all this work into building a friendship, and then your friend moves away. We've all been there, and it's hard to cope with. It can make people not want to bother investing in a friendship, because moving is so common.

These days, many people live far from their hometowns. They move away from their family and friends and settle down elsewhere. Then they have to start all over and make new friends and support networks from scratch.

Moving a lot can make it more challenging to find friends. It's hard to keep putting down roots only to pack up and move again and start all over a few years later.

Being rigid about friendships

Because many adults have such little free time, some are rigid or picky about friendships and who they spend their free time with. This means that they're often looking for a potential friend who checks all their boxes, and they're less willing to consider someone who only checks some of them. This can result in being exceptionally choosy about meeting up. They're often less willing to give new people a chance, and if they don't feel a connection after one get-together, some won't give a person a second chance. This can make it extra challenging to make new friends.

Have you ever heard the well-known quote by Jim Rohn: "You are the average of the five people you spend the most time with"? Many people want to surround themselves with friends who are positive influences or who bring something they value to the friendship. This could be someone with whom they have common interests, someone who works in the same field, someone who can teach them something, someone who has the same fashion sense, someone they can network with, someone with a sense of humor, or someone with similar values. Some people make a snap judgment about whether you have a quality they value based on your outward appearance or how you present yourself, and they can disqualify a potential friend without having all the information.

TIP

What can help is expanding your idea of what a friendship must be. Instead of wanting one best friend you can do everything with, keep in mind that a friend doesn't have to check *all* your boxes in order to hang out with them and have a good time. Instead, focus on having some friends who are activity partners you meet up with to do specific activities. For example, you may have a yoga friend, a golf friend, a friend you shop with, and a friend you try new restaurants with. The friend you play golf with may have no interest in shopping, but they can be your golf buddy and you can enjoy the conversations you have with them in that specific setting. Having friends for different activities can help expand your social circle.

TIP

One of the best ways to make new friends is to join a social hobby/interest group. You'll meet others who share your interests and who are also looking to make new friends who share those interests. You'll also have plenty to talk about, which will make easing into a friendship easier. (See Chapter 5 for more on joining groups.)

REMEMBER

Because many adults can be picky about friendships, rejection is a fact of life when you're looking to make new friends. Rejection stings, but it behooves you to mentally prepare yourself for this. Remember that rejection is something that everyone goes through, whether they're looking for platonic friends or romantic partners. You won't like everyone, and not everyone will like you. Many people have trouble coping with rejection, but remembering that it's part of the process and that making friends is a numbers game can help you bounce back quicker. Reframing negative self-talk about rejection into more neutral self-talk, and keeping a growth mindset ("I haven't made a new friend *yet*") are helpful ways to cope with rejection.

Being apathetic

Another common challenge for adults trying to make new friends is apathy. People can be apathetic and don't feel like taking the initiative with new friendships. Sometimes it's easier to just stay home than it is to reach out to a new friend to set up a get-together.

If you're proactive about reaching out to friends and setting up get-togethers and other people are apathetic, it can feel frustrating and disappointing.

Have you ever been told, "Let's get together soon" and then you never heard from the other person again? Or when you did try to set something up, has the person not responded? This complaint is a frequent one from adults trying to make new friends. They feel like they're always the one who has to initiate everything and take the lead on planning get-togethers. It's disheartening to feel like you always have to make the first move, or else the friendship withers.

TIP

When trying to make new friends, try to say yes to social invitations and opportunities more often. If you go, it's likely you'll have a great time. You never know what social opportunities you'll discover just by saying yes more often and being more open-minded.

Navigating trust issues

By the time you're a full-fledged adult, you've probably had some friendships where there have been trust issues. It's often harder to trust people as you get older, because some people have been burned before, and now are hesitant to trust again. It's also often harder to be vulnerable with new friends as you get older.

Having trust issues can make someone less willing to consider being friends with someone new, and instead stick with their tried and true. It takes a lot of time for some people to build trust. They can be slower to open up and keep people in the acquaintance stage for a long time, before they feel comfortable.

TIP

If you have a hard time trusting others, take things slow with a new friend.

Being hampered by social anxiety

Another reason why adults have a harder time making new friends is because social anxiety can sometimes get in the way. *Social anxiety* is an intense fear of being watched, judged, and scrutinized by others, and it can make people avoid social situations because they worry about feeling embarrassed or humiliated.

REMEMBER

Social anxiety can make it harder to put yourself out there, be yourself with others, and take the steps necessary to make new friends. If you're feeling a level of anxiety in social situations that's causing you distress and negatively impacting your functioning, it can help to talk with a therapist or other mental health professional. (See Chapter 8 for more on coping with social anxiety.)

Having fewer opportunities to make new friends

Another reason why it's harder to make new friends as an adult is that adults in general have fewer opportunities to make new friends. Children, teens, and college students are in school with their peers for many hours each day. Plus, they may do extracurricular activities and go to summer camp, and they have time to hang out casually with friends after school. Adults, by contrast, typically have fewer regular places where they see people and socialize. Because they have less free time, they have less of an opportunity to join clubs or other social activities where they may meet new people.

TIP

Because adults generally have fewer opportunities to make new friends, it can be easier to try reconnecting with old friends. To start, think of which of your old friends (or friends of friends) may be receptive to your reaching out. Look through your social media contact lists as a good starting point for deciding who you could contact.

Having rusty social skills

Adults' social skills can diminish over time, and there are several reasons why. Social skills can atrophy if you work from home and don't see your coworkers often, or if you have more of a solitary office job. We get so used to being in our houses all the time, working and socializing from home, that thinking about inviting a friend to meet up in person can be daunting. Then, because we're out of practice, it can become harder to make new friends.

Additionally, all the hours spent behind screens and on social media don't improve people's social skills. When you're sitting passively behind a screen, just scrolling along and liking and commenting on posts, instead of catching up with friends in person, your real-life social skills can get rusty.

Social skills aren't explicitly taught in school, but many kids pick them up naturally, in school and on the playground. These days, however, kids and teens are interacting frequently via screens, whether by texting their friends instead of talking in person or playing video games and interacting socially online. They're spending less time interacting in person, and some aren't learning crucial social skills.

Have you been to a restaurant lately and noticed a table where everyone is on their own devices and not talking to their table-mates? It's a discouraging sight to see.

TIP

Participating in a hobby or interest group can help you further develop your social skills. That's because you have an activity to keep busy with while you're socializing, so the focus isn't fully on talking. For example, if you're hiking with a hiking group, you can focus on the nature around you while having conversations versus sitting across from someone in a coffee shop, which can be anxiety-producing.

Having smaller social circles due to the pandemic

Another reason why it's harder to make friends as an adult is because the pandemic narrowed many people's social circles. After a year or two of being relatively isolated at home, some people continued to keep their social circles small, and there wasn't as much of an appetite to get outside to socialize and meet new people. People got used to their social circles being small and insular, especially when "pods" were common for schoolchildren and their families. Plus, many people went from working in person to working from home during the pandemic, and people generally became more isolated. Some of these preferences to keep a smaller social circle are persisting even several years later, which can make it harder for adults to make new friends.

Even though things seem to have gotten back to normal, some adults are finding that their once-robust social circles have dwindled, their interest in socializing and entertaining has diminished, and some of their previous friends have moved away. They're also noticing that their social skills have gotten rusty after being isolated so long during the pandemic.

TIP

If your social circles diminished during the pandemic, you can replenish them by joining groups such as hobby/interest groups, religious congregations, volunteer groups, sports leagues, in-person classes, and newcomers' groups, which are some of the best places to make new friends. Look for social-focused groups or classes that meet weekly so you see the same people on a regular basis.

Exploring How Common It Is to Struggle with Friendships

If you're struggling to make new friends as an adult, and finding it surprisingly and unexpectedly challenging, you're far from alone. It's common to want more robust and fulfilling friendships but not know how to go about getting them or where to find them. It's also common to feel disappointed and dissatisfied with the friendships you have but feel daunted by the idea of going out and making new friends.

Adults often feel like they need more friends than they actually have. A 2016 study published in *Royal Society Open Science* found that people have the most friends they'll ever have by age 25, and then those numbers decrease until age 45, when they level out. Friendships have been dwindling in the United States over the years. In 1990, only 3 percent of people said they had no close friends, but in 2021, that number increased to 12 percent, according to research done by Gallup and the American Perspectives Survey. This is a big difference, and it helps explain why people are feeling so starved for friendships these days.

In the following sections, I explain why loneliness is such a pressing issue for many adults, and the reasons why many people feel so socially isolated.

Exploring the epidemic of loneliness

If you've been feeling lonely lately, it helps to understand where that feeling is coming from and how common it is. According to the U.S. surgeon general, Dr. Vivek Murthy, loneliness is a public health epidemic in the United States. In May 2023, the surgeon general issued an 85-page advisory that described how significant a scourge loneliness has become. According to a 2018 survey by insurer Cigna, 46 percent of Americans feel alone. The Cigna survey also found that younger adults, ages 18 to 22, tend to be significantly lonelier than older adults 72 and older.

Feeling lonely is very common, even though most people don't talk openly about it. Loneliness is a subjective, emotionally painful feeling of wanting to be around people but not being able to find friends or connections. It's a feeling of wanting to share your life and experiences with another person but having no one to share them with. It can feel like an emptiness and a feeling of not being seen or valued.

When you're unable to have the kinds of friendships you want, you can feel lonely. You can feel lonely even when surrounded by friends and family if you're not connecting meaningfully with anyone.

Loneliness can also make it more challenging to make new friends. Lonely people tend to stay in more, and if you don't leave the house often it becomes harder to socialize and meet new people. Lonely people can also find that their motivation for making new friends has diminished, because of all the rejection they've dealt with over the years.

Why are so many people lonely these days? There are many possible theories. Working long hours and not having enough free time or energy to socialize, not knowing neighbors due to frequent moves and relocations, lingering feelings of isolation from the pandemic, and getting our social interaction fix online instead of in person are some of the reasons why loneliness is so pervasive.

Social media is another big factor in people's loneliness, as well in as our challenges in making friends. Social media makes us feel lonely because we're sitting behind a screen, passively consuming information about other people's lives and events. Social media can make it seem like everybody else is having an amazing time, constantly getting together with friends, because that's all they post online (no one's posting photos of themselves sitting home alone). Plus, when you're following dozens or hundreds of people, it can feel like all those people have a ton of friends, but if you look at any one person's social media, you may see that they actually only post photos once in a while. You're being inundated daily by the sheer quantity of photos from a huge group of people, and that's what makes it *seem* like they're all having fun without you.

Social media makes it easier to stay in touch with other people, because we can share our news with many people simultaneously, instead of having to tell the same updates to each one. But it also makes people feel like they've already caught up with others, by seeing the photos from their events and activities, so there's less need to catch up in person.

Many people don't even go to their high school reunions anymore because they feel like they've caught up with what their classmates are up to via social media.

But using just social media to socialize makes it harder to have fulfilling, enriching friendships. We're missing out on connecting face-to-face. People now prefer to sit at home and text their friends to catch up instead of gathering in person to chat about the latest goings-on. This is causing their social skills to diminish, which makes it harder to nurture actual friendships.

Another factor in our loneliness is working long hours and not having enough leisure time to socialize. People aren't spending as much quality time together anymore, because catching up over texts or emails is quicker and easier than meeting in person. When you have limited free time to fit in all your chores and errands during the week, connecting in the way that's the most efficient can seem the most appealing, but it's really causing people to stay more isolated.

TIP

Aim to meet up with friends in person in order to make and maintain optimal friendships.

EXPLORE

If you've been feeling lonely, could you find more time for socializing if you wanted to? Think about how you spend your nonwork hours. Could you cut back on some of the things that aren't essential and fit in more in-person time for friends?

Understanding social isolation

Many adults feel socially isolated because they have small social support networks and don't get together with other people in person very often. Here are some of the reasons for this pervasive sense of social isolation:

>> **People move far away.** With many people moving far from their hometowns and settling away from family and the friends they grew up with, it can be difficult for adults to build new social networks from scratch. People's friends and family are scattered all over the country or the world. It's also hard not to be able to rely on the village they grew up with, where they felt known in the community they grew up in.

>> **People don't join clubs and groups as often.** In the past, group/club membership was a significant way that many people made friends and socialized. They would join community and service groups or invited others over for a weekly card game or poker night. Now people join online groups more often, including support groups and hobby/interest groups.

>> **Long hours leave little energy for socializing.** With people working full-time, their spouse/partner working full-time, having little vacation time, and not having a village to help out, they're exhausted and they don't have the energy to go out and meet new people. In the past, people had more time and energy to socialize. They talked with their neighbors regularly, joined clubs, hung out on porches, and hosted dinner parties. Today, people rely more on online connections, because they're quicker and easier.

>> **We don't know our neighbors as well.** With many people moving frequently for new jobs and new opportunities, getting to know our neighbors is harder. We also don't have the need to go to someone's house to ask to borrow a cup of sugar anymore, because grocery stores are close by or we can order anything we need and have it delivered. And with people working long hours, there's less time to leisurely sit on the front porch with a drink and chat about what's new.

>> **We live in a disposable society.** With so many items today being made of plastic and inexpensive materials, we throw things away rather than fix them, and that mindset sometimes extends to friendships. People are quick to shed friendships that aren't working instead of trying to work things out. That's part of why ghosting seems to have gained in popularity — people think it's okay to just get rid of friendships without explanation.

>> **We're staying in more often.** Today, people enjoy staying home more, and going out can seem like a hassle. We're at home more because so many people work remotely, and also because our homes have every convenience. People can stay in and get their social needs met through social media, online groups, or video games.

Identifying New Turning Points

Even though making new friends as an adult can be generally challenging, there are a few turning points in life where people feel more of a need to make new friends.

When people go through a major life change, whether it's moving to a new area or becoming a new parent, they tend to be more eager and receptive to making new friends. When you go through these turning points, you want friends who can relate to you and who can join you on your new journey. These are the times when you should make an extra effort to attend hobby/interest groups, put yourself out there, follow up, and reach out to new people regularly. Soon you'll be expanding your social circle in no time.

In the following sections, I walk you through some of these major turning points when you can more easily make new friends.

Moving to a new city and starting over

Most people feel a lot of anxiety about moving to a new city and starting over. It's hard to make such a big change and not know many people in your new area. But moving to a new city is a great opportunity to build a whole new social circle from scratch.

TIP

Most people who've recently moved are eager to meet new people and make new friends. Joining a newcomers' group can be a great way to meet other newcomers to an area.

When you move to a new city, try to get to know your new neighbors as soon as you can. Not only does getting to know your neighbors help ease the transition to your new area, but they can also help you with recommendations for new doctors, dentists, and hairstylists. There's a window of time when it's best to introduce yourself to your new neighbors — try to do it within the first three months of moving in. (It can get a little awkward if you wait too long.)

Try to meet your new neighbors by catching them when they're outside or doing yard work. If they don't come by to welcome you, you can always ring their door-bell to introduce yourself and exchange contact information (which can come in handy if they ever need to get a hold of you). Consider inviting your new neighbors over for tea or coffee, or even a cookout or housewarming party if you're feeling up to it. Neighbors can end up becoming great friends because of their proximity, because you see them so often as you're coming and going. Proximity is an important ingredient in new friendships (see Chapter 5 for more on proximity).

Becoming a new parent

Having a baby and becoming a new parent is another turning point where people are eager to meet others and make new friends. As a new parent, you want to meet other parents to share the parenting journey with who are in a similar life stage with similarly aged kids.

REMEMBER

Being a new parent lends itself well to meeting other parents, because you'll often find yourself at kid-friendly places like playgrounds where everyone else is standing around watching their kids play. Striking up a conversation with a fellow parent in this kind of casual setting can feel easier than walking up to someone you don't know at a party or networking event. There will also be plenty of playdates where you'll make small talk with the other parents while your kids play.

There are lots of groups for new parents to join, too. You can find groups for parents of babies through your hospital or ob-gyn's office, or through Meetup (www.meetup.com) or Facebook groups (www.facebook.com). Sometimes just having same-aged kids and going through similar life stages gives you enough in common to form a friendship.

New parents are often tired and stressed, but you can find ways to make socializing work with young children, like inviting friends over to your house after the kids are asleep for board games or going out after the kids' bedtime for a ladies' night out while your spouse or partner watches them.

Getting divorced and having to create a new social life

Getting divorced is another life turning point where many people need to rebuild their social circles. Sometimes people lose many of their friends who were their ex-spouse's in a divorce, which can be painful. Others want to make new friends who are also divorced for support as they go through the divorce process.

TIP

Joining DivorceCare support groups (www.divorcecare.org) and new hobby/interest groups can be a good way to make new friends who can relate to what you're going through. Turn to Chapter 16 for more on navigating friendships through divorce.

Being widowed

Being widowed is another turning point where people feel lonely and are looking to make new friends. Sometimes they lose their spouse's circle of friends because they drift away after the person passes away. A widowed person may also be uncomfortable socializing in groups with couples and prefer to look for new friends who are single.

TIP

Joining an in-person grief support group can be a good way to make new friends who understand the journey you're on.

Retiring and leaving friends behind at work

When you retire, it's another huge turning point in your life. You leave behind your coworkers, many of whom you've worked with for decades. Saying goodbye to these coworkers and transitioning into the unstructured free time of retirement can be difficult, especially if you didn't have friends outside of work.

TIP

Retirement is an ideal time to make new friends. Attending programs at a senior center, joining new hobby/interest groups, and joining retirement support groups are all ways you can make new friends.

Outgrowing your friend group

People outgrow their friend group for a variety of reasons. Maybe you've done some intense personal development lately and feel like you've outgrown your friends, or perhaps you've started on a major life change (like getting married or starting a family) and feel like your friends can't relate. Regardless of the reasons why you feel you've outgrown your friend group, it's a good time to make new friends. Think about making new friends by joining hobby/interest groups, attending new events, making small talk with new people, and putting yourself out there.

Working from home

If you've started working from home instead of going into an office, this is another good opportunity to make some new friends. When you work from home, it can be helpful to make some new friends who are available for daytime lunch breaks or coffee get-togethers, to make working from home feel less isolating. You can find these new friends by looking for daytime get-together groups or work-from-home support groups, or by posting in local social media groups looking for daytime friends and get-togethers.

Understanding Why Adulthood Is a Great Time for New Friendships

Now that you know many of the reasons why adults find it hard to make new friends, you may feel like the cards are stacked against you. But the good news is, there are many reasons why adulthood is actually an *ideal* time to explore new friendships:

>> You know yourself better than you did when you were younger, and you've had years of experience with friendships, so you know what you're looking for in a friend.

>> You have a stronger grasp of what you want and don't want, based on past experiences with other friendships, which will help you find the best friendship matches.

>> You may have well-developed hobbies and interests and want to spend time with others who share them.

>> You're more self-confident and you can more effectively advocate for your needs in a relationship.

>> You understand better how to work through friendship conflict without resorting to ghosting or cutting off a friendship.

>> You have better communication skills now and can express your thoughts and feelings to your friends more effectively.

>> You know why you'd make a good friend and what you can offer a new friend.

IN THIS CHAPTER

» Understanding why men have a harder time making friends

» Exploring why LGBTQIA+ people have a harder time making friends

» Discovering why parents of older kids have a harder time making new friends

» Exploring why older adults have a harder time making new friends

» Understanding why neurodivergent people have a harder time making friends

Chapter **2**

Discovering Why Some People Have a Harder Time Making Friends

M any people find making new friends challenging, but some groups of people have a harder time with it than others. This may be because of a variety of reasons, including societal stigmas, being typecast a certain way, difficulties with social skills, or a lack of opportunities to meet others. Whatever the reason, finding the friend-making journey to be an uphill battle can be frustrating and disappointing. You aren't alone, though — many other people also feel this way.

In this chapter, I discuss some of the challenges that men, queer people, parents with older kids, older adults, and neurodivergent people have when it comes to making friends. I also offer strategies that can help with being more successful in the friend-making process.

Seeing Why Men Have a Harder Time Making Friends

Many men are struggling with friendships. According to a 2021 American Perspectives Survey report, 15 percent of American men say they don't have any close friends. The same survey found that only 21 percent of men receive emotional support from friends in a given week. The survey additionally found that only 48 percent of men are satisfied with the number of friends they have. These statistics are troubling and point to the fact that many men don't have the close friendships they want and need.

Men's friendships are declining, and many men are struggling with significant loneliness. Part of the problem is working long hours and not having as much free time to devote to friendships. After dealing with a long day at work, spending time with their spouse/partner and children, and taking care of household tasks, there's very little time for finding and nurturing new friendships. One of the best ways to make friends is to join groups to find others who share your interests, but it takes a lot of time and energy to find, join, and participate in these groups.

Even though men can be friends with men *and* women, men often prefer the male bonding they get from male friendships. Plus, friendships with women may bring in the complications of physical attraction, which can muddy the waters.

It can be hard for men to have close, intimate friendships with other men. One reason for this challenge is that when boys are growing up, society discourages them from being emotionally vulnerable with their friends because it isn't considered manly to do so. Instead, they're told to be tough and to rely on their own inner strength to get through difficult times, instead of sharing their struggles and getting emotional support from other boys. As a result, boys' and men's friendships tend to be more surface-level, rather than deeper and closer, the way girls' and women's friendships tend to be.

REMEMBER

To satisfy their need for emotional closeness, many men rely more on their romantic partners. However, if they're single, divorced, or widowed, many men feel completely alone in the world because they haven't taken the time to nurture and sustain male friendships.

Doing things side by side

Many men tend to prefer talking to their friends by doing activities side by side, like going to a sports game, playing sports, or working on a project together rather than sitting and talking face-to-face over lunch or coffee.

Years ago, men would often join fraternal organizations (which are no longer as popular), meet for weekly poker nights, or join sports leagues to hang out with friends. Today, with so much of modern life having shifted to online interactions, many men are mainly interacting with their friends online instead of in person. They're playing video games together or discussing different topics in online communities, because it's easier and more convenient than finding time to get together with their friends. However, this is limiting the closeness of men's friendships, because they aren't seeing their online friends in person. They aren't benefiting from in-person get-togethers as much as they used to.

Having smaller social circles

The movie *I Love You, Man* (starring Paul Rudd and Jason Segel) explores the challenges of men not having enough close friends. In the movie, the main character is getting married and doesn't have any friends to be his groomsmen, so he befriends a random guy and they become close friends. Many men can relate to the challenge of not having any close friends to be in their wedding or throw them a bachelor party, or not having anyone they can confide in or rely on.

Many men look to their jobs to fulfill their social needs. Some men get to know their coworkers, but they may shy away from having close relationships with coworkers because that can become problematic. Outside of work, some men don't have any close friends and don't have the time or inclination to join groups or nurture hobbies so they can meet more people. Many men just want their alone time when they're not out working because they're stressed and drained from the workday's demands. They need and value their alone time and value that over socializing with friends.

REMEMBER

Many men have small social circles, or just one or two casual friends. Some men have female platonic friends but this becomes more difficult if one or both parties have a significant other, because jealousy can arise. Men also tend to rely heavily on their spouses or partners for their emotional needs.

REMEMBER

Friendships are important for men because they provide companionship, give men a way to share their feelings by confiding in someone, enhance emotional and physical well-being, reduce feelings of loneliness and isolation, and give men a way to manage their stress more effectively and decompress from the day if they can hang out with friends and participate in a favorite pastime.

Making friends if you're a man

Because men often prefer to spend time with their friends doing activities side by side, such as playing sports, they can make new friends by joining hobby/interest groups. Sports leagues, like a weekly bowling club, golf club, biking group, or basketball club, are a good way to make new friends. Hobby groups (like a beer-brewing club, birding club, or car enthusiasts group) are other good ways for men to make new friends.

TIP

If you don't have a hobby or interest, be open to trying new things in order to find one.

Here are some other ways men can make new friends:

>> **Join groups that tend to interest other men.** You don't have to find men's-only groups (there aren't many of those), but joining groups that mainly interest men are good bets. Examples include a golf league, beer-brewing club, or Dungeons and Dragons (D&D) group. Join one or two of these groups to start, and see if you click with anyone. If you do, get to know them better and then invite them to meet up to do a related activity in a smaller group or one-on-one.

>> **See if you have any coworkers you get along with.** If so, see if you can get to know them over lunch or a coffee break at the office. If you then discover you have some things in common, invite them to meet up for drinks after work sometime.

>> **Join men's groups at your religious congregation.** They can be great ways to meet other men. Or you can join groups or committees at your congregation and get to know other men that way.

>> **See if any existing friends of yours have friends you can meet.** It's often easier to make new friends that are friends of friends rather than making new friends from scratch. If you've recently moved to a new area, put out a request on social media and see if anyone can match you up with someone you have things in common with.

>> **If you're in a relationship, see if you can get to know the other men from your couple friends and hang out with them on their own.** Or if you don't have couple friends, maybe ask your partner if their female friends have any brothers or brothers-in-law or even male coworkers they could introduce you to.

Understanding Why LGBTQIA + People Have a Harder Time with Friendships

LGBTQIA+ adults can have a challenging time making new platonic friends. If they want to make queer friends, it can be harder to find a friend who is strictly interested in a platonic friendship. Many queer people specifically seek queer friends because they want to be with someone who can relate to their lived experiences.

There are several reasons why it can be harder to make friends if you're queer:

TIP

>> **Romantic vibes can get in the way.** It can be challenging to find strictly platonic queer friendships because sexual tension can make things complicated, and it can be hard to find someone who only wants a platonic friendship.

What can help is making it crystal clear that you're looking for platonic-only friendships. Many queer people who seek platonic friendships have success making friends with both members of a queer or straight couple, making friends with a queer person who is in a committed relationship or married, or making straight friends.

>> **Some queer people find that they try to make platonic queer friends and then they find out that their friend is only looking for a "friends with benefits" situation.** This situation can be frustrating and disappointing, but continue to keep meeting new people until you find the kind of friend you want. Some queer friendships spring out of having a romantic relationship first and then downshifting to just being platonic friends.

>> **Finding enough places to meet new platonic queer friends can be tough.** Joining hobby/interest groups, volunteering, participating in queer-friendly sports clubs/teams, joining a religious congregation, and taking in-person classes are ways to start.

>> **Sometimes a partner can become jealous and discouraging of platonic queer friendships, because they're worried about sexual attraction getting in the way.** If your partner shows signs of jealousy, make sure to be transparent with them about your friendship. Always invite them to join you and your friend when you're getting together.

TIP

Consider making friends with straight people where romantic vibes won't get in the way of platonic friendships.

REMEMBER

When looking for queer friendships, it's important to have more in common than the fact that you're both queer. Often, that's not enough to have in common to create a long-lasting, close friendship. Look for someone who also shares your interests. You can find them in hobby/interest groups, at your religious congregation, at gyms, at in-person classes, and in Meetup (www.meetup.com) groups.

Distinguishing between platonic vibes and romantic vibes

Sometimes when trying to make queer friends, it can be difficult to distinguish between platonic and romantic vibes, because sometimes the line can be blurred.

If you notice your friend is flirting with you, the vibes may be more romantic. However, flirting can be subtle. For example, do they touch you more than to give a hug hello or goodbye or the occasional touch on the arm or shoulder? Do they try to put their arm around you, try to hold your hand, hold eye contact in a flirtatious way (longer than usual), or say romantically suggestive things? Do they make it a point to seek you out and sit next to you at gatherings, or do they pay you more attention than they pay anyone else? Do they go out of their way to spend time with you? See if they're doing this with others or only you. Do they suggest going back to their place at night? If so, they may be romantically interested in you. You can let them know what you've noticed and remind them that you're only interested in a platonic friendship.

If you only want a platonic friendship, and you've made that clear to your friend (especially when you've told them multiple times), it can be frustrating, annoying, and disappointing when they keep trying to come on to you. If they're persistent in trying to pick you up and not respecting your wishes, reiterate your boundaries again to see if they can respect them. Or you may decide to end the friendship if they aren't being respectful and understanding.

Making friends when you're queer

TIP

If you're queer and having trouble making platonic friends, try the following:

>> **Consider making friends online, through online queer communities, such as on Discord** (https://discord.com) **or other sites.**

>> **If looking for queer friendships, do activities where you may meet more queer people.** For example, join a queer-friendly sports league, volunteer at queer-focused nonprofit organizations or advocacy groups, look for queer-friendly groups on Meetup, or start your own group if you're not finding what you need.

>> **Check out apps for making gay friends such as JACK'D** (www.jackd.com) **and Lex** (www.lex.lgbt). Or you can use queer dating apps to make friends by making it clear you're only looking for friends.

TIP

Let your new friend know right away that you're only looking for a platonic friendship. Clear boundaries are key. Clarifying your expectations up front makes it less likely for romantic vibes to become an issue later.

REMEMBER

You can increase the chances of finding a strictly platonic queer friendship by meeting potential friends through hobby/interest groups, rather than in places like bars where people tend to be looking for something more.

Exploring Why Parents of Older Kids Have a Harder Time Making Friends

When you have young children, it feels like the opportunities to make new parent friends are endless, between playdates, parents-and-me activities, parent groups, preschool socials, and kids' sports and other activities. Because parents of young children have to stay with their kids at any kind of event, there are lots of opportunities to make small talk with other parents on the sports field, while waiting for their children at swim class or on the playground. Many parents value the opportunity to make friends with other parents in order to have others in a similar life stage to go through the parenting journey with. They enjoy having others to talk with about their kids' classes and academic journey, their extracurricular and camp resources, and issues facing that particular age group.

However, when kids are in upper elementary school, middle school, and high school, it becomes more challenging for parents to make new parent friends. You drop your kid off at their friends' houses and birthday parties, so you're no longer staying to make small talk with other parents. When friendships are still parent-directed, it's easier to make parent friends. But when kids start making their own social plans, you're no longer the go-between, so there is even less opportunity to get to know other parents. Some parents of older kids end up only meeting their kids' friends' parents once or twice, with little to no opportunity to form a friendship. This situation can be tough for parents who want to have parent friends.

REMEMBER

Although it's helpful to have others to go through the parenting journey with, think about whether you and the other parent actually have things in common besides the fact that you're both parents of same-aged kids.

TIP

If you find that you don't have much in common, you may want to enlarge your social circle and try to meet people through hobby/interest groups, volunteering, or a religious congregation. Although it's very convenient to make other parent friends, especially for parents who work full-time and have limited free time to meet new people, it can be limiting to only make friends with other parents.

Dealing with an empty nest and lost friendships

Many parents find it challenging to deal with an empty nest, but also find it difficult to deal with the loss of parent friendships they've had since their kids were younger. When kids leave home or go off to college, often those parent friendships fade.

TIP

Getting mentally prepared well ahead of time for this change can help. It can also help to figure out ways that you and your parent friends can keep in touch and still see each other, even though the kids have left the nest. A monthly coffee or lunch get-together can be a good way to maintain those connections. Also, consider making new nonparent friends and adding in new hobbies and interests when you have an empty nest.

Making friends if your kids are older

TIP

If you want to make friends with other parents, the best way to do it is to try to chat with them at drop-off or pickup, invite them specifically to meet up for coffee, or make friends with other parents on the sports field during kids' sports practice or events. Also, you can volunteer with their sports teams by being a coach, picking up snacks, or helping with fundraising. Also, consider other ways to volunteer at the school to meet other parents, either on the parent–teacher association (PTA), as a library volunteer, as a field trip chaperone, as a room parent, or on a school committee.

Understanding Why Older Adults Have a Harder Time Making Friends

Many people believe that retirement is the best time of life, where you have endless free time, a packed social calendar, the opportunity to take fun classes, time for hobbies you've always wanted to try, and meaningful time spent with your grown children and grandchildren. However, some older adults find themselves in the disappointing situation of having a much sparser social calendar than they anticipated, feeling lonely, and wanting to make new friends.

Many older adults feel lonely in their golden years. One research study from 2012, published in the *Archives of Internal Medicine*, found that 43 percent of people over the age of 60 in the United States felt lonely. Older adults feel lonely and have a harder time making new friends for a variety of reasons:

» **They've retired and left all their friends behind at work.** Many people make their closest friends at work, and when they retire, they leave those friends behind and don't have many friends outside of work to spend time with. They end up not seeing their work friends often after retirement because those friends are still busy with work.

» **They've relocated to be near their grown children.** When older adults relocate, they usually leave behind their established social networks and have to make new friends. Making an entirely new social circle from scratch can be challenging.

» **They're empty nesters.** Being an empty nester means not being able to make friends through their children, which is a significant way that many parents make new friends. They may also be struggling with loneliness caused by their children leaving the nest.

» **They may have a spouse or partner who still works and is on a different schedule from them.** They may feel lonely during the day while their spouse is at work because they don't have anyone to get together with.

» **Their neighborhood may be changing.** If neighbors they've known for decades are moving away, they may have a harder time making friends with new, younger neighbors. Similarly, they may have downsized and moved away from the neighborhood themselves, which means they have to find new friends. If they've moved to a retirement community or assisted living home, they may have a hard time making new friends due to established cliques.

» **Their community may not offer many classes or programs for older adults.** Especially if they live in a small town or rural area, it can be difficult to find groups or classes where older adults can meet other seniors due to limited program and group offerings. Even if their community does offer opportunities for older adults, many people don't want to participate because they think the other participants are "too old."

» **They may be homebound due to temporary illness or a chronic condition.** Being homebound can be isolating and can make it harder to make in-person friends.

» **Their long-time friends may have gotten sick or passed away.** Losing friends can leave an older adult feeling very lonely.

» **Their spouse or partner may have died, or they may have gotten divorced.** Suddenly finding themselves single later in life may result in loneliness and shrinking social circles.

» **They may have spent most of their lives focused primarily on work and family, only to enter retirement and realize they never made friends.** Now the idea of making new friends is daunting, and their social skills may be rusty. As a result they may feel too socially awkward to try to make new friends, and end up isolating themselves.

TIP

What can help with this feeling is building up self-confidence by putting themselves out there in small ways. Making small talk with neighbors can be a good first step for older adults to practice their small talk skills and get used to socializing again.

Identifying why friendships are important for older adults

Having friends is important at any age, but especially for older adults. Friends enrich seniors' lives, ease loneliness, help give them a sense of purpose, and make their days brighter. Here are several other reasons why friends are important for older adults:

» **Friends provide an important support network.** Having a support network is important for older adults, especially *solo-agers* (those who have no spouse/partner or children to rely on as they age). Older people need friends they can rely on in case of an emergency, to provide meals if they're ill, or to provide support if they have a chronic condition.

» **Socializing frequently with friends is good for mental and physical well-being.** According to a 2011 study published in the *Journal of the International Neuropsychological Society,* frequent socializing reduces cognitive decline by 70 percent!

» **Friends help give older adults a sense of purpose, especially older adults who don't have any local family nearby.** Spending time with friends and helping each other can give life more meaning.

» **Friendships provide seniors with more fun and joy.** This is especially important for older adults who struggle with chronic health conditions.

Making friends when you're older

TIP

Older adults have many avenues available to them if they want to make new friends and expand their social circles. Here are several ideas for how older adults can make new friends:

>> **Join a gym or take fitness classes for seniors through a community center.** Weight lifting, dance classes, pickleball, water aerobics, and yoga classes are great ways to socialize and meet new people.

>> **Join the older adults group at your religious congregation.** This kind of group offers a variety of activities to make new friends.

>> **Attend events through their local library system.** Libraries often offer language classes, knitting workshops, or book clubs.

>> **Make friends through pets.** Get a dog and meet your neighbors while walking around the neighborhood, or volunteer with your pet at a retirement community or library program. If you can't have a pet where you live, or you just don't want to make the commitment, consider fostering a pet who's waiting for their forever home or volunteer at a local shelter — shelters often are looking for animal lovers to help out.

>> **Join a group through Meetup aimed at people 55+ to meet new people.** Good examples are walking groups, brunch groups, pickleball groups, or singles groups.

>> **Attend programs at your local senior center to meet new people.** If you worry that everyone at the senior center will be "too old," try to attend three or four different events before making a judgment. You may be pleasantly surprised!

>> **Join a travel group for older adults in order to have people to travel with.** You can also sign up for tours geared toward older people.

>> **Take in-person or online learning classes tailored to older adults.** You'll meet people who are interested in the same things you're interested in.

>> **Join an in-person or online support group for a physical or mental health condition you're struggling with.** If you feel as though your life is dominated by a health condition, it can be hard to find friends who understand. A support group can connect you with people who understand what you're going through.

>> **Volunteer with a community organization or a cause you feel passionate about.** Whether you want to help animals, clean up a local park, or mentor a child, you're sure to find a group that needs volunteers.

Understanding Why Neurodivergent People Have a Harder Time Making Friends

When someone is *neurodivergent*, their brain functions differently than someone who is considered *neurotypical*. Whether they have autism, attention-deficit/hyperactivity disorder (ADHD), a learning disability, or another condition like sensory processing disorder, neurodivergent people can have a harder time socializing and making new friends.

Some neurodivergent people don't want to socialize and have friends, which is perfectly okay, but others do want to make friends and just have challenges with the process. Those who want to make friends may feel that socializing is too difficult, too stressful, or too much work because they have a hard time understanding the thoughts and behaviors of others, as well as difficulty reading social cues. Every person who is neurodivergent is different and will have unique experiences, preferences, and challenges.

There are many reasons why neurodivergent individuals sometimes struggle with relationships and making new friends:

>> They may have difficulty reading social cues, facial expressions, and reading between the lines to determine how to act or respond in a social setting.

>> They may have had challenges in the past with bullying, social rejection, social isolation, and lack of friends in their grade-school and young adult years, which has caused them to be anxious about putting themselves out there.

>> They may have a lack of motivation to pursue friendships because they're content doing things solo. They may have a preference for being alone instead of going to a group social event like a party due to the stress of socializing.

>> They may have difficulty making conversation and not know how to initiate and maintain conversations.

>> They may feel like they can't fully be themselves in social situations and need to mask.

>> They may have difficulty expressing emotions on their face and having good eye contact, which can make them seem unfriendly or unapproachable.

>> Social anxiety can get in the way of reaching out to others or initiating friendships, which is common in people who are neurodivergent. (See Chapter 8 for more on social anxiety.)

>> They may have challenges with sensory issues or sensory overload in certain social environments, like loud restaurants or parties.

>> They may have had experiences with social rejection in the past, making them hesitant to put themselves out there again.

>> A lack of experience with socializing can cause their social skills to be underdeveloped.

Seeing why friendships are important for neurodivergent people

Many neurodivergent people want to socialize and make new friends, whereas others are content having small social circles or no friends. Not every neurodivergent person wants to make friends or change their social situation. For those who *do* want to make friends, here are several reasons why friendships can be beneficial:

>> Having friends who accept and value you the way you are, without trying to change you, is validating.

>> Friendships provide emotional support, as well as support when navigating personal or health challenges.

>> Having close friendships helps reduce loneliness.

>> Friendships help you practice the skills of reading between the lines and deciphering social cues.

>> Having friends who truly get you is comforting.

>> Friendships give you a greater sense of belonging.

>> Friendships help you improve your conversation skills by going beyond small talk into deeper conversation and keeping a conversation going (see Chapter 10).

Making friends when you're neurodivergent

If you're interested in making new friends, here are several ways you can do so:

>> **Bond with others over shared interests.** Join a hobby/interest group that is social in nature and meets regularly. You can join groups through Meetup or other social groups. Focusing on the hobby or interest while socializing can take the pressure off talking, which can be too intense for some people.

» **Build up your social self-confidence slowly and in small ways.** You can do this by starting slowly and taking small steps when you're ready, such as practicing smiling at people first to gain confidence. After you feel comfortable with that, you can smile at people and make good eye contact. Eventually, by building up your self-confidence slowly and over time, you'll feel comfortable approaching new people to make small talk.

» **Determine your preferences for meeting new people.** Would it be more comfortable for you to meet people one-on-one, like through a friendship app, or would you do better joining a hobby/interest group and trying to get to know people in a group setting?

» **Make friends online.** You can meet people through social media, through Discord or Reddit (www.reddit.com) groups, or through online gaming communities.

» **Join a support group for people who have autism, ADHD, or sensory processing disorders.** You can find these support groups by asking your doctor or therapist for some recommendations, doing an online search, or going on the *Psychology Today* website (www.psychologytoday.com) and searching for support groups.

» **If you have a special area of interest, go to conventions or conferences around that interest to meet other people.** For example, if you're really into music or movies, go to SXSW (www.sxsw.com); if you're into comic books, head to Comic-Con (www.comic-con.org); or if you're into science fiction, head to Worldcon (www.worldcon.org).

» **Work on conversation skills, both small talk and deeper conversations.** Chapters 7 and 10 are great places to start.

» **Join social skills groups for adults.** You can find them at community centers and mental health clinics.

» **Try a friendship app that is specifically geared toward making friends.** Bumble For Friends (BFF; https://bumble.com/bff) is one app. Hiki is a friendship app specifically for neurodiverse people who want to make new friends; find out more at www.hikiapp.com.

» **Try volunteering.** VolunteerMatch (www.volunteermatch.org) is a great way to find a volunteer opportunity that matches up with your interests.

» **Take an in-person or online adult enrichment class in an area that interests you.** You'll enjoy the class, and if you make a friend in the process, all the better!

Chapter **3**

Assessing Your Friendship Needs

Before you take the first courageous steps on your new friendship journey, it's helpful to do some self-reflection to better understand what you're looking for in your new friendships. Because making new friends takes so much time and energy, it's important to consider your own friendship needs so that the effort you invest feels worth it.

Because there are many ways to make new friends, assessing your friendship needs now can help you clarify your friendship preferences and further narrow down the kind of friends you'd like to meet. Doing a self-assessment can help you reflect on why you're looking for new friendships, decide how many friends you'd ideally like to make, and identify the qualities you're looking for in a new friend.

Adult friendships sometimes happen organically, but most of the time, people need to be intentional about finding and making new friends. Clarifying your needs and preferences will facilitate being more intentional. When you know what you want, you'll have a more accurate road map that will efficiently lead you to your friendship destination.

In this chapter, I discuss why friendship is so important for adults and cover its many benefits for health and well-being. Then I explore the concept of how many friends a person needs. I cover introversion and extroversion and how these personality traits impact the ease of making new friends. Finally, I discuss how to do a friendship self-evaluation and provide many questions throughout the chapter for self-reflection.

Exploring Why We Need Adult Friendships

Many people would agree that adult friendships are one of the best things in life. Friendships enhance our lives, bring us joy, are important for our mental health and overall well-being, keep us healthy and active, and help give meaning and purpose to our lives. Our friends support us when we need an extra hand and celebrate our successes and milestones with us. Life is simply sweeter when we enjoy the company of others we love and care about.

In the following sections, I explain how friendships impact overall well-being, the benefits of friendships for health and longevity, and how friendships help you feel more supported.

The importance of friendship for overall well-being

Friendships are vitally important for overall well-being and a high quality of life for adults of all ages. Many research studies have been done on the benefits of friendships for people's wellness. A 2023 study published in *Frontiers in Psychology* found that adult friendship is predictive of overall well-being. The study also found that the more friends we have, the greater our well-being.

Friends lift our mood, provide invaluable social support, and help us be our best selves.

REMEMBER

Knowing that you have someone who cares and asks how you're doing makes you feel valued and improves your well-being. People need human connection and companionship in order to thrive, and when we don't have it, our health and well-being suffer.

Friends also boost your mood and give you someone to have fun with. People who don't have the connections they want or need often become lonely and depressed.

The benefits of friendship for health and longevity

Friendships benefit health and well-being in many different ways. First, friendships have tremendous benefits for people's mental health. Multiple research studies have shown that people who have strong friendships have lower incidences of depression, anxiety, and loneliness. Friendships help people reduce stress and weather life's challenges more effectively, because they know they have supportive people to rely on.

Friendships also benefit physical health. Multiple research studies have found that people who have strong friendships have stronger immune systems and are able to fight off illness better. They also live longer. A 2017 study in the journal *Personal Relationships* found that adults, especially older adults, who valued friendships had better overall health and functioning. A 2010 study in *PLOS Medicine* found that people who had stronger friendships had 50 percent increased longevity.

WARNING

A lack of friends also is associated with significant health risks, especially for older adults. Seniors who don't have friends face a higher risk of dementia, cardiovascular disease, and stroke. Researchers in a 2015 study in *Perspectives on Psychological Science* found that loneliness is just as bad for health as smoking 15 cigarettes per day.

How friendship provides a circle of support

Having social support through a network of friends is beneficial in many different ways. Having social support gives you a feeling that you're valued and cared for, provides emergency backup, and lets you know you're not alone in navigating a sometimes stressful world. It's important to have friends who have your back and who you can count on if you need help. It's important to your overall well-being to have someone there for you when life gets tough, who shows up for you and provides a shoulder to cry on, and who you can rely on. Having no friends to provide support can make you feel alone, which can lead to feelings of anxiety.

REMEMBER

Having a support network of friends is especially important when you don't have local family or you have a small family. Friends can help fill in the gap and make you feel cared for and less alone.

EXPLORE

Do some self-reflection about what your ideal social support network would look like. How many people would be in your support network? How would they ideally support you? How often would they keep in touch? How would you feel if you could attain this type of social support network?

Contemplating How Many Friends You Really Need

As you begin your friendship quest, think about how many friends you need in order to feel socially fulfilled. Do you want a huge social circle who you have group texts with all day long and with whom you hang out as a big group? Or do you prefer a smaller circle of close friends where you mostly get together with people one-on-one?

There are no right or wrong answers — just think about what feels right. Multiple research studies have looked at the number of friends a person has and its impact on their well-being. A 2021 *American Perspectives Survey* found that 49 percent of Americans have three or fewer close friends. A 2023 study in *Frontiers in Psychology* found that the more friends an adult has, the greater their overall well-being. A 2012 study in the *Journal of Epidemiology and Community Health* found that having five or fewer friends in your mid-40s was associated with lower levels of psychological well-being.

EXPLORE

Think back to a time when you were the most socially satisfied. How many friends did you have at that time? Looking back, do you think that was an ideal number for you? Is there anything you can learn from this exercise to apply to your current life?

Regardless of the number of friends you'd ideally like to have, it's important to ask yourself if you're able to put in the necessary time and effort to nurture each relationship. Ponder how much time and space you have in your life right now for new friends. How much energy do your job, family, pets, household tasks, and eldercare responsibilities require? Nurturing a new friendship is like planting a seed and caring for it as it turns into a plant — to get the healthiest plant, you must fertilize it, give it the proper amount of light, and water it regularly.

REMEMBER

If you have very little mental energy available to nurture a friendship right now, you may want to factor that into your ideal number of friends. Instead of making five new friends, maybe one or two is a more realistic plan for now.

EXPLORE

Think about your longest-lasting friendships. How many of these friendships do you have and how long have you had them? How much time and effort do you put into tending these friendships daily, weekly, or monthly?

REMEMBER

Sometimes our longest-lasting friendships run on autopilot, because these friends have been in our lives for so long. You can often go months without connecting, and the relationship remains strong because you have such a robust history together. If you haven't talked in a while, you can start back up right where you left off. More recent friendships, on the other hand, need more work and maintenance to give them a strong and healthy start.

In the following sections, I explain the concept of friendship turnover, and why we replace some friends in our social group every seven years, as well as the concept of Dunbar's number, which explains how many relationships we can handle at one time.

Exploring friendship turnover

Some friendships last a long time, but other friends are in your life just a short time. These friendships are more situational — for example, if you make some good friends at work, but then you change jobs and those friendships fade out. Turnover in friendships is common.

Just as our skin cells renew, we also experience friendship turnover as a natural part of the friendship process. In fact, research conducted by sociologist Gerald Mollenhorst in 2009 in the Netherlands found that, every seven years, our friend group experiences turn over — we end up replacing nearly half of our friends every seven years.

Here are some reasons why friendship turnover is common:

>> People drift apart as their life circumstances and values change.

>> People stop putting the effort into friendships, and the friendship fades.

>> Friends move away, and maintaining a long-distance friendship is difficult.

>> Priorities change — people may start valuing other things over the friendship.

>> Some people like to constantly meet new people and have an ever-changing friend group.

>> You leave the situation that brought you together, and the friendship naturally fades away.

REMEMBER

Making new friends and having some friendships gradually fade is natural and to be expected, but impulsively cutting off ties to friends or ghosting them regularly is another situation altogether. If you find yourself frequently "unfriending" people in your life, it can help to do some self-reflection, either alone or with a therapist, about your need to vigorously prune your social circle.

EXPLORE

What has your experience been with friendship turnover? Are there any turning points in your life that stand out when you had a significant friend turnover? How have different episodes of friendship turnover affected you? Do you find that your friend group experiences transition every seven years?

Understanding Dunbar's number

Have you ever wondered about the extroverted people who seem to have countless friends and social media followers and wondered how they seem to maintain such close ties to them all? Despite the way things may seem for these social butterflies on social media, one friendship researcher found that there is actually a cap on how many relationships a person can maintain at one time.

Robin Dunbar is a British anthropologist and psychologist who came up with the concept of *Dunbar's number*, which states that humans can only maintain friendships with at most 150 people. The reasoning behind Dunbar's theory is that the *neocortex* (the part of the brain that's responsible for social relationships) is large enough to handle only 150 meaningful relationships at a time.

REMEMBER

To avoid feeling intimidated by this large number, keep in mind that not everyone even *knows* 150 people, let alone has that many friends. Having a much smaller social network, even with just a handful of people, can be more than enough.

Clarifying Why You Want More Friends

Another important step in assessing your friendship needs is to clarify why you're looking to make new friends. Do you want to go out for dinner or to a play but always end up going alone? Or do you feel disconnected in your city and want to finally find "your people"? Clarifying why you want new friends is also important because it can help you decide where to look. Are you looking for activity partners to do things with? If so, joining some groups to meet others who share your interests would be a good way to make these kinds of friends.

In the following sections, I cover several reasons why people want to make new friendships, including having more people to do things with, feeling more connected in a general sense, reducing loneliness, and developing a social support circle.

Having more people to do things with

Many adults want to make more friends in order to have more people to do things with. They don't necessarily need a best friend, but they want activity partners who are up for getting together to do things like going to an exercise class, taking an art class together, or going to theater performances in their area.

TIP

Having activity partners is helpful, because you don't need to rely on one friend to satisfy all your friendship needs. You can have friends who complement different areas of your life, which makes for a more well-rounded friend group.

In order to find activity partners, try joining groups based on your hobbies and interests. After you've found one or two groups that you like, and you get to know some of the people in the groups, you can invite the ones you've connected with most during group meetings to meet up outside the group to do the activity. For example, after your birding group meets, you can invite a fellow birding enthusiast to meet up for coffee while you discuss your favorite feathered friends.

EXAMPLE

Kendra loved pickleball and wanted to find a pickleball activity partner, but she didn't know anyone who was interested in playing. She joined a community pickleball group and met another woman who she enjoyed talking to. The two of them started getting together outside the group to practice more often, playing singles pickleball after work, and had a great time socializing and getting exercise.

Feeling more connected

Another reason you may want to make friends is to feel more connected to your community. If you've lived in your area a while, but it doesn't yet feel like home, not having friends can be one reason why. You may start out by broadening your network of local acquaintances, and see which ones you can turn into friends. There are several good ways to do that:

>> Join groups based on your hobbies/interests.

>> Meet more people in your neighborhood.

>> Join networking groups in your career field to meet new people.

>> Take in-person adult enrichment classes.

>> Join your school's alumni association and see if they have a local chapter (or start one if they don't) to feel more connected to both your college and your local area.

Reducing loneliness

Many people want to make more friends in order to not feel lonely (see Chapter 18 for more on coping with loneliness). Loneliness is a feeling of wanting to be with others and wanting to feel more connected, but having no one available to connect with. Increasing your number of connections and filling your social calendar with events can be good first steps to tackling loneliness.

To meet more people, join groups based on your hobbies/interests, join a religious congregation and get involved, and attend community events to get out and about more often. Local library systems, for example, usually have extensive event calendars filled with book clubs, language groups, arts-and-crafts workshops, and author events. Feeling a little busier by packing your social calendar with events is something you can start doing now (without needing to have any friends) to help manage lonely feelings.

Developing a circle of support

Some people want to make more friends in order to create a social support network. This is especially important for people who have no local family or no family at all. Having a support network provides comfort and security in knowing you have people who will support you in good times and bad. Having a circle of friends who are willing to help you if needed, step up in an emergency situation, and serve as emergency contacts can go a long way toward helping you feel like you have a network of people who care.

Determining Whether You're an Introvert or an Extrovert and Knowing Why It Matters

It can be helpful to know whether you're an introvert or an extrovert before you start on your friendship journey. Introversion and extroversion are personality traits that have to do with where you get your energy from (internally or externally) and how you prefer to recharge.

In the following sections, I help you figure out if you're an introvert or an extrovert and explain what that means for your goal of making friends.

Discovering your type

Introverts get their energy from being on their own and enjoying their own company, and they feel drained and depleted by too much socializing. They usually recharge by being by themselves in a quiet place. *Extroverts*, on the other hand, get their energy from being around other people, enjoy bustling environments, and love to socialize. They feel depleted by being alone too much and recharge by going out and socializing. *Ambiverts* have characteristics of both introverts and extroverts, and their personalities fall somewhere in the middle.

You probably already have a general sense of whether you're an introvert or an extrovert (or an ambivert), just based on those descriptions, but if you want to dig deep into the subject, there are a few different ways to determine which type you are:

>> **You can do some self-reflection after taking an online quiz to find out which type you are.** Check out the quiz on *Psychology Today* at www.psychologytoday.com/us/tests/personality/extroversion-introversion-test.

>> **You can read books about personality types.** Some books to start with include *Quiet: The Power of Introverts in a World That Can't Stop Talking*, by Susan Cain (Crown); *Do What You Are: Discover the Perfect Career for you Through the Secrets of Personality Type*, by Paul D. Tieger, Barbara Barron, and Kelly Tieger (Little, Brown Spark); and *The Four Tendencies*, by Gretchen Rubin (Harmony).

>> **You can take a personality test.** The most well-known personality test, which measures introversion and extroversion among other traits, is the Myers-Briggs Type Indicator (MBTI). You can take this test online for a fee (it takes about 45 minutes to complete), or you can schedule an appointment with an organization or professional (like a career coach) who can give the test to you. You can find more information about the test, plus sign up to take the actual test, online at www.mbtionline.com.

If you don't want to spend the money to take the official MBTI, you can take free quizzes online that can help you determine your levels of introversion and extroversion, as well as your personality type. Some examples include 16Personalities (www.16personalities.com), PersonalityPerfect (www.personalityperfect.com), or bigfive-test.com (https://bigfive-test.com).

Determining the impact on friendships

Introversion and extroversion both have positives and negatives, but introverts can sometimes have a harder time making friends. There are many reasons for this, but one explanation is that when you're perceived as being more quiet and reserved, and don't like to be the center of attention, you can sometimes be overlooked by people who are seeking more outgoing friends. Additionally, introverts can sometimes take a little extra time to get to know, and they can be private people. Busy adults who are in a hurry to make new friends may find it easier to get to know someone who is more extroverted.

On the other hand, many introverts are perfectly content with smaller social circles and prefer having a few super-close friendships instead of a larger network of more casual friendships. They also prefer to spend time with their friends individually or in small groups, having deep conversation. Introverts are also known for being excellent listeners — not only do they listen intently to their friends, but they also remember important details to bring up in a thoughtful way later. They also tend to value deep, meaningful conversations, and prefer those over more surface-level discussion.

Extroverts, who are often seen as "the life of the party," tend to get noticed more often. They shine in group settings and often like to be the center of attention. People want to be around them because they're often outgoing, charming, bubbly, and funny. Extroverts can be charismatic, are great at networking, and are often great leaders. Because they're so personable, they often have an easier time making new friends and tend to have larger social circles. However, they can struggle with time alone and can have a hard time enjoying solitude. They can also become lonely if they're not socializing often.

Doing a Friendship Self-Evaluation

Before going out and looking to make new friends, it can be helpful to take a close look at your existing social network and do a friendship evaluation. A friendship evaluation involves looking closely at and evaluating each of your current friendships to see whether they're working for you. This will help you determine whether you're looking to make one or two new friends or an entirely new social circle.

TIP

You'll think about the friendships you have and whether each person adds value to your life. You'll also think about whether they've been a good friend, whether they've been there for you when you've needed them, whether they're putting the same amount of energy into the relationship that you are, or whether they're lacking in some of these areas.

If you realize that your friends haven't been stepping up, you may want to reevaluate whether they're still worth holding on to, whether you want to put less energy into those friendships, or if you should find some new friends. If you want to hold onto these friends, it's a good idea to advocate for your needs in the friendship. Think about how you'll communicate to them that you'd like to see some changes (see Chapter 15). Be gentle and kind when you let them know, but be confident in advocating for yourself. If they can't or won't change, it may be time to refresh your social circle.

EXPLORE

On a piece of paper, write down all your current friends. Write down the last time you saw them, how frequently you see them, and a yes or no for whether you're overall happy with the relationship. Think about how each one adds value or enhances your life. If you're unhappy with the friendship overall, think about whether the friendship is worth holding on to. Are the things you're unhappy with realistically changeable? If yes, you may want to advocate for your needs and talk to your friend about what you'd like to see change.

REMEMBER

Evaluating your friendships is important, but it also goes both ways. Remember Ralph Waldo Emerson's saying that "The only way to have a friend is to be one." It's also important to do some self-evaluation to make sure that *you're* being the type of good friend you want to be for others. Do some self-reflection and ask yourself the following questions:

>> Have you been as good a friend as you could be in the past year?

>> Have you been as supportive as you could be?

>> Are you there for your friends and do you show up for them?

>> Have you remembered your friends' milestones and important events?

>> Have you put in the work to nurture the friendship?

>> Have you been good about keeping in touch?

It can be hard and somewhat painful to take an honest look at yourself and realize you're coming up short in the friend department. But figuring out how you can improve is very doable. After you've done that, create an action plan. (Turn to Chapter 13 for more on how to be a good friend.)

EXAMPLE

Monique did some self-reflection about whether she was being the best friend she could be to her two closest friends. She realized that her friends often complained about the fact that she was always late, and she knew that made them upset, like her time was more important than theirs. She also knew that she hadn't been reciprocating social invitations as much as she should — she just got busy and kept meaning to plan events and invite her friends but never got around to it. Monique resolved to be a better friend in these ways in the coming year.

EXPLORE

Do some self-reflection about your ideal social life. What would it look like? Would it involve having a packed social calendar every week, with plenty of parties, barbecues, and dinners on your calendar? Would it include meeting with a close friend weekly for a walk? Would it include hanging out with friends at your local watering hole every Saturday night? Think about whether you can have your ideal social life with the friends you have now, or whether you'll need to make new friends who want to do the kinds of things you do and are on board with how often you want to get together.

Determining How Often You Want to Meet Up with Friends

Another aspect of assessing your friendship needs is determining how often you want to meet up with friends. Think about your ideal frequency for meeting up, based on your current schedule and other commitments. Would you like to meet up with friends weekly, monthly, or a few times a year? Are your current friends matching up with your frequency needs, or do you differ in your ideas of how often you should get together?

There can sometimes be resentment and frustration when friends have different needs and expectations for their get-togethers. It can be hard to navigate having a fulfilling friendship if one friend is content with getting together twice a year, and the other wants to meet twice a month.

REMEMBER

If this is a chronic frustration in your friendship, it's helpful to advocate for yourself and let your friend know that you would prefer more frequent get-togethers. A compromise would be best, but if that can't be worked out due to mismatched schedules or other factors, then it's healthy to recognize that some friends you meet with a few times a year, some you meet with once a month, and others you meet with more frequently. If your needs for getting together aren't being met by one friend, then try to get to know new people who are able to meet up more often. That way, you can still meet up with your old friend when they're available.

If you need more frequent in-person contact to build the relationship, it can be worthwhile to share your feelings. You could use an *I* statement, which is a great way to share your feelings and needs with others (see Chapter 15 for more on *I* statements). Here's an example:

> I wish we could see each other more than two or three times a year. I'd love to see you more often! I know you're busy, but do you think we could get together more regularly? Maybe we could take a weekly workout class together? Or join a monthly book group and go for coffee after?

Living Your Best Life

Now that you've done some valuable self-reflection and you're about to start your friendship journey, it's important to remember that your friendship quest can take a while. Remember to play the long game and be patient while you seek out new friends.

In the meantime, work on living your best life while you're waiting to make new friends. This can involve doing all the things you want to do with a friend, but doing them solo. Going out for dinner (go to a restaurant, sit at the bar, and take a book), going to a movie, and going to a museum can all be done on your own, even if you wish you had someone to go with you. (See Chapter 21 for more on how to live your best life while you're waiting to make a friend.)

When you're in a good place and content with yourself, it will make finding the type of friends you're looking for much easier. People are interested in making friends with other people who are upbeat, optimistic, have a positive outlook, and are inspiring. If you're not in a good place yet but you want to make friends, try to take some time first to work on your mental health and well-being so you can be your best possible self while putting yourself out there.

IN THIS CHAPTER

» Reflecting on your ideal
  friend's qualities

» Setting short-term and long-term
  friendship goals

» Writing a friendship
  mission statement

Chapter **4**

Manifesting Your Ideal Friend

A n essential part of the friend–making process is envisioning your ideal
friendship. You'll want to think about all the qualities and characteristics
you'd like your potential new friend to have, from their age or life stage to
their hobbies and interests. If you can imagine the type of friend you want to
meet, it's more likely you'll be able to actually find that type of person when
you're out and about meeting new people.

Manifesting your ideal friend can take various forms that you explore in this
chapter: setting short–term and long–term friendship goals, creating a vision
board with images of your ideal friendship, and writing a friendship mission
statement.

This chapter is self–reflective in nature. It helps you explore the qualities you'd
like to find in a new friend, narrow down the characteristics that you do and don't
want in a friendship, and create positive friendship affirmations.

Reflecting on Important Friendship Qualities

Before you go out and meet new people, it's helpful to do some self-reflection on the qualities you want in a friend. Being clear on these qualities will help you be more effective in finding the ideal friends who embody these qualities. Read through the following list, and ask yourself if each quality is one that you value in a friend. If so, note it down so that you can refer to your list later when getting to know new people.

>> **Conversation skills:** Is having a friend who's a good conversationalist important to you? Someone who is a good conversationalist never has problems coming up with things to talk about, asks good questions, and keeps the conversation moving smoothly.

TIP

This trait can be helpful if you prefer outings that lend themselves to conversation, like getting coffee or tea or going for a walk. It's also helpful if you yourself are a good conversationalist, because you may want a friend who's also very chatty.

>> **Warmth:** Many people look for warmth when making new friends. Someone who is warm makes you feel good about yourself, as well as valued and appreciated. A warm friend may always be enthusiastic to see you, tell you how much they missed you, and offer a hug or be affectionate.

WARNING

If you're not used to warmth or you find it too overwhelming or cloying, you may prefer a friend who is more stoic or neutral.

>> **Responsiveness:** Many people value responsiveness in their friends. A responsive friend responds to texts or messages quickly, which makes you feel like you're valued and appreciated. If you call them and leave a message, they'll return it in a timely fashion. When they respond quickly, it communicates that they care and see you as a priority, which is a good feeling.

>> **Loyalty:** A loyal friend always has your back and supports you no matter what. They're there with you through thick and thin and can always be counted on to take your side. It can feel comforting to know that you have such a loyal friend, especially if you feel all alone in the world.

>> **Supportiveness:** A supportive friend is there for you through good times and bad. You know they'll show up whenever you need them. It's comforting to know that you have someone who supports all your ideas and celebrates your wins with you. It's nice to have a cheerleader-type friend who shows their support in many different ways.

>> **Generosity:** Many people value a friend who is generous with their time and energy. If you say you had a rough day and need to talk, they'll drop everything to be there for you and give you their time. Friends who are stingy with time and energy don't make you feel valued. Someone who is very giving with their time makes you feel like you're one of their top priorities.

>> **Proximity:** Many people value having friends who live close to them. It's helpful for a friend to live nearby, because it makes everything easier and more convenient. You're more likely to spend time with those who live nearby because you see them frequently. When a friend lives nearby, it's easier to fit a quick hangout into your schedule, which makes it more likely that you'll spend time with them often (as opposed to someone who lives a 30-minute drive away).

>> **Time and space:** Many people are looking for friends who have the room in their life to make a new friend. Some people's dance cards are already full — they have all the friends they need and no room for any more. It's helpful to find a friend who is eager to put in the time and attention that a new friendship needs to blossom.

>> **Life stage:** Some people are looking for friends in a similar life stage. Being around the same age or going through the same life milestones or transitions can help you be more in tune with each other and give you lots to talk about. Being in a similar life stage can also help you relate to them better because you're going through the same things at the same time.

>> **Interests:** Some people value having friends with similar interests. They want to find someone with whom they have a lot in common and a lot to talk about.

TIP

It's easiest to meet people with similar interests when you join a hobby/ interest group or take a class.

>> **Sense of humor:** Some people are looking for a friend with a good sense of humor. Lots of people enjoy being around lighthearted, funny people. Humor often helps lighten the mood and helps people cope more effectively with life's challenges.

EXPLORE

Make a list of the top five most important qualities you think your new friend should have. To make this list, think about whether you prefer that your friend be similar to you or different from you in terms of personality. After you've made your list, you can file it away to take out when you start getting to know someone, to make sure that your new friend has at least some of the qualities on the list. Nobody will have *every* quality you're looking for, but you can probably find someone who has a few of your most important qualities.

REMEMBER

Remember that you can have multiple friends with different traits that you value. Maybe one of your friends is extremely supportive, responsive, and caring, and another friend is a great conversationalist with an amazing sense of humor. Both friends complement your life in different ways and bring their own set of friendship strengths.

Thinking like a real estate agent

When you're searching for new friends, it can be helpful to be intentional about new friendships. Being intentional means really thinking about what you're looking for in a new friendship instead of leaving things up to chance and being willing to be friends with anyone. When you're intentional about your friendships, you're more likely to find friends who are the best match, which is important for busy adults who don't have a lot of free time.

It can be helpful to think like a real estate agent when considering the qualities you're looking for in a new friend. What's on your friendship must-have, nice-to-have, and definitely-do-not-want list? To figure this out, divide a piece of paper into three columns, and do some self-reflection about which friendship traits fall into these three categories for you.

TIP

Sometimes it helps to write it all out and see it on paper to help you clarify your thoughts. If you're a person who thinks better out loud, you can create this list with your spouse or partner or with your therapist.

After you've created your list, think about how you can seek out new friends who have these qualities you're looking for. Ideas include joining new groups to meet people who share your interests, looking for friends in a similar life stage through various groups like new parent groups, meeting new people at your religious congregation, or looking for friends while volunteering.

Considering what qualities make you a good friend

During your friendship journey, it's also helpful to think about the qualities you have that make you a good friend. If you have difficulty with this task, think about how others who are close to you would describe you. Make a list of the most important qualities that make you a good friend. This can help guide you as to what type of people would be your best match. It's helpful to be intentional about making new friends and not just befriend anyone who comes your way.

Preferring a friend who is similar to you or different from you

While you think about your best friendship matches, it's helpful to think about whether you prefer a friend who is similar to you or different. Do you tend to get along better with people who are similar to you? Or do you thrive off the synergy that comes from learning new things from different people? For example, being in the same life stage as your friend means you have more in common and more to talk about. Alternatively, you can gain new perspectives and wisdom from friends who are in different life stages.

Remembering the Ghosts of Friendships Past

When making new friends, it can be helpful to think back to old friends that you've made in the past, and remember what was positive about those relationships and what didn't work out. Learning from past relationship challenges can help you avoid making those same mistakes this time around.

Think about your closest friends from elementary school, middle school, high school, and college. What did you like about those friends? How did you make your closest friends? Have you been able to find other close relationships recently with people who share similar qualities?

Were there any friendships from your earlier years that didn't work out but where you learned valuable lessons that you can apply to future friendships?

Your first best friend

Think back to your very first best friend. Our first best friends are often some of our most special friendships. You probably still remember that friend very vividly and remember some of the special times you spent together.

What was your friend like? Where did you meet them? What are some of your best friendship memories with that person? It can help to write down some details on a piece of paper to remember these special times with your friend.

Here are some other questions to ponder as you take a trip down memory lane:

>> What did the two of you like to do together?

>> What made the friendship so special?

>> Have you stayed in touch? If not, what happened to that friendship?

>> Have you considered trying to get in touch with your first best friend? If so, they'd probably be thrilled to hear from you!

Friendship mistakes you don't want to repeat

When thinking about friendships from the past, friendship mistakes may come to mind. Were there any of your friendships that ended badly? If you could go back in time, is there anything you would do differently with those friendships?

TIP

Thinking back to past friendship mistakes can help you make different choices with new friendships now.

Having Multiple Friendship Baskets

Ideally, it's helpful to have friends for different areas of your life. You can think of this as having multiple "friendship baskets" where you have friends who you do different activities with or who are from different times in your life. For instance, you may have a running friend, a friend from church, a work friend, and a friend from college who you still stay in touch with.

REMEMBER

The benefits of having multiple friendship baskets are that you don't rely too much on any one friend, which can drain some people. Instead, you spread your time and attention across multiple friends, which is healthier.

Some people have one best friend who they do everything with, which can be very meaningful, but it's usually harder for adults to make a brand-new best friend who they do everything with. If adults have a best friend, it's usually from an earlier time in their life, like a high school or college friend they still keep in touch with. Instead, having friends for different areas of your life can help satisfy your need for deep, whole friendships.

Having multiple friendship baskets is another way to diversify your social network with friends of all ages and stages — you could have "couple friends" who you and your spouse hang out with, a parent friend who's the parent of your kids' friends, and a neighbor friend who you do backyard cookouts with.

TIP

Additionally, by having friendship baskets, if you have a falling out with one friend, you don't feel totally adrift and alone because you have other friends to turn to. This can help decrease anxiety if there's a huge blowout with a friend. You'll know that you have other friends to spend time with who are not connected with the friend you had a falling out with, which can be comforting.

Here are a few friendship baskets you may want to fill:

» **Neighborhood friends:** Neighborhood friends are great to have if you want to just chat casually with someone, because you can go outside and run into a neighbor to chat with. It's also helpful to have neighborhood friends if you want to meet up with someone last minute or if you need a small favor, like someone to water your plants while you're out of town.

» **Activity partners:** It's helpful to have activity partners to get together with when you want to talk a walk, go to an exercise class, or try a crochet group. You can meet activity partners by taking a class or by inviting someone to join you for an activity. You can socialize and do an activity with your activity partners, which can lead to meaningful friendships.

» **Work friends:** Many people have friends who they only see at work, but who end up being close friends. Work friends make the job more enjoyable, can help you with your career, and can support you if something goes awry at your job.

Setting Friendship Goals

As you prepare to start out on your friendship journey, one helpful step to take is to consider your friendship goals. Having friendship goals helps you to be more intentional in the way you go about making new friendships. Some questions to ask yourself are:

» What kinds of friends would you like to make, and how many?

» How much work are you willing to put into finding your new friends?

» Where are you willing to look for new friends? Are you willing to join new groups or try new activities?

Setting short-term friendship goals

Short-term friendship goals are those that will take place in the next few weeks to few months. Short-term friendship goals are more important than long-term friendship goals because they focus on the present, when you're most focused on trying to find the right friend matches.

Your short-term friendship goals depend on whether you're starting from scratch and trying to make an entire new social circle. If you're starting from scratch without any friends yet, then your short-term goals should focus on meeting people first. (Turn to Chapters 5 and 6 for more on the best ways to meet people.)

Your short-term goals will be different if you already have acquaintances that you'd like to turn into friends. In that case, you'll want to focus on spending more time with your new acquaintances and deepening these relationships. (Check out Chapter 11 to learn more about how to turn acquaintances into friends.)

Here are some examples of short-term friendship goals that may resonate with you:

>> Turn one acquaintance into a new friend over the next three months.

>> Make small talk with three new people this month.

>> By the end of the month, get back in touch with four Facebook friends who I rarely see.

>> In the next two months, reach out to five acquaintances to see how they're doing.

>> Know at least three people to invite to a Friendsgiving get-together next year.

>> In the next six months, have at least three people I can ask to join me if I want to go out and do something.

REMEMBER

These goals are just starting points, and they may not apply to you. Maybe you already make small talk with new people all the time, or maybe you're not on social media. Maybe you want to host a Friendsgiving event with a dozen people, or maybe you want a birthday get-together with only two or three friends. Use these sample goals to get the creative juices flowing and help you think of your own. The key is to be clear about how many people you're talking about and by when — that way, the goal is specific, measurable, and time-bound (three of the hallmarks of a solidly written goal — see the nearby sidebar for more).

SETTING SMART GOALS

One of the best ways to effectively set goals is to make them SMART:

- **Specific:** The more specific a goal is, the better your chances of being able to achieve it because you know exactly what you're trying to do. For example, "Talk to more people" isn't very specific; "Stop and chat with at least one neighbor every week" is.

- **Measurable:** When you set a number to a goal, you can easily measure whether you've reached the goal. For example, "Make small talk with three new people this month" is better than "Make more small talk" because you can measure it.

- **Attainable:** It's great to aim high, but you don't want your goals to be so unrealistic that you're setting yourself up for failure. If you don't have any friends, setting a goal to host a party with 25 friends next month isn't attainable. Instead, a more realistic goal could be to make one new friend in the next three months.

- **Relevant:** Make sure your individual goals will get you one step closer to your big-picture goal of making friends. Setting a goal to read more books isn't relevant to your friendship-making goal; setting a goal to join a book club (where you can meet other book-loving friends) is.

- **Time-bound:** Make sure to set a deadline for every goal. Maybe you'll make small talk with three new people *this month* or know five people to invite to a Friendsgiving event *this year*.

These guidelines apply no matter what kind of goals you're setting, including friendship goals.

Setting long-term friendship goals

Long-term friendship goals are those that will take place in a year or more, or even several years down the road. It's not too soon to set some general long-term friendship goals, even before you make a new friend. Thinking about your long-term friendship goals can help you clarify what you're looking for in a friendship and help you be more intentional about making new friends.

As one idea, you can come up with long-term friendship goals based on upcoming milestones or events that you'd like to have made some friends in time for. For example, you may want to have a few friends to invite to your 40th birthday celebration in three years or have enough friends to invite to your 20th anniversary party in five years.

Here are some ideas of long-term friendship goals to help you brainstorm:

>> Within three years, make two friends I would feel close enough to confide in.

>> Make a friend who would be interested in traveling with me within two years.

>> Within five years, make one close friend who is there for me in good and bad times.

>> By the end of next year, make enough good friends that my city or town finally feels like home. (The number of people it'll take varies from person to person. Some people need just two or three friends for a place to feel like home, and other people need ten or more friends to feel this way.)

>> Have two friends to put down on an emergency contact form by next year.

>> Within two years, have three friends I can call in a crisis.

Keep your friendship goals SMART (see the sidebar earlier in this chapter). And don't get hung up on the details of these examples — use them as jumping-off points for setting goals that make sense for you!

Determining Your Overall Friendship Strategy

When thinking about being intentional in making new friendships, it's also a good time to think about your overall friendship-making strategy. How do you want to go about making new friends? Do you want to take the more organic approach and just put yourself out there and see what happens? Or do you want to be intentional about joining groups that interest you, making small talk with people, reaching out, and inviting them to do something with you? Either approach is fine, but the latter may be a more efficient way to make new friends.

Writing a friendship mission statement

One part of your overall friendship strategy can include writing a friendship mission statement. Some people create mission statements for other areas of their lives where they want to narrow their focus and outline a purposeful plan. They may have a personal mission statement, a family mission statement, or a mission statement for their small business. Likewise, you can create a friendship mission statement that captures the essence of what you have to give as a friend and all the things you're looking for in a friendship.

Your mission statement can have the following elements:

>> Statement of your goals or intentions

>> Reflection of your values

>> Description of your greater purpose

>> Explanation of why you want to have friends

EXAMPLE

Here's an example:

I will be a loving, kind, generous friend who always treats my friends well. I value responsiveness, so I'll always make sure to respond to my friends quickly and make sure they know I value and appreciate them. I value diversity in my friendships, so I'll seek friends from a variety of backgrounds. I'll also seek friends who share my values of adventure and travel and who want to go out and explore the world together. I also want friends who are looking for friends who are like family and will help me build my sense of community.

Taking on a new friendship challenge

If you're someone who likes to be challenged, taking on a 30-day friendship challenge may be just the thing that gives you extra motivation to get out there and meet new people.

You may be familiar with the concept of the 30-day challenge, where you choose a personal area of interest to work on (for example, exercise, water intake, reading, or flossing) and work on improving it for an entire month.

TIP

You may have tried a 30-day challenge in the past, because it's an inspirational way to get yourself to do something you've been putting off. A 30-day challenge also helps you overcome inertia, by giving you a reason (completing the challenge) to stick with something difficult. It can also help you evaluate different approaches to a task, to see which one is most helpful or effective.

A reading challenge, for example, can take the form of seeing how many books you can read in a single month. A running challenge can take the form of seeing if you can run every day for a month and increase your physical fitness. A flossing challenge can take the form of seeing if you can floss consistently every day.

REMEMBER

A 30-day challenge is supposed to be fun. The enjoyable part of a 30-day challenge is that a little dose of competition (even with just yourself) can turn something that you've been dreading or procrastinating into a fun exercise in self-discipline.

If you choose to take on a friendship challenge, you can be creative with how you'd like to implement it. Here are some different ways you could structure a 30-day friendship challenge:

>> Try out one new friendship strategy from this book each day for a month, and see which one is the most effective.

>> Plan a friend date with one new acquaintance each day for a month.

>> Reach out to a different Facebook friend every day for an entire month.

>> Meet a different friend or acquaintance for lunch every week for a month.

>> Try new ways to meet people every day for a month (for example, taking an exercise class, signing up for a friendship app, or joining a new social group), and see which one is most effective.

>> Set the goal of making two new friends in one month.

>> Set the goal of making four new acquaintances in one month.

>> Attend one new networking event each week for a month.

If you find that your 30-day friendship challenge is going well, you can extend it another month (or more). You can also get your new friends on board; perhaps they have friendship goals they'd like to work on, too. Sometimes turning an activity into a challenge can be just the thing to get you motivated and invigorated in working toward your goal.

Designing Your Friendship Vision Board

Have you ever created a vision board for the new year or for a specific goal you want to work toward? It's a fun and inspiring activity that helps you flex your creative muscles. Vision boards are trending right now — there are even classes you can take that teach you how to make them. Vision boards are also a fun friend bonding activity, so consider inviting all your new pals to join you for an upcoming vision-board-making session.

Creating your vision board

Take a piece of poster board or other large paper and create a collage out of magazine images or online printed images that represent the friendship goal or vibe you're working toward. You can also do this online with images from sites like Pinterest (www.pinterest.com).

For example, if you were making a New Year's vision board, you could include cutouts of vacation destinations you want to go to in the new year, a new job you want to apply for this year, books you want to read this year, or images of your dream wedding if you're getting married this year. Your vision board can include cutout images; specific words that resonate with you, like *joy* or *calm*; or personal photos. It's a creative exercise in turning your goals, hopes, and dreams into a tangible, visible form that you can look at every day.

The power of a vision board is that it gets all the goals that may be floating around chaotically in your mind onto paper in a tangible form so you can start to visualize them and work toward them more effectively.

Deciding what to include

Your friendship vision board can include anything that supports your goal — images of friendships that inspire you, words about friendship, or even images of places you'd like to go with your friends. Here are other ideas that your friendship vision board can include:

» Activities you'd like to do with friends

» Foods you'd like to eat with friends

» Places you'd like to go with friends

» Milestones that you'd like to celebrate with friends

» Images of you and your friend laughing together or other images of what you would like your friendship to be

» Friends of different ages, if intergenerational friendships are important to you

Creating Positive Friendship Affirmations

One helpful strategy for increasing your confidence around making new friendships is to create positive friendship affirmations. Affirmations are positive statements that you can say to yourself (either out loud or in your mind) that focus on your strengths, to help you feel more empowered and uplifted during your friendship journey.

Creating positive affirmations

Positive affirmations help you nurture more positivity toward yourself, which is especially helpful when you're feeling down or discouraged during your friendship journey or if you're feeling rejected. Positive friendship affirmations can take a variety of forms, but they're usually in a statement format.

Here are several examples of positive friendship affirmations:

» I am positive and interesting and people enjoy my company.

» I am kind and generous, and I have a lot to offer a new friend.

» I am doing everything I can to make new friends.

» I will make someone a great friend for many reasons: I'm nice, I'm thoughtful, and I'm kind.

TIP

You can repeat your affirmations during any stressful parts of your friendship search, use them to give yourself a pep talk before meeting new people, or use them to comfort yourself if you experience rejection. Make sure to use present, as opposed to past or future tense, when saying your affirmations — they're more empowering that way.

Using positive affirmations

Here are several ways you can use positive friendship affirmations:

» Write them down on index cards and carry them in your purse, briefcase, or backpack for when you need a pep talk.

» Repeat them to yourself if you've suffered a rejection.

» Write them on sticky notes and place them where you'll see them, like on your bathroom mirror, on the fridge door, or on top of your phone.

» Repeat them to yourself silently before going up to someone new.

» Write them down on strips of paper and put them in a jar to pull out at home when you need a lift.

2

Discovering How to Make New Friends

If you've struggled to figure out exactly how to go about making a new friend, this section will really resonate. In this part, you learn the most effective groups to join to make new friends, discover all the ways to approach someone new, explore how to make small talk with new people without losing your mind, and get the secrets of becoming more personable. You'll also learn how to cope effectively with shyness and social anxiety and how to turn acquaintances into friends.

Chapter **5**

Finding Friends in New Places

At this point in your friend-making journey, you've done all the foundational work for making new friends: You've decided that you're in the market for new friends, you've assessed your friendship needs, and you've set some exciting friendship goals. The next step in the process is knowing where to find potential friends.

Some people find this step to be particularly challenging. They may not know where to look for new friends or what social opportunities exist in their area. Never fear! The good news is that there are many places to find new friends, and this chapter shows you exactly where to start and what to do.

One of the most tried-and-true ways to find new friends is joining a group. Groups allow you to meet other people who share your hobbies or interests, engage in a fun activity for your own personal enrichment, and socialize with people you probably have several things in common with.

In this chapter, I help you understand a few important predictors of friendships, including proximity and frequency, the types of groups to join for maximum friend-making success, and how to start your own social group if you want.

Knowing What It Takes for Friendships to Happen

Two important predictors of friendship are essential to keep in mind as you decide where to look for new friends: proximity and frequency.

Proximity: Keeping your friends close

One of the most important predictors of friendship is the *proximity effect*, first identified by a scholar named Theodore Newcomb. According to the proximity effect, the people who are geographically closest to you become your friends because you see or interact with them the most. This is the reason why kids in school make friends so easily with the kids they're in class with, and it's why college kids often become best friends with the people in their dorms — they see each other daily and have frequent connections. This is also why people tend to become good friends with their neighbors — you see them all the time, while getting the mail or walking your dog. It also explains why it's less likely that you'll become friends with a coworker who lives 40 minutes away — you may see each other all day at work, but you live too far away to easily meet up outside of work. The more you see someone, the more likely it is that you'll become friends. And you're more likely to get together with someone if they're geographically closer to you (because doing so is easier and more convenient).

A 2022 study on classroom seat proximity, published in *Frontiers in Psychology*, found that school-age children who sat near each other were more likely to become friends than those who sat farther apart. This makes sense — students who sit near each other have more casual opportunities to socialize and get to know each other than they do with a kid all the way across the room. Have you ever had the experience of becoming better friends with your cube mates at work, whereas the people who work down the hall you don't know as well because you don't see them as much? You're more likely to ask your cube mate how their weekend was or ask to borrow a pen, and these repeated, casual interactions often lead to friendships. This is the proximity effect at work.

Problems with proximity are among the reasons why adults have such a hard time making new friends. Because work takes up so much of a person's day, theoretically, it would be one of the best places for them to make new friends. However, these days, because many people either work from home (and therefore don't know their coworkers as well, if they even have coworkers) or have long commutes, proximity doesn't work in their favor to make new friends through work.

The takeaway here is that you're more likely to become friends with someone who lives near you, because you'll see them more, than someone who lives far away. So, when you're looking for new opportunities to make new friends, look closer to home. If you're going to join a tennis class with the goal of making new friends, look for classes that are within a mile or two of your home, as opposed to classes that are clear across town. The easier it is for you to get together with your new friend outside of class, the more likely it is that a friendship will blossom.

Frequency: Making time

Another important predictor of friendship is how often you see someone. The more often you see them, the more likely it is that a friendship will form. Seeing them weekly is better than monthly, and seeing them monthly is better than seeing them a few times per year. For instance, if you're volunteering and you see the same person on your shift every week, it's more likely that a friendship will form than if you only see that person once a month. The more often you see someone, the more interactions you have that can lead to a meaningful friendship.

Frequency is especially important with brand-new relationships, because a friendship can't take root if you're only seeing each other once in a blue moon. According to a 2018 study in the *Journal of Social and Personal Relationships*, it takes 80 to 100 hours to turn a casual friend into a friend. That's a lot of hours! If you're only able to meet up with a new friend twice a year for coffee, it's going to take a *really* long time to become good friends. On the other hand, if you can meet up with a friend once a week for coffee, it may only take around two years to rack up enough hours to turn that casual friend into a good friend.

Lack of frequency is another reason why adults have such a hard time making new friends. Between work, family, household responsibilities, and walking the dog, many just don't have the time in their schedules to see a new friend frequently. As a result, many adults have a ton of acquaintances and superficial connections but they never have the opportunity to turn them into good friends.

Making a new friend at a one-off event like an art gallery opening or open-mic night will be a lot more challenging than joining a group that meets every week. You may exchange phone numbers with someone at the open-mic night, but it'll take a lot more work to initiate and coordinate get-togethers, as opposed to knowing you'll see the same person at regular group events. One of the benefits of joining a group is knowing that everyone has already made time in their schedules for the group meetings, so you have a guaranteed opportunity to socialize.

Branching Out from Your Regular Routine

Before doing a deep dive into finding new places to meet friends, it's important to think about how this part of the process may be a new change for you. Up until now, you may have always tried to make friends in the same ways, perhaps through work or with neighbors. Maybe you've never thought about joining a bowling league or had time to consider volunteering, or maybe the idea of being a *joiner* (someone who joins groups) doesn't appeal to you.

However, sometimes you need to change up your routine to make new friends. For adults, new friendships take intentional effort. Are you willing to branch out from your regular routine to try something new? Can you spare a few hours a week to put in the time to make new friends?

EXPLORE

This is a good time to do some self-reflection about the pros and cons of trying something new and different versus sticking with what you've done in the past. For this reflection exercise, make a list of the new activities or events you've tried in the last year or two. Reflect on how it felt to try something new and the new people you met or new skills you gained. Do you have space in your life right now to add another new activity, or are you content with the way things are? If you haven't tried anything new in the last year, it can be helpful to reflect on why. Sometimes putting yourself out there and trying new things can be difficult, but it's usually worth it.

TIP

Be open-minded about making friends in new places — being flexible and open to new experiences will broaden your social horizons. You'll connect with a variety of new people, learn some new skills, and probably have fun in the process.

You can be open-minded during this part of your friendship journey by trying any of the following things:

>> Joining a new group

>> Giving that new group a chance, before judging it

>> Being willing to make small talk with a lot of people, even if they don't seem like potential friends at the time

>> Asking people questions about themselves to learn more

>> Getting to know people a little bit before deciding they aren't friend material

>> Frequently initiating get-togethers

>> Being willing to go out on lots of friend dates

Joining Groups to Make Friends

One of the most effective ways to make new friends is to join a group or find a social hobby. But not just any old group will do; you need to be strategic about what kind of group you join. When you want to make friends, the best group for you to join has the following characteristics:

>> It's based on one of your interests or hobbies.

>> It's conducive to socializing.

>> It meets frequently.

>> It's relatively near your home.

According to a 2017 Pew Research Center survey, 57 percent of Americans participate actively in a group. Of those surveyed, 11 percent are active in four or more groups!

Joining a group is a helpful friend-making strategy for several reasons:

>> It gives you and the other members something to talk about (because you have a common interest).

>> It helps you build community and a sense of belonging.

>> It provides a less awkward way to get to know people when you're all engaged in a common activity.

>> It guarantees dedicated weekly (or monthly) time for socializing with members of the group.

For example, if you love knitting and join a knitting group, you'll automatically have things to talk about with your fellow group members, so that makes getting to know people much easier. Also, many people find that making casual small talk is easier when you're engaged in an activity (it makes things less awkward) versus standing around at a cocktail party where there's not much else to do. So, if you and your group mates are happily knitting away, it takes the pressure off to be constantly making small talk and getting to know people can feel more organic and natural.

Joining a group is also helpful because it ensures that you'll have at least one thing in common with the group participants: You all share a mutual interest in the group's topic, whether it's crafting or pickleball.

And having something in common will give you plenty of fodder for small talk, which makes your friend-making mission easier!

In any city, there are hundreds of groups you could potentially join, which can feel overwhelming. Sometimes it's hard to narrow things down and know which groups are the right fit. Look for a group that interests you, is social in nature, meets frequently, and is near your home. If your group meets these characteristics, you're golden.

REMEMBER

It's also helpful to join a group to explore or deepen a new hobby or interest *regardless* of whether you make friends. Don't join a group assuming that you'll definitely make a new friend there. If you join a group that's interesting to you, and you don't end up making a new friend, at least you'll have enjoyed your experience in the group and it will have felt like a good use of your time.

Knowing what to look for in a group

When you're looking for a group to join, you'll find all kinds of options, but not every group will set you up to make friends. You need to find the right group for you — one based on your interests, one that meets regularly, and one where socializing is the focus.

Looking for groups that mesh with your interests

The first step in finding a group to join is to take stock of your hobbies and interests. Whatever your hobby or interest is, there's almost guaranteed to be a group out there of fellow enthusiasts.

COUNTRY MOUSE: WHAT TO DO IF YOU LIVE IN A SMALL TOWN OR RURAL AREA

If you live in a small town or a rural area without a whole lot of options, look for any groups offered by your local library, community center, or religious congregation that may be the right fit. If you're sporty, you could also find a local adults' sports team to join or see if you can coach youth sports. Alternatively, you can look into online groups that may fit your needs better, or you may be willing to drive to a neighboring town to join a group that's of interest.

Don't forget that you can always start your own social group on any topic that interests you, which may be a perfect option if you have a specific interest. You can start your own group easily through Meetup (www.meetup.com) or Facebook groups (www.facebook.com).

EXPLORE

Jot down a quick list of your top five hobbies and interests. Think about which of these may lend themselves to a group. If you already have a hobby that you love, such as reading, think about how you can make it more social. If you love to read, you can join a book club, which turns reading into a social hobby! If bird-watching is your jam, find a bird-watching group to join, so you can join other birders every weekend to chat about feathered friends.

The best place to find groups that match your interests is on Meetup or through Facebook groups. Meetup and Facebook are both free to join. Just create an account and search for new groups, join groups, RSVP for events, and even send messages to fellow participants in your new groups.

If you have no interests or hobbies, don't stress! Now is a great time to develop some and experiment. If you're having trouble thinking of ideas, do an online search to find articles and lists of different hobbies to browse through. Chances are, at least one hobby on the list will resonate with you. Or ask family and friends about their hobbies — you may find that your uncle's interest in woodworking sounds interesting, so you can ask him for more information on how to get started.

When you have a few hobbies in mind, choose the one that seems most appealing and the most social and then look for a group around it that you can join.

Zeroing in on groups that meet regularly

The best kind of group you can join to make friends is one that meets regularly. Meeting monthly is good, meeting twice a month is even better, and meeting weekly is the holy grail!

Meeting more frequently is better is because of the frequency concept discussed earlier in this chapter: The more often you see people, the more likely you'll become friends. There is actually a scientific reason for this, and it's called the *mere exposure effect*. This concept was developed by a scholar named Robert Zajonc, who did a variety of experiments in the 1960s involving language to show that the more often we come into contact with something that's familiar, the more we start to like it and the more we prefer it. In other words, if you attend a group and keep seeing the same person every week, just by repeatedly seeing that person over and over, you start to like them, because they become more familiar to you.

What kinds of groups tend to meet regularly? Exercise groups (like a weekly yoga or water aerobics class), groups through religious congregations, language classes, or volunteer activities. Groups that meet less often tend to be book clubs (which usually meet monthly), committees for various things that meet as needed or quarterly (like a school's parent–teacher association [PTA] or your neighborhood homeowners association [HOA]), and cooking clubs tend to also meet monthly or less often.

Prioritizing groups where socializing takes center stage

The best type of group to join to make new friends is one where most of the focus is on socializing. That way, there will be plenty of time to chat with your fellow participants. Examples include ballroom dancing, knitting, crocheting, walking, running, a sports league, or a book club. A yoga class would be an example where there is less opportunity to socialize (because there's no talking, other than before and after the class).

Or you can take whatever hobby/interest you already have and figure out how to add a social dimension. Here's another way to think about it: Writing is a great hobby, but by itself it isn't social and it's difficult to make friends through it. However, if you join a writing or critique group, that adds the social dimension to your hobby, because you're getting together with fellow writers for camaraderie, feedback, and conversation.

An example of a group that wouldn't be considered as social and, therefore, wouldn't be a good choice for making new friends would be volunteering on a committee that meets primarily to conduct business and where there is little to no opportunity to socialize.

REMEMBER

When you're looking for new groups to join, evaluate their opportunities to socialize.

You may not realize right away whether a group is going to be a good social outlet. If you can, go to a few meetings to evaluate the group while you're deciding whether to commit.

Committing to the group for three sessions

You've found a promising group to join. Yay! Now you need to go to your first meeting or event. Try to commit to the group for three meetings before you decide whether it's for you. The reason behind this completely unscientific number is that going to just one session isn't enough to make an effective judgment about the group. If you bail after the first meeting, you're not giving the group enough of a chance to show you what it's all about and you may end up missing out. But if you attend for three sessions, you'll have a good grasp of the overall vibe of the group and know if it's a good fit. Three meetings is a good balance between giving it a fair chance and committing too much time and energy when it's not the right match. So, remember the rule of three!

Seeing who you connect with

When you join a new group, think of it as an opportunity to chat with people and see who you connect with. Your goal for the first few meetings shouldn't be about making friends (that would be too much, too soon). Instead, your goal should be to talk with as many people as possible, get to know them, and learn about them. Even if you don't find anyone you connect with, it's not time wasted — look at it as good practice making small talk and putting yourself out there.

When you get to your first group meeting, grab a nametag (if there are any) and start smiling at people. When you feel ready, go up to someone who seems nice and approachable and start making small talk (see Chapter 7 for more on making small talk). If you're struggling with what to say, you can start out with something simple and friendly like: "Hi, I'm new here! This is my first meeting of the badminton club. Have you been in this group long?" That should get the conversation off to a good start. From there you can ask the person about how long they've been interested in badminton, if they've joined other clubs, and how often they play.

TIP

Here are some tips to keep in mind:

>> Making small talk with new people can feel awkward at first, but with practice, you'll get better at it and it'll feel more natural. Practice makes perfect!

>> Keep your expectations low, so you don't get disappointed. If you join a group expecting to make a best friend right away, you're bound to be disappointed. Keeping expectations low leaves room for you to be pleasantly surprised if you do end up making a connection.

>> When you find someone you connect with, decide if you would like to exchange contact information. Depending on the type of group, you could hand them your business card or give them your phone number, email, or Instagram *handle* (username). Many people these days exchange social media handles instead of phone numbers.

If you're tech-minded, there's even a handy phone app called Blinq (`https://blinq.me`) that acts as a digital business card. The other person scans your QR code, and your contact information is automatically downloaded to their contacts, which makes keeping in touch quick and easy.

Identifying the Top Places to Find Like-Minded Friends

You can explore many new places to try to make new friends. Some of the opportunities listed in this section are groups; others are places that you can go to meet new people. Read through these ideas and make a note of one or two you're interested in trying in the next few weeks.

Meetup groups and Facebook social groups

One of the best ways to meet new people is to join a social group. Social groups are everywhere, on every topic imaginable. Meetup is a well-known site where anyone can create a social group that others can join, or find events and activities to go to. There are tons of groups on Meetup in every city and state (as well as internationally), ranging from puppy-playdate groups to board-game groups to running groups and everything in between. You can also find groups by age range and life stage (like brunch groups for people in their forties and fifties, new moms groups, or trivia nights for twentysomethings).

Joining Meetup is easy and free. You just create an account, enter your geographic location, and start adding groups that interest you. The site will then show you groups that are near you and meet your criteria. After you explore a group online and see if you're interested, you can RSVP to an upcoming event. To join, just click the RSVP button and you'll be automatically added, and the event listing will make it clear where to meet and when, as well as telling you who else signed up. Meetup makes it easy to see your upcoming social calendar with all your group events on it as well. Some groups charge a nominal fee to offset the organizer's costs in running the group, but many groups are free to join.

There are other ways to join social groups besides Meetup. Facebook also offers free social and networking groups. To join them, you'll need a Facebook account. After you log in, type some words in the Search box to describe what you're looking for (such as "San Francisco women's groups") and then browse the groups that come up in the search results. You can see the public groups right away, but many groups' privacy settings are set to private, so you'll need to apply to join them (which usually just consists of answering a few questions). After you're in the group, feel free to make a post to introduce yourself and start connecting with people online before your first in-person event. You can also RSVP to events within these groups or ask questions within the group.

One great thing about both Meetup and Facebook social groups is you can get to know participants online and chat with them through direct messages before or after meeting up in person for your first event.

Senior centers

Senior centers are places where older adults (usually 60+) can meet other seniors, participate in activities, listen to speakers, take trips, and more. Most communities have a senior center, which may be independent, county-run, or attached to a local community center. Senior centers offer lifelong classes, enrichment activities, speakers, and trips, and many include lunch. Senior centers usually charge a nominal fee for participation in daily activities. You can go to one to try it out for the day and see what you think. Most senior centers allow participants to pay by the day and attend as they want. Many senior centers post their activity calendars online, which you can check out to get a sense of what a typical day would be like. These centers are perfect for older adults who are looking for community and intellectual stimulation.

EXAMPLE

Steven recently moved to be near his daughter and her family. He didn't know anyone in his new area and felt quite lonely. He decided to try out his local senior center to see if he could meet some other retirees. Steven decided to try a whole day at the senior center to see what he thought. He ended up taking some interesting classes, hearing a good speaker, and having lunch the day he attended. At lunch, he met another man who was also new to the area and didn't know anyone, and the two became friends.

Gyms and exercise classes

Joining a gym or going to a weekly exercise class is another good way to participate in a healthy activity and meet new people. There are many types of gyms to choose from in all price ranges, from town or county-run rec centers to private gyms like Planet Fitness (www.planetfitness.com) or Gold's Gym (www.goldsgym.com). Additionally, there are smaller boutique gyms and fitness studios for activities such as weight training, dancing, biking, rock climbing, yoga, Pilates, and barre. Many boutique gyms for fitness enthusiasts cultivate a community feel with social activities for members.

TIP

When you go to a gym at the same time every day or take the same class every week, you'll likely see the same people over and over and have the opportunity to get to know them. Try making small talk with another gym-goer while waiting in line for a machine or before a fitness class starts.

New parents groups

Having a baby is a great time to make new friends, because new parents tend to want to befriend other new parents who are in their same life stage to go through their parenting journeys together. There are many types of new parents groups to join, through Meetup, Facebook groups, your hospital, your ob-gyn's office, as well as local community center groups.

If you can't find any suitable groups, you can also post on your local Facebook or Nextdoor (https://nextdoor.com) community site to inquire about recommendations for any new parents groups for your child's age. One benefit to these types of groups is that new parents groups usually meet quite often (weekly or even several times a week), so you have many opportunities to get to know other people and make new friends. I started and ran a local Meetup group for new moms that grew to more than 400 members and made many new friends through the group. At the time, I planned three or four events per week, so there was ample opportunity to meet new people.

REMEMBER

Many new parents value the sense of community and support system that they find in new parents groups, because being a new parent can be overwhelming and lonely. Having people you get together with regularly can provide a much-needed sense of support.

Newcomers' groups

One effective way to make new friends if you're a newcomer to an area is to join a newcomers' group, which is a group specifically meant to help people who are new in town make new friends and connections. You can be new in town (or new in spirit — there are usually no rules about just how new you have to be). People who are new in town are usually eager to make new friends, because they don't know anyone. In fact, it's a good friend-making strategy in general to focus your friendship-making efforts on people who are new to your area and don't know many people yet. There is more of a chance that they'll be open to new friendships as opposed to someone who grew up in your area and has deep roots there.

You can find newcomers' groups on Meetup, on Facebook groups, or by doing an internet search.

Religious congregations

Religious congregations are another good place to make new friends. According to a 2017 Pew Research Center survey, 19 percent of Americans are members of a church or other religious group. You already have something in common with the other members in terms of your shared religion, so making connections should be easier. If you join a congregation, there are usually a lot of events and activities to choose from. You can go to weekly services, join a special interest group, serve on a committee, or volunteer.

For example, you could join a small group fellowship community for weekly Bible study and get to know the other members. Or you could join the synagogue's sisterhood or brotherhood or teach at the religious school. Congregations often have groups for different ages and stages, from new parents to older adults, so there's usually something for everyone.

You can do an online search for congregations in your area, or you can ask neighbors or post on Nextdoor or community Facebook groups for recommendations.

Advocacy groups

There are many groups you can join if you're passionate about a particular cause, whether it's a nonprofit animal rescue group, an environmental advocacy group, or a political advocacy group. These groups offer the opportunity to work alongside other dedicated volunteers who share your commitment for a particular cause, so you have something in common already. Advocacy groups have meetings, events, and volunteer opportunities where you can meet others and form connections. To find them, heat to VolunteerMatch (www.volunteermatch.org) or Idealist (www.idealist.org).

Online social groups or discussion forums

If meeting people in-person is not your preference right now, online groups are a great alternative. Online friends can be great friends, and you can keep those friendships online or meet up in real life at some point (see Chapter 11 for an in-depth discussion of turning online friends into real friends). Online groups like Nextdoor, Facebook social groups, Instagram (www.instagram.com), Discord (https://discord.com), or topic-specific discussion forums are good ways to meet new people online. You can read and respond to others' posts that interest you or create your own posts to make new connections. Some people who struggle with friendships feel more comfortable making friends online first. This can be a great way to build your self-confidence and grow your community. Making online friends may also be especially useful if you live in a rural area and don't have access to as many in-person group options.

REMEMBER

You can write your own "friend ad" in online groups and list what you're looking for in someone you'd like to meet. Your friend ad can be a few sentences or a paragraph or two describing you, your age, your interests, and the type of person you'd like to meet. Most likely, you'll get some enthusiastic responses from other people feeling the same way who would also like to connect. People can send you a private message to connect with you, and you can chat online one-on-one with them before deciding to give them your contact information or meet up in person. When you do meet up with a stranger from the internet, remember to meet at a public place like a restaurant or coffee shop.

In-person or online adult learning

Who says that adults can't go back to school? Taking an adult enrichment class is an excellent way to meet new people and make new friends. You can take in-person classes through your local parks and rec department, adult education center, community college, or university that offers continuing education classes. Many colleges and universities offer adult learning classes specifically for older adults, which is a great way to meet others in your same life stage. You can even find in-person classes at art studios, martial arts studios, and cooking schools. Look for classes that aren't a one-time event in order to have the best chance at making friends. Many adult ed classes meet weekly for six to ten weeks.

You can even take online classes for fun and enrichment, though it's harder to make friends this way, unless the online class has group office hours where you can chat and hang out with other participants. Many online classes also offer a private Facebook group for participants where they can meet other participants.

Neighborhoods

Your neighborhood is one of the best places to make new friends, because of the proximity effect (see "Proximity: Keeping your friends close," earlier in this chapter). Neighborhoods are such fertile ground for friendships because you see your neighbors regularly, during casual encounters like walking your dog, strolling around the neighborhood, taking out the trash, or getting the mail. Over time, you start to get to know your neighbors, and friendships can blossom.

TIP

If you feel that you don't know anyone in your neighborhood, it can help to be proactive and reach out to your neighbors. Consider inviting a neighbor for coffee or tea or hosting them for a backyard barbecue. At the holidays, think about taking your neighbor a plate of cookies or sending a holiday card. There are many ways to reach out and be neighborly, and your efforts are sure to be appreciated and maybe reciprocated.

If you find it difficult to meet neighbors organically, consider joining your neighborhood HOA or social committee, if there is one, or find another way to get involved in your neighborhood. You could organize a block party, organize a community food drive for a local nonprofit, or even set up a lemonade stand with your child and chat with passersby.

Having a dog really helps your socialization efforts, because everyone likes to stop and meet an adorable dog. If you have kids, the neighborhood bus stop can be a great way to meet neighbors. If your neighborhood has communal amenities, like a playground, pool, tennis courts, or clubhouse, these are also great places to meet your neighbors and build community.

Book clubs

Book clubs are a fantastic way to make new friends, because they provide both a structured activity (talking about the book) and the opportunity to socialize, and you already have one thing in common with the other participants: a love of reading. Book clubs generally meet monthly, either at one of the members' homes or at a coffee shop or restaurant, and discuss the book of the month. Most book clubs have a theme, such as historical fiction, romance novels, or nonfiction books. You can find them on Meetup, on Bookclubs (https://bookclubs.com), through your local library, on Facebook, and by asking for recommendations online and from neighbors.

EXAMPLE

Carmen loved to read, but she couldn't find a book club in her area that met when she was free. She ended up finding a great book club at her local library that met monthly. The library appealed to Carmen because she preferred meeting at a central location that was convenient for her. Not only did she love the book discussions, but she enjoyed the camaraderie of meeting people who lived close by for monthly book chats.

Sports leagues

Adult sports leagues are another good way to make new friends. These leagues often meet weekly, which is great for seeing the same people over and over and getting to know your fellow teammates. Also, having something fun and active to do while socializing makes for an easier time getting to know people. Plus, many teams go out for drinks after the game, which is a good opportunity to socialize. You can find adult sports leagues at your local rec or community center, or through specific sports venues such as ice-skating rinks.

Alumni groups

Alumni groups (either from high school, college, or graduate school) are an excellent way to meet new people in your area who you have something in common with. Many alumni groups host periodic events throughout the year like trivia nights, lectures, or reunions for all alums from the school, and it can be nice to reconnect with classmates from long ago.

If you don't know of any alumni groups in your area, contact the alumni department of your alma mater and find out if there are any local alumni groups you can join. If not, consider starting one.

Professional networking organizations

Professional networking organizations, such as women-in-business organizations or local chambers of commerce, are great ways to network with others in your specific field or other small business owners. These groups often offer networking breakfasts before work, monthly networking events with a speaker, or other mix-and-mingle events where you can socialize and network with others in your profession. To find them, research your field's national association to find local chapters, or do an online search for local networking and professional organizations in your field.

EXAMPLE

Yvonne was having difficulty meeting other women who shared her professional and personal interests. She joined a networking group for women business owners and started attending their monthly lunch speaker series. Soon Yvonne was networking with other attendees in the group and ended up making a new friend who was also a female business owner.

Friendship apps

Another great way to make new friends is through friendship apps like Bumble BFF (https://bumble.com), Friender (https://frienderapp.com), Hey! VINA (www.heyvina.com), or Peanut (www.peanut-app.io). These are good ways to make new friends because you know that everyone on the app is actually looking to make a new friend, which can be helpful. Sign up, create a profile, and then start looking for friend matches.

A drawback of trying to make friends online is that people can be enthusiastic to chat with you at first but then flake out when it's time to meet up in real life. So, keep your expectations low when trying these, and you may be pleasantly surprised!

Volunteer activities

Volunteering is one of the best ways to make new friends and build a sense of community at the same time, all while giving back. Volunteering also lets you build new skills or improve your résumé, so there are a lot of additional benefits. Volunteering can even open the door to an entirely new career. You may make a friend who is also volunteering on your shift, or you may get to know some of the regular employees when you go to an organization to volunteer.

It's easy to get started — most organizations are eager for volunteers and don't have many requirements to sign up. To find local volunteer opportunities, look at VolunteerMatch, Idealist, or your local county or town website to find volunteer opportunities. You may have to submit an application and a few references to be considered, but it's usually a quick turnaround between submitting your application and being able to start volunteering.

Starting Your Own Social Group

If you don't find a group that fits your interests or your schedule is super busy and you can't find any groups that meet when you're free, consider starting your own social group. Starting your own group has several benefits:

>> You get to create the exact group you wish you could find and join.

>> You get to schedule the meetings when it fits your schedule.

>> You gain valuable organizational skills when you plan and host events.

Starting a group may sound intimidating at first, but it's actually quite easy. There are just a few simple steps involved. You can start a group easily on Meetup (though there is a fee to start groups as the organizer) or start a group for free through Facebook groups. Just click the button to start your own group, and the site will walk you through the process.

Over the past 20 years, I've started multiple social groups, mainly on Meetup and through Facebook groups. Here are a few of the groups that I've started and managed over the years:

>> A women's walking group

>> A drawing group

>> A women's brunch group

>> A baby and toddler playgroup

>> A working moms coffee group

>> A women's book club

>> A moms'-night-out group

I hope this list will help inspire some ideas for starting your own group! You can start any group that you want, and after it's up and running, you'll probably be surprised by how much interest there is in your group.

Deciding what type of group to start

Consider what your interests are and which of them would lend themselves to a social-type group. Or, consider the types of people you'd like to meet. Do you want to meet art enthusiasts or car lovers? If so, consider starting a group that people with those interests would want to join. For example, if you love knitting, consider starting a knitting circle. If you love to fish, consider starting a weekend fishing get-together at your local pond or lake. Almost any interest can lend itself to a group format.

Also, think about which of your interests may have fewer groups available — they may draw more interest because they're unique. For example, there are lots of book clubs around, so you may have a harder time getting your book club noticed, but there are probably fewer origami groups.

Knowing how to start your own group

When you determine the topic or theme of your group (such as a forties and fifties women's running group, men's bowling group, or holiday crafting group), decide whether Meetup, Facebook, or another online provider is the best place to host your group and get the word out about it. Then create a name for your group, follow the online prompts to set up your group, and start planning your first event. The website that hosts your group will get the word out about your group, but you can also advertise it by posting information about the group on social media.

Hosting events to find friends

When your group is up and running, it's time to plan some events. Events are the most important part of your group because that's where you're going to meet people and make friends. Plan events for your group that you think would interest others.

TIP

Make sure when planning your events that you choose days and times that would work for your group participants. For example, if you think most of your group participants work full-time, then planning events in the evenings or on the weekends would be best. If your group participants are stay-at-home parents, daytime events would be ideal. Think about your typical group member and what would be most convenient for them. If you're not sure, you can poll your members to get ideas.

When you have a good idea for an event, you can enter your event's specifications into the event-planning tool. Then you can invite everyone in the group to your event and wait for the RSVPs to roll in. When the event rolls around, try to show up a few minutes early to find a good spot or grab a table, especially if your venue is crowded. Make sure to have a sign so people can find you.

One benefit of starting your own group is that you can fill your social calendar with your group's events, because they'll all work with your schedule. This is especially helpful if you don't have friends to do things with but really want to socialize.

EXAMPLE

Amber had just moved to a new city and didn't know anyone. She felt lonely and was finding it hard to make friends. Weekends were especially hard for her, and she often found herself sitting home alone. She got the idea to start a dinner club for women 40+ and scheduled all her events on Friday and Saturday nights. After scheduling a dinner every weekend, Amber was thrilled to finally have a full social calendar.

TIP

The following tips should help make your new group a success:

» **When you're planning your first events, think casual.** People tend to feel more comfortable at short, casual events like coffee or a walk, versus long, formal events like dinner on a Saturday night (unless your group is a dinner club).

» **Bring a list of icebreakers to your events.** Icebreakers help people feel more comfortable. After you do general introductions, fun icebreakers include going around the table and sharing a fun fact about yourselves, sharing your favorite places in your city or town, and playing two truths and a lie.

» **If you're meeting a group of strangers, it helps to have a sign.** You can scribble a sign on a piece of paper or print one out, but some sort of signage is helpful so your group members can find you more easily.

WARNING

People can be flaky. Don't take it personally if you get ten RSVPs to your event and only two people show up. That's par for the course of being a group organizer. People don't necessarily feel a commitment to the event, especially if it's their first one and they don't know anyone yet. So, if they don't feel like going, they just don't show up and often don't bother to change their RSVP. Just carry on and keep on planning events. As people start to meet each other and as your group gains momentum, people will usually become more reliable and no-show less often.

You can even host an event within a group if you don't want to start your own actual group. For example, if you're a member of a local community group, you can plan a one-time event for members of that group. If you're a member of a local women's community group on Facebook, consider organizing a craft night, game night, or coffee date for all the members of that group. That way, if you want to see what it's like to host an event, but you don't want to commit to the responsibility of running an entire group, you can plan an event once and see how it goes.

Chapter **6**

Approaching New People

I f you want to make new friends, you have to routinely go up to people you don't
know and make small talk. Some people find it nerve-racking to approach total
strangers and try to make conversation in the hopes of forging a connection.
Many people worry about coming across as awkward, saying the wrong things, or
being judged. Most of all, they fear rejection.

Although approaching new people is a necessary part of the friend-making process, it doesn't have to be scary and stressful. This chapter gives you everything
you need to know to approach new people and have it be a positive experience. In
no time, you'll be a pro at figuring out who to approach and what to say, and you'll
be initiating interactions with confidence and enthusiasm.

This chapter covers how to determine the most receptive people to approach,
deciding whether someone is open to new friendships, and the cautionary signs to
heed that indicate someone isn't interested in being approached. It also covers
where you can approach new people (and where not to), the specific steps to take
when you approach someone new, and how to ensure that your interaction goes
smoothly. You'll also discover how to avoid any miscommunication and make it
clear you're looking for platonic friendship.

Leaving Your Comfort Zone

For many people, approaching someone new involves leaving their comfort zone. It can be scary and nerve-wracking to put yourself out there and take a social risk. Risking rejection is stressful and makes many people, especially introverts, uncomfortable. But if you don't put yourself out there, nothing much will change for you. It can be worth going out of your comfort zone and taking that risk.

Building up your courage

Building up your courage is one of the main strategies that helps you take a social risk and leave your comfort zone. You can do this by not avoiding the things that seem stressful or hard (which actually increases anxiety), but instead taking small steps to build up your self-confidence. When those small steps go well, you'll have the courage to keep going.

For example, if it feels too overwhelming and stressful to approach a stranger and introduce yourself, instead, as a baby step, consider smiling at the person from a distance. Then, if that goes well, and if you're feeling braver, you could try making good eye contact with them while smiling. If that step goes well, you could practice visualizing going up to them and saying hi. Then you could work your way up to introducing yourself to a stranger by gradually increasing the complexity level of each step until you're able to confidently approach them.

Risking rejection

Many people fear rejection, but if you put yourself out there, you'll inevitably be rejected at least sometimes. Not everyone will like you, just like you won't like everyone you meet. Dealing with rejection is tough, but it's a necessary part of the friend-making process. You have to learn to be okay with the possibility of rejection — otherwise, you'll never reap the reward of making new friends.

TIP

Here are several strategies for dealing with rejection:

>> **Remember that rejection is a part of life, and not necessarily personal.**

>> **Develop a thicker skin.** Try not to let the rejection get to you. You can do this by putting things in perspective — everyone gets rejected, and friendship is a numbers game. But it's important to keep trying — eventually if you keep meeting new people and putting yourself out there, you will succeed!

>> **Use positive self-talk to remind yourself of what a great person you are, and that rejection doesn't define you or mean you'll never make a friend.**

>> **Develop resilience.** Rejection is painful, but is there another way to look at it? If you can reframe the rejection as a learning experience instead, you can apply what you learned from the experience to improve your chances of making a new friend next time. This will allow you to bounce back from rejection more quickly instead of stewing in the injustice of it.

EXPLORE

Think about a time when you put yourself out there and were rejected. How did you handle the rejection? Was the outcome as bad as you thought it would be? Were you able to take what you learned and apply it to other social situations?

Understanding the importance of positive self-talk

Using positive self-talk is helpful when venturing out of your comfort zone. It gives you a pep talk before doing something hard. Telling yourself that you're doing something good for your social life by approaching new people, and that they're going to like you and you'll eventually make a friend will be more helpful than negative self-talk, such as "I shouldn't bother talking to them because they're not going to like me."

TIP

What we say to ourselves in our inner monologue is extremely important. Here are some examples of positive self-talk that you can say to yourself to get pumped up for approaching new people:

>> "I have a lot to offer a new friend."

>> "I'm making the first move so I can talk to the people I want to."

>> "People have liked me in the past, and they'll like me now."

>> "I haven't found my people yet, but I will."

Deciding Who to Approach in New Settings

The first step in meeting new people is to approach them. This seems obvious, but you'd be surprised how many people don't take this step and wonder why they can't make friends. Many people take a passive approach to friend-making: They wait for others to approach them and shy away from making the first move.

If you wait for others to approach you, you may be waiting a long time — and you may never be approached. You'll be left wondering why no one was friendly to you at the party or gathering you attended. Instead, be that friendly person who puts themselves out there. Gather up your courage and make the first move! At the very least, you'll make someone's day a lot brighter, even if you don't end up making a new friend.

Even though it sounds easy, it takes a lot of courage to put yourself out there and approach someone you don't know. Many people feel self-conscious and awkward, which makes it difficult for them to approach someone new. They worry about being judged, ignored, or rejected, so they don't go up to anyone at all. Instead, they hang out alone or stick to the one person they know at group events or parties, and they miss out on many wonderful friend-making and networking opportunities. Don't be that person — work up the courage to walk up to someone and make some small talk. Ask yourself: What's the worst that can happen? If the other person doesn't want to talk to me or rejects me, can I handle that? Most likely, you can.

Here are some of the reasons why people are hesitant to approach others:

>> They are shy or feel socially awkward.

>> They struggle with small talk and making conversation and don't know what to say.

>> They fear being rejected or judged.

>> They have low self-confidence and assume the other person won't want to talk to them.

All of these are valid reasons why people are hesitant to approach others, but they're all conquerable with some practice, a social skills refresh, and a self-confidence boost.

TIP

After reading this chapter, there are two other chapters that will help you with the essential skills you need in approaching new people. Check out Chapter 7 to learn more about making small talk with new people and Chapter 8 for more on handling shyness and social anxiety.

Looking for newcomers

When you're at a social group, in a class, or even in your own neighborhood, one of the best ways to make new friends is to look for other newcomers (even if *you're* not new to your area). Newcomers are among the best people to befriend because they're new to the area and often looking to make new friends. Because they don't know anyone, as compared to people who have lived there a long time and may already have plenty of friends, they're usually eager to meet new people and go out and do things.

If you're making small talk with someone and you find out they're new to your area, jump on that opportunity! Let them know that you'd love to meet up for coffee or a drink sometime, and that you're happy to provide any recommendations or resources about the area they need. Newcomers are always interested in recommendations for doctors, dentists, hairstylists, and good restaurants near them. You could even offer to be their tour guide!

Finding friendly people

Look for people who appear friendly. Those who are smiling, laughing, or talking to others are your best bets. They're the ones who will probably be the most open to chatting and getting to know you and who won't make you feel intimidated.

Finding others who are similar to you

When you're approaching new people, for the best chance of making a new friend, look for people who have similarities to you. Many research studies have shown that people prefer to make friends with, and are most drawn to, people who are most like themselves.

A great way to find others who are similar is to join a social group, a hobby/interest group, or a religious congregation. That way, you'll find others with similar interests and you'll always have the topic of the group to talk about, whether it's knitting, yoga, running, or having religious views in common.

Meeting others in a similar life stage

Finding others in a similar life stage is one of the best ways to meet new people. Others who are in the same life stage may be able to connect with you better, because you'll have plenty to talk about and you're sharing the same experiences. For example, if you're newly retired, finding others who are also newly retired will give you a lot of things to connect over, and if you're a new parent, finding other new parents will be a great way to bond over the chaos of having young children. So, look for others in a similar life stage for an increased chance of making a connection.

Connecting with others who seem lonely

Trying to find other people who seem lonely can be another way to find new people to approach. At an event or gathering, look for people who are standing off by themselves and aren't talking to anyone or who seem a bit lonely. Go up to them and start a conversation. They'll probably be relieved and grateful that you approached them first, and you may make a new friend this way!

EXPLORE

Think about the last time you were at a social event and approached someone new. How did you decide who to approach? What characteristics or qualities did you look for? How did the interaction go?

Deciding If Someone Is Open to Meeting New People

Before you approach someone new with the goal of interacting, increase your chances by doing a quick read of their body language and social cues to see if they seem open to new friendships. There are a few subtle signs that can indicate that someone is open to making friends.

Demonstrating positive body language

Look for people who have positive body language — they're more likely to be open to new friendships. According to *Body Language For Dummies* by Elizabeth Kuhnke (John Wiley & Sons), positive body language is considered to be a more open stance and includes having their arms at their sides, leaning toward you, having an open torso, looking forward, making good eye contact, and pointing their feet toward you. Someone with open body language like this is communicating that they're open to new opportunities and new connections.

Conversely, someone with negative body language is communicating that they're not open to new connections. According to *Body Language For Dummies*, closed body language is more inward facing and people appear more closed off, which can be off-putting. Closed body language involves having crossed arms, slouching or hunching, pointing their feet away from you, and looking down at the ground. If you see someone with negative body language, they're probably not the best person to approach. Instead, find someone who has more positive body language, which will give you a better chance of having a successful interaction.

Having an approachable demeanor

Another good way to find people to approach is to look for those with an approachable demeanor. Those with an approachable demeanor may be smiling, having a friendly look on their face, and be chatting with others. Approach these people because they'll make you feel more comfortable and at ease than someone who is frowning or looks angry or bored.

TIP

Keep an eye out for eye contact. If someone holds your gaze and has good eye contact, they're likely approachable. If they catch your gaze, look away, and avoid eye contact, they most likely don't want to be approached.

Hanging out solo

Approaching someone who's hanging out by themselves is easier than walking up to a group of people who are talking and laughing. People in a group can be more intimidating to approach than someone who's solo. Look for someone who's standing alone near a buffet table or on the outskirts of the action but whose positive body language is sending off signals that they're approachable.

If you want to approach someone in a group, walk up to the group with a smile, and wait for an opening to introduce yourself. While you wait for the opening, try to listen to what they're talking about so that you can interject a comment about it. When there's a pause, make a lighthearted comment to ingratiate yourself with them and be invited into the conversation.

Don't try to switch topics when you've just entered a group — wait until the conversation flows more naturally. You don't want to dominate the conversation of a group you've just joined.

Having a friendly attitude

Look for people with a friendly, interested attitude to keep talking with. A friendly attitude can include being positive, being a good conversationalist, and showing interest in others. Someone with a friendly attitude may ask you questions, show interest by asking follow-up questions, and have an overall demeanor of friendliness versus boredom or annoyance. They're enthusiastic about talking with you and are making it clear they want to get to know you, as opposed to looking all around the room for the next person to talk to.

Knowing when someone doesn't want to be approached

Sometimes people are in a bad mood, are under the weather, or just don't feel like talking. There are certain key signs that someone doesn't want to be approached:

- >> They have earbuds in or headphones on.
- >> They're immersed in a book.
- >> They're talking on the phone.
- >> They see you approaching and they move away or turn away from you.
- >> They look upset, are crying, or look like they're having a hard time.
- >> They're consoling a crying child.

EXPLORE

If you're not in the greatest mood and you don't want to be approached while out somewhere, how do you signal this? Think about the signals you put out that you want to be left alone. Those are the same signals other people give off, too.

Exploring the Best Ways to Approach People

You've decided to take the initiative and approach someone new. But how exactly do you do that? Follow these steps to approach someone with confidence and enthusiasm:

1. **Scan the room and decide who you're going to approach.**

   Look for someone who seems friendly and approachable (see "Deciding Who to Approach in New Settings," earlier in this chapter).

   Before approaching, remember to read their body language (see "Demonstrating positive body language," earlier in this chapter). Do they seem like they would welcome your approach or does their body language indicate they want to be left alone?

2. **Give yourself a pep talk to encourage yourself to make the approach.**

   Remind yourself that you're ready to meet new people and have a lot to offer a new friend, but it's not the end of the world if they don't want to connect with you.

3. **Demonstrate positive body language (arms at your sides, relaxed posture, face the person, feet toward them) and smile!**

4. **Introduce yourself and make small talk.**

   Be friendly and enthusiastic. If you're at a loss for what to say, make a comment or ask a question about the setting you're both in — for example, "Is this your first time at this book group?" or "How do you know the host?" Or make a comment about the weather.

REMEMBER

Respect the other person's personal space, and stand a comfortable distance away from them (usually about 2 or 3 feet for Americans — this distance varies in different cultures). Standing too close to someone you don't know makes people uncomfortable. If you notice them stepping backward to create more distance between the two of you, that means they're uncomfortable, so don't step closer to them to decrease the distance — they'll only keep stepping back and start to feel annoyed. Make sure not to touch them either — a friendly touch or a hug is reserved for closer friends and family.

5. **Keep a close eye out for any signs that the other person wants to end the conversation, is getting bored, or feels uncomfortable.**

   These can include not making eye contact, looking around the room, having short answers and not elaborating, seeming bored, or pointing their feet away from you. Nothing good comes from trying to prolong an interaction that the other person's just not into. If you notice these signs, wrap up the conversation quickly, let them know you enjoyed meeting them, and find someone else to talk to or take a breather and get something to eat or drink.

6. **If your interaction went smoothly, decide if you're going to ask for their contact information or just end with a friendly closing like, "It was great chatting with you! Have a great rest of your day!" or "Hope to see you again soon!"**

7. **If your interaction went well, give yourself a pat on the back!**

   If it didn't go well, use this as a learning experience to figure out what to do differently next time. Reframe any negative self-talk about the interaction not going well into positive self-talk.

Identifying the benefits of approaching first

Most people wish that others would approach them more often. It can be a drag to feel like you're always the one reaching out and taking the initiative. Hopefully in time, more people will approach you. In the meantime, however, if you want to make new friends, you need to seize the day and reach out to others first.

TIP

There is actually huge benefit in being the one to approach others first. You get to choose who you want to talk to, which gives you more control in the situation than being approached by someone else, who may not be your cup of tea. Having more control over social situations is a big benefit of reaching out first.

Understanding where you can approach new people

There are certain places where it's customary and common to expect that people will approach you to socialize and other places where it's not. Places where people may expect others to come up to them include:

>> Group events

>> Parties

>> Social events

>> Religious congregation events

>> Standing in line at different places

>> The gym, pool, or an exercise class

>> Elevators

>> Kids' activities and sports

>> Volunteer opportunities

>> Bars

>> Dog walks

EXPLORE

Given your lifestyle and interests, do some self-reflection about the best places to approach new people. Then commit to approaching one new person the next time you're there.

Identifying places where you shouldn't try to meet new people

Think about the last time you were at a doctor's office. It's probably the last place you'd expect someone to come up to you to try to make a new friend. You'd likely be annoyed and confused, and you'd find the gesture off-putting.

There are certain places where people don't expect someone to approach them and it probably won't be welcomed:

>> **Doctor's office waiting rooms:** People are often stressed waiting for the doctor, or they feel sick.

>> **Hospitals:** People are usually stressed, waiting for their loved one to get out of surgery, or ill themselves.

- » **Restrooms:** Get in, do your business, and get out — absolutely no socializing here!

- » **Grocery stores:** People are usually focused on shopping and are wary of being approached by strangers. But small talk in the checkout line is perfectly okay.

- » **Out on the street:** People may be wary of being approached by scammers or thieves — it's a safety issue.

- » **Restaurants:** People are busy eating and don't expect to be approached by random people. The exception to this is if they're eating or drinking alone and seated at the bar (as opposed to a table). Sitting at the bar is more social.

- » **Airports:** People are often stressed and tired in airports.

- » **Libraries:** The library is a quiet space, and you're supposed to whisper or talk quietly, which makes it hard to have a good conversation. The exception to this is library events. Many libraries offer a full calendar of events, like children's story times, book clubs for adults, and language classes. Feel free to make small talk with people at these kinds of events!

- » **Locker rooms:** No one wants to make small talk with a random person while they're changing clothes or showering.

- » **Running or biking:** People are engaged in a strenuous activity and out of breath, so being approached to make small talk would feel odd.

Always try to read between the lines to determine if someone is open to your coming up to them to chat versus wanting to be left alone. Here's how you'll know if the other person is open to connecting with you: If they respond in a friendly, interested way, and elaborate on their responses, they're open to being approached. If they avoid eye contact, respond with curt answers, and look around the room or seem uncomfortable, they're not. In that case, just say something like, "I need to get going now. It was nice chatting with you. Have a great day!" and walk away.

REMEMBER

Sometimes other people have things going on in their lives that may be preoccupying them or bringing them down, and those things have nothing to do with you. Just accept that they aren't up for connecting right then, and find someone else who is more receptive to talking.

Approaching new people without giving off dating vibes

People have very different opinions about whether platonic gender-diverse friendships are a good idea. The movie *When Harry Met Sally . . .* famously broached this subject when Harry (played by Billy Crystal) said, "Men and women can't be friends because the sex part always gets in the way."

TECHNICAL STUFF

The term *gender-diverse* is more inclusive and doesn't limit this conversation to straight men and women. A gender-diverse friendship is a platonic one with someone who's the same gender as people you're sexually attracted to. So, if you're a straight man, a friendship with a straight woman (à la Harry and Sally), but also if you're a gay man, a platonic friendship with another gay man, or if you're a lesbian, a platonic friendship with another lesbian.

Some people believe it's important to have platonic gender-diverse friends; they value the benefits they get from these friendships. Other people have no interest and feel that these friendships will just cause problems.

It's common to wonder what gender-diverse friendships are like, especially if you've never had one. Platonic gender-diverse friendships have several benefits:

>> They can provide a fresh perspective on male/female interaction.

>> They can help you expand your social circle to include new people.

>> They can provide the opportunity to do new activities that your other friends or partner may not be interested in.

However, gender-diverse friendships can become problematic if one friend becomes attracted to the other friend, which muddies the waters in a supposedly platonic friendship. If things become awkward, the friendship isn't ever the same.

Clarifying your intentions right away

When approaching someone in the spirit of friendship, make sure to let them know in a subtle, but clear, way that you're looking for platonic friendships, so there's no confusion. This could look like chatting with someone at an event and then saying, "Hey, if you ever want to grab a drink — just a friends thing — here's my number" or "If you're ever looking for a dog-walking buddy, let me know!"

REMEMBER

If you're truly just looking for friends, you'll probably be conveying that subtly in the way you talk with the person. You're not going to be flirting with them the way you may be if you were looking for something romantic.

The takeaway here is to make sure to say something sooner rather than later that conveys, "It's just a friends thing," without having to directly spell out that you're seeking platonic friendships. If you have a spouse or significant other, let the person you're trying to befriend know this as well, to further clarify your intentions of a platonic friendship.

Hanging out in a group setting can be a good way to have friends of all genders. That way, there's less of a chance for romantic feelings to form if you're always hanging out in a group. It's also helpful to communicate with your friend in a group-text format so that you're not only communicating one-on-one with them, which can sometimes lead to problems if you (or they) have a jealous significant other.

Think about whether you preferred making friends of the same gender or different gender while you were growing up. Did you feel more comfortable with one or the other? How has that changed since becoming an adult?

Seeking out friendships

Most gender-diverse friendships happen incidentally — maybe you work together; maybe you're in the same car, cooking, or wine enthusiasts group; or maybe you live next door to each other. In these settings, you see each other a lot, so a friend-ship readily and organically forms. Usually, these friendships just happen when you meet someone — regardless of gender — that you click with.

If you're specifically looking to diversify your friend group, consider joining hobby/interest groups or volunteering, where you can find people of all genders who share similar interests.

Understanding the challenges of platonic gender-diverse friendships

If you're married, partnered, or dating someone, making friends with someone you might otherwise be attracted to can cause jealousy and resentment in your partner. Unintentional flirting and a lack of transparency can also become an issue with these friendships.

Making platonic friends is usually easier for single people than married or part-nered people. Your spouse may not feel comfortable with you calling, texting, or hanging out solo with the other person. It's a different story if you've had the friend since high school or college, but it can be a problem when making new friends who are gender-diverse, because your spouse may wonder about your motivation for wanting to be friends. Your spouse may worry that something is missing from your relationship to cause you to need this type of friendship. Your partner may start to become insecure about your friendship, and may want a play-by-play of what happened at every get-together.

Here are some additional challenges of gender-diverse friendships:

>> Your friend may express romantic interest in you, which makes things awkward and uncomfortable if you don't want that.

>> People may assume that the two of you are a couple.

>> You may feel certain activities with your friend are off-limits, like going out for dinner just the two of you or going to a bar together, because your spouse/partner may feel that it's inappropriate.

>> Your significant other may be jealous.

>> You may run into issues with sexual attraction that you don't want to deal with.

Although these challenges can be formidable, with some careful planning and partner reassurance, you'll likely be able to have successful gender-diverse friendships. Here are some tips for having a successful friendship:

>> Hang out in groups instead of individually.

>> Be transparent with your spouse or significant other about the friendship. When you're hanging out with your friend, always invite your spouse/partner to join, too.

>> Stick with meeting up with your friend at a public place instead of hanging out at each other's homes.

>> Let your significant other know that they're free to read your text messages to your friend at any time.

>> Don't plan activities with your friend that could be construed as romantic, such as dinner for two at a nice restaurant on a Saturday night. Stick to daytime lunches, coffees, walks, or going to activities together.

EXPLORE

Do some self-reflection about your past experiences being friends with someone of the gender you're attracted to. How has it gone for you? Did the friendship present challenges within your relationship?

Acing Your First Impression

First impressions are important. Research has shown that first impressions are made in seven seconds. This thought can be disconcerting — if you inadvertently mess up your first impression, it can have long-lasting consequences. But you can set yourself up for success by being mindful that first impressions count and by making the best first impression you possibly can.

Understanding why first impressions matter

First impressions matter so much because people make snap judgments that can last a long time and can't be undone easily. Right or wrong, these first impressions can impact their interactions with you long-term.

In a first impression, people decide if they like you or don't like you, and if you'll be a potential friend. It's important to make the best impression you possibly can.

Setting yourself up for success

You can improve your chances of making a great first impression by putting some effort into your appearance. Doing so will help you feel more confident, which will come across to the people you meet and will make them more interested in getting to know you. Consider doing some of the following to make the best first impression:

>> **Make sure your clothes are clean, well-fitting, and pressed.** Give your clothes a once-over and make sure they don't have any rips, holes, or tears (unless they're intentional, like jeans that come with holes or rips). If you look put together, you'll likely feel more confident, and this confidence will come across in your interactions with people.

>> **Make sure you have good personal hygiene.** Brush your teeth, take a shower, wear deodorant, trim your nails — basically take care of all the things your parents pestered you about when you were a kid.

>> **Make sure your hair is clean and styled the way you want.**

>> **Smile and exude positive energy.**

>> **Have a firm, confident handshake or fist bump.**

>> **Look approachable.**

>> **Be enthusiastic.**

EXAMPLE

Cindy doesn't put much effort into her appearance. She sometimes brushes her hair, doesn't wear makeup, throws on whatever outfit happens to be around, and often forgets to brush her teeth. She wants to make friends but has noticed that when she approaches people, she tends to get a lot of lukewarm responses. Cindy decides to try an experiment one month. She makes more of an effort with her appearance and tries to look more put together. She styles her hair, brushes her teeth, and puts some thought into her outfits, making sure they fit well and are ironed. Cindy feels more confident because she feels more put together. As a result, she got more interest when she approached new people, and they were more interested in getting to know her. Cindy decided that she liked her improved self-confidence and started being more put together when she would go out to group meetings and events.

UPPING YOUR RIZZ: HOW TO BE MORE CHARISMATIC

People are often drawn to others who are charismatic. Being charismatic — or having rizz, if you're up on the current slang ("How do you do, fellow kids?") — means having a certain presence, being charming and enthusiastic, being a good speaker, telling great stories, and making others feel good when they're with you.

Not everyone can be naturally charismatic, but everyone can learn a skill or two from charismatic people to help them feel more confident and less awkward when approaching and getting to know new people.

Here are several ways you can increase your level of rizz, er, charisma:

- **Engage in friendly banter.** It helps to be a good conversationalist when you're trying to make new friends. Charismatic people have topics of conversation in mind and cycle through them. It also helps to be witty and playful in your conversation — witty banter is fun and memorable for many people.

- **Listen well.** Charismatic people are good listeners. To be a good listener, when you're trying to get to know someone, talk 30 percent of the time and listen 70 percent of the time. Also, ask good follow-up questions to show that you're paying attention.

- **Develop your sense of humor.** You don't need to be a comedian, but you can improve your sense of humor by learning a few good jokes, having a few funny stories to tell, laughing easily at others' jokes, and poking fun at situations in a lighthearted way when you can. Watch interviews with comedians to see how they skillfully incorporate humor into conversations, or watch funny movies. People like to be around others who make them laugh, so think of ways to do that more often.

- **Make the other person you're talking to feel like the only person in the room.** Charismatic people are able to do this effortlessly. Having good eye contact and focusing on the other person without distractions shows that you're interested in what they have to say. Put the phone away or put it on silent when you're talking to someone. Give them your full attention. Make sure your eyes don't wander while you're talking to them, which gives off the impression that you're bored. When you make them feel like they're the only one in the room and you're giving them your full attention in an enthusiastic way, you'll stand out.

- **Remember important details.** Charismatic people listen intently and remember important details that they bring up later to show interest. For example, you might mention your upcoming vacation to Greece during one interaction, and the next time they see you, they'll ask how your vacation went. Remembering small details like this makes people feel valued and cared about. This is a great skill to have when approaching new people.

- **Be inclusive.** If you're talking in a group and someone new comes up, a charismatic person will make sure to include the newcomer in the conversation and not leave them hanging out on the sidelines, which can feel isolating.

- **Look for similarities and connections.** Charismatic people look for the things that bring people together instead of focusing on their differences. They can create new connections that way.

Figuring Out If You Click with Someone New

While you're approaching someone and talking with them, you'll be having many thoughts. One of your main thoughts is likely wondering if this person is someone you feel a connection with and would like to get to know better.

There are several ways to determine if the person you've approached is a good match for you, which I explore in the following sections. If at the end of the interaction you'd like to see them again, you can ask to exchange numbers, emails, or social media handles; give them your business card; or let them know you'll look forward to talking with them next time at a future group meeting or event.

Experiencing friend chemistry

Sometimes you approach someone new and feel an instant click. This feeling is *platonic chemistry*. When you click with someone, it feels like you mesh really well together and you're on the same wavelength. You may feel as if you've known them for a long time, and you want to spend more time with them. Clicking with someone is a euphoric feeling, but it only happens once in a while — not with every new person you meet. When you do feel it, though, you know you've found someone special.

When you click with someone, the conversation feels easy and natural, and you feel drawn to them. You want to get to know more about them, and you find them incredibly interesting. Here are some other ways to know when you're feeling chemistry with someone:

>> You want to keep talking to them and feel like you could talk for hours. The conversation flows easily.

>> You're both actively engaged in the conversation, and you both want to get to know each other better.

>> You feel like you've known them forever.

>> You feel drawn to them.

>> You laugh a lot with them and have fun.

>> The interaction feels easy and effortless.

>> You find that you have many things in common.

EXAMPLE

Celine met Marianne at a book club. Right away she felt a click with Marianne. They both love to read the same types of books, they're both from the same town originally, and they both like to play the piano. Celine liked Marianne's energy and found herself talking and laughing with Marianne more than she had with anyone in a long time. By the end of the first book club, Celine felt like she had known Marianne for years. They had a special connection, an instant friendship chemistry.

Determining how you feel around them

Another way to determine if you're clicking with someone new is figuring out how you feel about yourself when you're around this person. Some people make us feel good about ourselves, and other people make us feel badly about ourselves. You'll know that you click with someone when they make you feel good about yourself and they like you for who you are. You can have an authentic connection with them and feel like you can be fully yourself. You may also be thinking, "I like who I am around this person" or "I like the way they make me feel."

WARNING

You'll know it's not a good connection when you feel badly about yourself around them, they put you down or make you feel incompetent, or you feel like you have to hide parts of yourself from them.

EXPLORE

Think about the last time you met someone who made you feel bad about yourself. How did they go about making you feel bad about yourself? How did you end up handling the relationship? What did you learn from this experience?

Sharing mutual interests in common

Another way to determine if you click with someone is by figuring out if you share mutual interests in common. When people share many interests in common, they have a lot to talk about. When they don't have much in common, the conversation can feel forced, awkward, or strained, because you're searching for things to discuss.

TIP

The best way to find people with whom you share mutual interests in common is to meet them in hobby/activity groups, your religious congregation, your school alumni association, or through volunteering.

Keeping in Mind That You're Not Going to Like Everyone

As you reach out and approach new people, it's important to remember that not everyone you meet is going to be your new best friend — you just won't click with some people. That's a fact that *everyone* has to deal with as they make new friends. It can be a tough fact to swallow, especially when you find someone you'd love to have as a friend, but they're not interested.

It's important to make peace with the idea that not everyone is going to like you, and then be able to move forward. Instead, feel confident about meeting new people and also be resilient when things don't work out, knowing that making new friends is really a numbers game: The more people you meet, the more likely it is that you'll eventually find your people. And when you think about it, it's okay that not everyone will like you because you don't like everyone you meet either. Some people will appeal to you for certain reasons, and others won't.

Assuming that people like you

When meeting new people, your energy and overall vibe matter. Ideally, you'll have a friendly and positive vibe toward people. Assuming that people like you helps to further foster that vibe.

When you assume people like you, you tend to act warmly toward them, show interest in them, and project a welcoming energy — and, in turn, it's more likely that they'll end up becoming a friend. When you assume people *don't* like you, you can consciously or unconsciously act withdrawn, cold, and aloof, which will likely not lead to your making any new friends. This phenomenon is also known as the *acceptance prophecy*, which was studied by researchers in a 2009 study in *Personality and Social Psychology Bulletin*.

TIP

When you assume people like you, it sets you up for success because it's a self-perpetuating cycle: You act friendly and warm, so people respond positively and warmly and like you back. This is a "fake it 'til you make it" situation — act as if you know people already like you, and you're more likely to make a connection.

Improving your self-esteem

Having a healthy self-esteem is important when approaching new people. Strong self-esteem helps you feel confident about putting yourself out there and helps you bounce back quickly when things don't go your way. A healthy self-esteem also helps you cope better with rejection.

The good news is that self-esteem can be strengthened. Having successful interactions with new people will improve your self-esteem and self-confidence, but there are several other ways to improve your self-esteem:

>> Remind yourself that you're a wonderful person with many amazing and unique qualities.

>> Remember that you've made friends in the past, even if it was years ago, and people *do* like you.

>> Remind yourself that the people who know you think highly of you, whether that's friends, family, or coworkers.

>> Think about all the positive qualities that you have to offer a new friend. Write them down and refer to them often, especially before meeting up with new people.

>> Have a positive affirmation you can say to yourself when you're feeling down about making new friends, such as, "I'd like to make friends — I just haven't met them yet."

Remembering that not everyone is looking for a friend

When approaching new people, it's important to remember that not everyone is looking for a friend. Many people's social calendars are already full, and they already have all the friends and family they need. The person you're interested in being friends with may be too busy or stretched too thin to make new friends right now. However, other people, especially newcomers, usually do have the time and space in their life to make new friends.

TIP

It can be disappointing when you want to make a new friend, but they're neutral or disinterested in the idea of a friendship. Don't take it personally! They may have stressful things currently going on in their life that makes it too difficult to make a new friend, or they may be content with the friendships they already have. Don't dwell on the loss — move on. There are plenty more fish in the friendship sea.

Being prepared to kiss a lot of frogs

Making new friends is a lot like dating. You have to approach a lot of new people, make small talk, go out on friend dates (that may or may not be successful), and keep initiating plans with others. It's a lot of work!

REMEMBER

You probably won't become friends with the first person you meet — you'll need to kiss a lot of frogs to find your people. It takes time. Through trial and error, you'll learn who you gravitate toward and where you can find those people.

Being patient

When approaching new people, remember to be patient. Making new friends can take a long time for busy adults. Not everyone you approach will be open to making new friends, so it can take a long time to find people who are open to new friendships. You may need to approach dozens of people before you find one who is enthusiastic about making a new friend. But if you keep at it, you'll find people to connect with — and they'll be worth the effort and the wait.

IN THIS CHAPTER

» Demystifying the importance of small talk

» Identifying some helpful conversation starters

» Understanding how to wrap up small talk gracefully

Chapter **7**

Making Small Talk with New People

Most people have made small talk at one time or another, and may have a love/hate relationship with the concept. For some people, small talk is a fun and easy way to get to know someone new and learn a little bit about them. Other people, however, absolutely dread the idea of small talk. Those in the "dislike" camp believe that superficial, getting-to-know-you conversation can sometimes feel like pulling teeth if the other person isn't receptive or chatty, so they avoid it whenever possible. But making small talk with new people is the best way to learn more about them, establish rapport, and decide if there is a connection. It's the next step on your friend-making journey, one that will bring you closer to finding a new friend.

In this chapter, I do a deep dive into why small talk is important, help you learn how to master the fine art of small talk, and go through some helpful exercises and examples to help you build your skills. I also run through some tried-and-true conversation starters and give you some pointers about how to remember people's names when you first meet them (and what to do if you forget).

Demystifying Small Talk

Small talk is light conversation about surface topics that anyone can answer. It involves asking a lot of simple, getting-to-know you questions and making brief comments to build a connection. You should also share a little about yourself while you make small talk to keep the conversation feeling natural and reciprocal. With a little practice and by incorporating the recommendations in this chapter, you can go from avoiding small talk to actually enjoying it (or at least not minding it too much).

Small talk is an important social skill and essential in the process of making new friends. Being able to make conversation with anyone, anywhere is an important skill that benefits everyone. It's also an essential strategy in your friendship-making toolbox.

Small talk often happens at parties, events, and places where you don't know many people. It often gets a bad rap because some people find it tedious and boring to rack their brains for basic questions to ask someone they don't know, and initiating conversation with a complete stranger can make people feel awkward. Small talk can be a way to pass the time so you're not standing around at a gathering feeling awkward and bored, or it can be a way to make new connections. After making small talk with someone for a few minutes, you may decide to move on or decide you're interested in a connection with this person and request to keep in touch or stick around for deeper conversation.

EXPLORE

To determine your own perceptions of small talk, think about the last few times you made small talk. Make a list of five things that made making small talk seem difficult or awkward, and five positives or benefits of making small talk. Are there any items on the difficult/awkward side that you're skeptical about overcoming? Keep this list nearby as you read to see if you feel more comfortable with any of these items by the end of the chapter.

Warming up

Think of small talk as a warm-up to more interesting conversation, similar to how you warm up first before exercising. When you first meet someone new, you want to take your time by learning more about them to determine whether you're interested in further connection. Don't jump into anything too deep, too soon — that can feel jarring. Instead, ease into it, and keep things light and fun. Later, when you know a little more about them, you can decide to introduce deeper, more meaningful topics of conversation (see Chapter 10 for more on deeper conversation).

Talking to strangers

We all know that small talk is important, and that we should make an effort to do it, but have you ever thought about why? There are several reasons:

>> **Making small talk helps to break the ice and helps you and the other person get to know each other a little better.** When you're meeting someone for the first time, they're a stranger and you don't know anything about them. Even if you wanted to make deep conversation right off the bat, you wouldn't know what types of questions to ask or where to go with it. As you learn more about the other person through small talk, it gives you more conversation fodder to help you ease into deeper, more interesting discussion later.

>> **Making small talk is a friendly and polite gesture because it shows others that you're interested in being sociable.** Sociable people are more likable because they're making an effort to be friendly. Small talk is especially useful if you're at a party, event, or gathering where you don't know many people (or anyone at all). Instead of standing around awkwardly or staring at your phone, making small talk helps you pass the time in a pleasant way, and it may even help you make real connections. Even if you don't make a new connection from making small talk, it can still help you practice your conversation skills and build your self-confidence in talking to strangers.

>> **Small talk helps lighten the mood.** Small talk can help reduce anxiety (both yours and the other person's) and make you feel more comfortable, because it puts people at ease. If you keep the discussion light and friendly — nothing too serious or intimidating — it will help people feel more comfortable with you. It also gives you something to do when you're feeling trapped at a party or event, which can help lower your anxiety.

REMEMBER

>> **Making small talk can help you make connections, both personally and professionally.** People who are good at networking are good at small talk, and they end up making professional connections at events or parties that can be beneficial down the road. You never know when a quick conversation about the weather will end up turning into a business lead or a job offer. You also never know when a five-minute conversation at a dinner party can end up blossoming into a wonderful friendship.

>> **Making small talk can help you gain useful information.** For example, you may get a restaurant recommendation or hear about events or activities in your area. You may come away from small talk with a new bakery to try, a new park to visit, or a new idea for your next vacation.

TIP

When you initiate small talk with someone, it helps them feel important that someone took the time to talk with them. Many people don't feel genuinely listened to or feel overlooked, so showing interest in what someone has to say can be very meaningful to them. It's a kind gesture and can make someone's day!

REMEMBER

After making small talk for a while, you may decide that you'd like to get to know the person better because you have things in common and you like their general vibe. Or maybe you'll realize that you don't have much in common and don't think there's any connection. If so, you can end the conversation politely and move on, which is perfectly okay.

Psyching Yourself Up for Small Talk

One of the hardest parts about small talk is approaching someone you don't know, saying hi, and then racking your brain about what to say next. Walking up to a random stranger and starting a conversation can be anxiety-producing, not to mention awkward. People fear rejection, and there's always the chance that the other person won't want to talk, will give you a terse answer, or will walk away. That's why you need to psych yourself up first.

First, give yourself a little pep talk about how most people will appreciate your making the first move, and that no one will notice if your voice is shaky or you mess up. Positive self-talk comes in handy here. Positive self-talk means saying something positive to yourself that motivates you or gives you the self-confidence to do something. You may say to yourself: "I'll just be friendly and talk to them for a few minutes, and if I run out of things to say, no big deal. There are plenty of other people I can talk to at this party."

EXAMPLE

Antonio dreaded making small talk because he felt like he was always getting stuck in boring conversations. The last time he went to a party, he made small talk with a guy at the hors d'oeuvre table who ended up talking his ear off about a sports team that Antonio had no interest in. Antonio found it hard to extricate himself from the conversation and felt trapped. Every time he tried to change the subject, the other guy just brought it right back to his favorite sports team. After 20 minutes, Antonio had had enough and ended up saying that he needed to use the restroom to escape from the boring conversation. Antonio didn't let this ruin the party for him, though. He used positive self-talk to remind himself that this was just one small talk snafu in the grand scheme of things, and that there were plenty of other people at the party he could try talking with. Antonio felt better and ended up making small talk with another guy in the buffet line whom he ended up having several things in common with.

Also, remind yourself that even if you stumble through your words or sound awkward, it's unlikely the other person will look down on you or think that you're socially inept. They'll probably be thrilled that you took the initiative to approach them! Remember that people don't focus on your mistakes or flaws as much as you think they do.

Here are several other important do's and don'ts of small talk:

>> **Listen closely.** Pay attention to what the other person is saying and ask follow-up questions.

>> **Show interest in what they're saying with a varied tone of voice or facial expressions.** A flat, monotone voice or a blank facial expression won't make a good impression that you're interested in them.

>> **If you liked the person and see them again in the future, try to remember something they mentioned during your small talk conversation and follow up about it.** For example, if they were about to leave for a vacation when you last talked, ask them how it went next time you see them. This will show that you were listening attentively, and it can lead to a stronger connection.

>> **Don't interrogate.** Interrogation is asking one question after another without stopping to make a comment or sharing your own experiences. Interrogation makes people feel like they're being interviewed or that you're prying for information, and it can make the conversation feel stilted and awkward. Make your discussion style casual and conversational. For every question you ask, make a comment or share your own experience to break things up.

>> **Don't look around the room too much while you're making small talk.** This gives the impression that you're bored or looking for someone more interesting to talk to. Instead, focus on making good eye contact.

>> **Don't have your phone out.** When making small talk, put your phone away and give the other person all your attention. This is respectful but also good manners. There's nothing worse than someone talking to you but also glancing at their phone or texting, which gives the impression that they're not interested in what you have to say.

Deciding when and where to make small talk

There are many places and situations when small talk is appropriate and welcomed. You can make small talk when you're:

» Standing in line at the grocery store or a shop

» At a party

» At a networking event

» At work

» At a playground or park

» Waiting for your kids at their extracurricular activities or school pickup/drop-off

» Attending a new group

» At a bar

» In an elevator

» Waiting for a class to start

EXPLORE

Practice makes perfect when it comes to small talk. As an exercise, make a list of three places or situations where you could practice your small talk skills in the next month. Ideas could include talking to other parents while waiting at your child's swim class, talking to a stranger in line somewhere, or starting a conversation with the person next to you at the gym.

Determining how long to chat

Small talk can last any amount of time, depending on the situation and venue, but most commonly it lasts between 5 and 20 minutes. If you're waiting in line at the grocery store and making small talk with a customer near you, you're only going to be chatting for a few minutes until one of you checks out and leaves. On the other hand, if you're at a dinner party or networking event, you could be making small talk for much longer, perhaps 20 to 40 minutes (or even more) with each person.

TIP

There are no cut-and-dried rules for how long small talk should last. Just see what feels right and go with the flow.

Mastering the Art of Small Talk

The first step in mastering the art of small talk is having a few tried-and-true conversation starters that you can practice and rely on to help you feel more confident and at ease. *Conversation starters* are standard ways to start basic conversations that you can memorize and keep using over and over with new people. Examples of effective conversation starters include making an observation about the weather, commenting on the venue you're both in, or giving a compliment. It also helps to add a short comment about your own experiences to help the conversation flow better.

TIP

Practice using these conversation starters with random people when you're in line or at your next social event, and soon making small talk will start to feel more natural:

>> **Comments about the weather:** "It sure is hot today, isn't it? I love summer. How about you?"

>> **How their day/week/season/holiday is going:** "How's your summer going so far? Have you taken any fun trips?"

>> **How you know the host of the event:** "How do you know Patrick? I met him through church."

>> **A question about jobs or career:** "What do you do for a living? I'm a hairstylist."

>> **A comment about the group or event:** "Have you been to other group meetings or is this your first one?" or "When did you first start coming to this group? This is my first meeting."

>> **Where you're from:** "Are you from here originally? I'm from Milwaukee, but I moved here last month."

>> **How long you've lived in the area:** "How long have you lived here? I can't believe I've lived here 15 years already!"

>> **Age of your kids (if you're at a playground or kid-friendly event):** "How old are your kids? I have two kids, ages 6 and 8."

Small talk can be tedious, but it doesn't have to be painful. Read on to learn five easy, no-stress tips that will help your small talk shine.

Giving compliments

Who doesn't love a compliment? Giving someone a compliment is one of the best conversation starters there is. Complimenting people makes them feel warmly toward you. Plus, because you've started the conversation off on a positive note, it makes it more likely that they'll be open to chatting with you. A simple compliment can also make someone's day — not everyone receives genuine compliments. It also opens the door for follow-up questions about where they got the item or asking for their advice on something. You can compliment someone on their outfit, accessories, jacket, or something else you notice (for example, "I love your glasses! That color looks great on you. Where did you get them?"). When you get to know someone more, you can compliment them on qualities or traits they have that you admire.

REMEMBER

Avoid complimenting someone's general appearance, like telling them they're handsome or beautiful, because that can be mistaken for a come-on and can make people uncomfortable. (It can also come across as superficial.) Instead, look for something specific they're wearing or an accessory and compliment that.

EXAMPLE

Mary Ann always struggled with small talk and worried about sounding stilted when she would try to make a comment about the weather or work to start a conversation with a stranger. Instead, she decided to try something new and started complimenting people on something she noticed about them and genuinely appreciated. She soon realized that the other person always responded warmly and seemed very enthusiastic about chatting with her. Mary Ann quickly saw that this was a more authentic way for her to make a connection with someone. As part of her new small talk strategy, she started wearing a conversation piece as part of her outfit as a way for others to start conversations with her more easily. Her favorite conversation pieces are colorful scarves, interesting broaches, and unique necklaces. Now, people come up to her all the time to compliment her unique animal-print scarves, and that starts an easy conversation.

Asking open-ended questions

Questions come in two main forms: open-ended and closed-ended.

Closed-ended questions can be answered by a yes or no response. An example of a closed-ended question is: "Did you just move here?" The person can answer yes or no and not say anything further, so the conversation may stall quickly.

Open-ended questions, on the other hand, can't be answered by a yes or no response — they invite more elaboration and explanation. For example, if you ask, "How do you like it here compared to where you moved from?," you invite a longer response. Open-ended questions are ideal for small talk because they encourage the other person to talk more. Plus, you can glean more information to ask follow-up questions and get to know the person better. That's why it's helpful to incorporate open-ended questions into your small talk repertoire.

A handy tip for remembering to ask open-ended questions is the rule of three: Ask how, what, or why to encourage the person to talk more and elaborate. Here are some examples:

>> "This seems like a great Ping-Pong group. How are you liking this group so far?"

>> "What are you doing over winter break?"

>> "Why did you move here?"

Asking about their work or hobbies

Many people enjoy talking about their jobs, which can lead the way to finding things in common. You can ask "What do you do for work?" or "How do you spend your time?" (because not everyone works). I like "How do you spend your time?" because it's an open-ended question that may lead them to talking about their job, their retirement, their hobbies, or being a stay-at-home parent. Ask them a few questions to get them talking, and then you can ask some follow-up questions, such as: "Your job sounds so interesting! How did you get into that field?" or "What kind of educational path does it take to get into your field?" People love to talk about what they love or hate about their jobs, so this is a great conversation starter.

Asking about hobbies and interests is another great conversation starter because it's a fun topic that most people can speak to. Plus, it gives you a glimpse into how they spend their free time, which can let you know if the two of you have some things in common. For example, you can ask, "What do you like to do in your free time?" Then when they specify an activity or interest, you can follow up with another open-ended question: "That sounds so neat! I've always wanted to learn more about growing roses. What do you like about gardening?"

When you're looking to make new friends, it's helpful to look for people you have some things in common with. After making small talk with someone for a while, if you don't share any hobbies or interests in common or you don't think what they do in their spare time sounds fun, then you probably won't have much in common to form a friendship.

Being a good listener

Lots of people like to talk, but fewer people are good listeners. Practice *active listening*, which means giving the speaker your full attention — good eye contact, body and feet facing them, and nodding or making positive, short comments to show interest, like "Wow, interesting" or "Tell me more." A guideline that many experts recommend is to listen 70 percent of the time and speak 30 percent of the time.

TIP

Ask follow-up questions, and remember something the speaker said so you can reference it the next time you see them. This shows interest and will make you really memorable to that person.

Asking for advice or recommendations

People love to be asked for advice or recommendations; it makes them feel important and like their opinion is valued. You can ask someone for their advice on a number of different topics, such as restaurants, local service providers, schools, activities, and travel recommendations. You can't use this strategy instantly when meeting someone, but you can put it into action after you know more about them, within a few minutes. For example, you may say, "Your trip to Maine sounds so interesting. We're traveling there this summer. Do you have any hotel recommendations?" or "That restaurant you're describing sounds so good. Do you have any other recommendations for restaurants in the area?"

WARNING

There are certain topics that are off-limits in small talk, namely politics, religion, sexual orientation, and family size. Stay away from anything sensitive as well, such as asking why someone doesn't have children or asking for their opinion on a controversial current event. You don't want to offend someone inadvertently or start an argument. Keep things light and fun when making small talk.

TIP

REMEMBERING PEOPLE'S NAMES

Some people have difficulty remembering a new person's name, especially if they hear the name just once. One trick for remembering names better is to repeat the person's name right after they say it. So, if they say, "Hi, my name is Henry," then say, "Nice to meet you, Henry." This will help to reinforce it in your mind. Then try to use Henry's name again in conversation later, to further build those neural connections. Saying someone's name in conversation has the added bonus of making them like you more, because people love to hear the sound of their own name.

If you completely forget their name, don't feel mortified. Just make a little joke out of it: "I'm so sorry, but I'm really bad at names. Can you remind me of your name again? My name is Bill." Most people will empathize and won't mind repeating their name.

Wrapping Up Small Talk

When you feel like you've finished talking to the person and you want to wrap things up, there are a few ways you can do it. It's important to end the conversation on a polite, friendly note, even if you're not interested in getting to know them better or you really want to escape. What isn't polite is to just stop talking and walk away or try to flee when they're looking the other way. You want to end the conversation with grace: Be tactful and kind, even if you're not interested in getting to know them. Politely wrap up the conversation before walking away or moving on.

TIP

Here are some ways to end small talk when you don't want to get to know the other person or invite further connection:

>> "It was really nice talking to you, but I've got to get going. Enjoy the party!"

>> "It was so nice meeting you. I need to go pick up my child now, but good luck with the rest of the soccer season."

>> "I'm going to get a drink. Have a great rest of your day!"

>> "I need to go chat with my friend for a minute, but it was nice meeting you."

>> "I need to [use the bathroom, get more food], but it was great talking with you. Have a good evening."

TIP

Here are some ways to end small talk when you *do* want to get to know the other person better:

>> "It was great meeting you. We seem to have a lot in common, and I'd love to keep chatting more. Can we exchange numbers and keep in touch?"

>> "It was so nice talking to you. I hope to see you again next week at the meeting."

>> "It was awesome talking to you. I'd love to learn more about that trip to Wisconsin you were mentioning. Can I email you if I have some other questions about it? What's your email address?"

TIP

If you enjoyed the small talk and felt like you made a connection, it's a good idea to ask for their contact information (and offer yours as well) so you can keep in touch, especially if you think you won't run into them again (like at a party or one-time event). Make sure to follow up later to set up a coffee date, walk, lunch, or other get-together.

Before the event, decide if you want to bring business cards or get set up with an electronic business card through Blinq (https://blinq.me); work-related events are usually perfect for those types of info exchange. If you're going to a more casual or nonwork event, you'll likely just exchange social media handles, phone numbers, or email addresses.

EXAMPLE

Ashandra went to a lot of networking events and felt good in general about making small talk. She sometimes connected with someone she wanted to get to know further, but her challenge came when it was time to ask for their contact information and she felt shy. Ashandra feared rejection, so she was hesitant to put herself out there. Finally, she decided she had nothing to lose — she probably wouldn't see the other person again anyway if she didn't ask for their number. Ashandra mustered up the courage to start asking people she connected with if they could stay in touch. She then asked if they could exchange numbers or emails. Ashandra has expanded her social network greatly with this method and has even made a good friend this way.

Exploring What It Means to Be "Bad at Small Talk"

You might have heard someone say in the past that they're "bad at small talk." What this usually means is they don't enjoy making basic conversation with others, aren't patient with the process, have difficulty thinking of what to say, or feel awkward while doing it.

Many people dislike small talk, because asking superficial questions and getting short answers can be boring, especially if the other person isn't a good conversationalist or doesn't seem interested. It's also hard to come up with enough questions to ask. If the other person doesn't seem interested in chatting, it can lead to a feeling of awkwardness as you both sit in silence. But it's important to remember that small talk is important to build a bridge to deeper conversations. You can't just dive right into deep chats without having some small talk first, especially when you're just meeting someone. It would be very disconcerting to have a stranger walk up to you and ask you something like "Where do you see yourself in five years?" if you haven't warmed up to that type of deep question first.

Never fear, you can become good at small talk very easily and you don't have to dread it. All it takes is having the conversation starters and other tips we discuss in this chapter in mind for your next event or gathering. You can write the conversation starters down and actually keep them in your pocket, if you need to take a quick look before or during the event.

TIP

Practice makes perfect when it comes to small talk. If you feel rusty at your small-talk-making skills, practice at the grocery store, in line when waiting, and with people at parties and events. Eventually it will get easier.

If you really dislike small talk, consider making small talk for a few minutes and then testing the waters with a deeper question, and see what happens. If the other person seems uncomfortable, switch back to small talk. If they seem to go with it, you can try continuing with deeper conversation.

TIP

Setting a specific goal for your small talk adventures at your next party or event can be a great way to feel that small talk is less of a chore. The next time you're attending a party or other gathering, think about a goal beforehand that you'd like to achieve with your conversational efforts. For example, your goal may be to talk to two people that night, make four networking connections, or talk to as many people as it takes until you find one person who you'd like to befriend. Having a goal can make the process of small talk feel less cringey and more meaningful for you.

Chapter **8**

Coping with Shyness and Social Anxiety

M any people want to socialize and make new friends, but challenges like social anxiety disorder and shyness can get in the way. Shyness and social anxiety disorder are two different conditions, though many people confuse them or incorrectly use the terms interchangeably.

Social anxiety disorder is an intense fear of being watched, scrutinized, and judged by other people. It usually leads to the avoidance of socializing, because people with the disorder have so much anxiety about talking to new people or being in social situations that they have a hard time functioning in social situations. Social anxiety disorder is a diagnosable mental health condition and can be treated with therapy (often cognitive behavioral therapy [CBT] or exposure therapy) and medication.

Shyness, on the other hand, is a personality temperament (not a disorder) that involves feeling awkward or uncomfortable in social situations. Shyness is not a diagnosable condition and doesn't have any formal treatment, though there are many ways to work on overcoming shyness, such as by improving self-confidence. Both shyness and social anxiety can prevent people from meeting new people, making new friends, and thriving in new social situations.

Both shyness and social anxiety bring people into therapy. Some people who have difficulty with socializing struggle with shyness or social anxiety, and if you're thinking you might as well, you're not alone. Shyness and social anxiety are relatively common, but they can be overcome and there are a variety of coping strategies to help.

In this chapter, I discuss shyness and social anxiety disorder, and help you understand what each is and how they differ. I also explain the signs and symptoms, help you understand how they can adversely affect making new friends, and provide helpful coping strategies that will empower you to courageously face future social challenges.

Understanding Shyness

Shyness is a feeling of being uncomfortable, awkward, or self-conscious when you're around other people. Shyness can always be present, or it can become an issue in new social situations, like when you're meeting someone new for the first time. Additionally, some people are shy in some situations but not shy in others. For instance, you can feel shy in group settings but do just fine with people one-on-one.

Shyness can make it hard to socialize and make new friends, because some people feel too shy to go up to new people, introduce themselves, and start a conversation. Others feel too shy to approach people they've met a few times before, because they fear rejection. Shyness can get in the way of making new connections.

REMEMBER

When you're shy, you're not necessarily overly worried about others judging and scrutinizing you, the way people are who have social anxiety disorder. But you can still feel self-conscious and insecure, which can get in the way of making connections. Shyness is less severe than social anxiety disorder because shy people are generally able to function normally, and they don't avoid most social situations, even though they may feel uncomfortable in them. They will go to social situations and interact with others, but they may experience uncomfortable physical symptoms like blushing, a shaky voice, or shortness of breath. Most people who struggle with shyness will be able to get through the interaction just fine, even despite these symptoms.

EXAMPLE

Maura grapples with shyness. At her first meeting of the investment club, she can feel herself blushing when everyone is going around introducing themselves. Her stomach is doing flip-flops and she feels a little shortness of breath while everyone goes around one-by-one and she knows it's almost her turn. Finally, it's her turn, and as Maura stands up to speak, she can feel herself turning red. Maura does introduce herself and, after the meeting starts, she starts making small talk with a few nice people sitting near her. At first, she feels herself stumbling over her words, but the other people put her at ease. By the end of the meeting, Maura feels more comfortable.

REMEMBER

Many people don't like to be called shy. They resent the term and find it embarrassing. The terms *quiet, demure,* or *reserved* may be more considerate ways of describing them.

Understanding when people feel shy

Can you think of a time when you felt shy? Maybe it was when you had to introduce yourself in front of a room full of people. A shy person may stumble over their name and feel nervous; they may also blush or start to sweat, and they don't like feeling everyone's attention on them — but they get through it.

Someone with social anxiety disorder, on the other hand, who had to introduce themselves in front of a group would probably leave the room, go into the bathroom, and maybe even throw up. Their hands may be shaking badly, and they may feel physically sick. They may have to leave work and go home. Social anxiety disorder is much more severe and debilitating than shyness.

Here are other examples of situations where you may feel shy:

>> Asking your boss for help

>> Making a toast for your best friend at their wedding

>> Raising your hand to ask a question in a large lecture hall

>> Attending a mixer and having to introduce yourself to strangers

>> Answering questions about yourself at your mother-in-law's birthday celebration

>> Asking a celebrity for their autograph at an event

>> Asking your doctor questions about your health

>> Ordering at a restaurant

Different people feel varying levels of discomfort from these situations, but shy people can still function well overall and can get through the social event without having severe stress.

EXAMPLE

Yolanda is at her twentieth high school reunion and really wants to mix and mingle and talk to some of her classmates who she hasn't seen since graduation. She feels too inhibited to go up to them as they're standing in a group, however, because she feels awkward and self-conscious. Even still, she tries to work up her courage to talk to the group and even starts to walk toward one woman she remembers from civics class, but then when she's halfway there, her palms start to sweat and she feels her face getting red, so she turns around and sits back down. Yolanda instead goes to talk to her best friend, Henrietta, and doesn't feel nervous at all. She decides to think about trying again later if her classmate is standing by the drink table by herself, which will feel less intimidating for Yolanda.

Exploring whether shyness is nature or nurture

Research has found that shyness is a result of both nature and nurture. Thalia Eley, a researcher at Kings College in London, has determined that shyness is 30 percent genetic and 70 percent environmental. This means that if a parent is shy, it's possible that their child will also be shy. However, situations a person experiences growing up, such as being bullied or rejected, can also contribute significantly to shyness, as can having low-self-confidence.

EXAMPLE

Peter's parents are both shy, and he is shy as well. Peter was also bullied in grade school, which made him want to fade into the background so as not to be noticed and picked on. Both his genetic heritage and his experience growing up contributed to his shyness.

Understanding the symptoms of shyness

People experience shyness differently, and there are multiple symptoms of shyness. These symptoms can include:

>> Challenges making eye contact

>> Stumbling over words or not being able to speak at all

>> Sweaty palms and armpits

>> Nervous pacing

>> Frequent throat clearing or dry throat

>> A racing heartbeat

>> Shortness of breath

>> Speaking in a very quiet voice

>> Feeling shaky

WARNING

The symptoms of shyness can make it hard to approach new people and make new friends. If you want to talk to someone but your hands and armpits are dripping with sweat, you feel shaky, and your heart is racing a mile a minute, it can feel like you're about to pass out. This can make it hard to regain your composure and go up to that person. Taking a break in the restroom to calm yourself, doing some deep breathing, and repeating some positive affirmations can help you overcome your shyness and successfully approach someone new.

Overcoming shyness

If you struggle with shyness, there are many ways you can cope. Shyness is a challenge to deal with, but it can be overcome if you're motivated to try some new coping strategies. If you find that, despite your best efforts to cope on your own, you're not able to overcome your shyness, consider finding a mental health therapist to work with who can provide some additional guidance.

TIP

Here are several coping strategies for shyness you can try:

>> **Come up with several positive affirmations.** *Positive affirmations* are empowering phrases that you repeat to yourself to psych yourself up and build your self-confidence. An example of a positive affirmation for shyness could be: "I'm a great person with a lot to offer, and I'd make an awesome friend." If you repeat this affirmation to yourself several times as a pep talk before approaching someone, it can improve your self-confidence.

>> **Change negative self-talk into more neutral or positive self-talk.** Negative self-talk focusing on self-consciousness and rejection can keep you stuck. Instead, reframe your negative self-talk into something more neutral or more positive. An example would be going from "She looks so confident and poised — she wouldn't want to hang out with someone like me" to "She looks confident and poised, but she's also here at a group to meet new people. I have nothing to lose by going up to her to say hi." The first statement is an example of negative self-talk, while the second statement is more neutral. The first statement makes you feel badly about yourself and will undermine your self-confidence, while the second statement will help you feel more confident.

>> **Remember that people are wrapped up in themselves.** When you're feeling shy or self-conscious, it's helpful to remember that most people are wrapped up in themselves and are thinking about their own problems and challenges — they aren't as focused on your shortcomings as you think. If you

worry that you'll say something embarrassing and they'll remember it weeks from now, remember that they'll likely forget all about it after your discussion, because they have their own worries.

» **Focus on the other person when you feel yourself getting nervous.** Focus on details about the other person, like their interesting eyeglasses or fun earrings. Ask them questions, and listen closely to their responses. Use empathy to put yourself in their shoes. If you can focus more on them, you'll focus less on yourself and your feelings of nervousness.

» **Practice deep-breathing exercises.** Deep breathing is an excellent coping strategy for shyness. The 4-7-8 technique has you breathe in for the count of four, hold your breath for the count of 7, and breathe out for the count of 8. Do this several times until you feel calmer. It can help to do this breathing exercise in the car before going into a new place or in the restroom if you need a calming break.

» **Build your self-confidence in small ways.** If the idea of going up to a random stranger at a party is too overwhelming right now, focus on building up your confidence in a smaller way. Talk to people at work or at group meetings who are acquaintances, and praise yourself when the interactions go well. Then work your way up to saying hi to random strangers at group meetings. Over time, you'll be able to build your self-confidence enough to approach new people without feeling as nervous.

TIP

Another coping strategy for shyness when you want to meet people and make new friends is to participate in social groups where there is an activity in addition to socializing. This will take the pressure off pure socializing. For example, instead of going to a dinner club where you'll be sitting across from people trying to make small talk, join a hiking group where you can focus on nature and the beautiful surroundings while you socialize. This gives you other things to talk about to take the pressure off just socializing — you can make comments or observations about the trees, the birds, and the weather. It also makes it easier to take a break from socializing and enjoy the forest if you need a little quiet time. An activity that would be more challenging for a shy person would be meeting someone they don't know for coffee, where you're sitting across from someone and you're expected to make a lot of eye contact and just focus on them.

Exploring Social Anxiety

Have you ever felt panicky before going into a social situation, and had your heart race, your stomach flip-flop, and your mind go completely blank? Maybe you're worried about saying or doing the wrong thing and feeling embarrassed, or maybe you're feeling anxious that people will scrutinize and reject you. That's some of what people who have social anxiety disorder go through every time they try to socialize, only they're feeling it so intensely that they usually end up avoiding the social situation altogether.

REMEMBER

Social anxiety is a type of anxiety disorder. It's a chronic mental health condition that causes people to worry about saying or doing something that will cause other people to dislike or judge them, and they also fear being watched and scrutinized. When someone has social anxiety, they overthink interactions and worry for a long time afterward about what they did or said, worrying that other people are going to judge them for it. They also tend to jump to worst-case scenarios, like catastrophizing for a long time about something minor they said or did.

REMEMBER

Unlike shyness, which is not a diagnosable condition, you can be diagnosed with social anxiety disorder. In order to be diagnosed with social anxiety, you need to have had the symptoms for six months or longer. Social anxiety disorder usually starts in the teenage years. A 2017 study in *Clinical Psychology Review* found that women are more likely to have social anxiety disorder and are more likely than men to have severe symptoms. The same study found that men are more likely than women to seek treatment.

EXAMPLE

Jorge has social anxiety disorder. He wants to go to a walking club to meet more people who share his interests in walking. However, he has anxiety about attending the walking club and ruminates for several weeks about whether he should go. With great trepidation, he does make it to a meeting. While there, Jorge believes that other people are scrutinizing him because he's gained 20 pounds in the last year. He can feel everyone looking at him and judging him for being overweight. Jorge gets so anxious about this that he starts to sweat profusely, his hands start to shake, and he starts to feel like he can't breathe. Jorge feels like he's going to faint and knows that he can't make it through the entire walk. While everyone is taking a break to look at a bird's nest, he quickly walks away in the other direction, without letting anyone know he's leaving.

Understanding how social anxiety affects friendships

Social anxiety disorder causes people to have challenges making and keeping friends because they worry so much about being watched or judged during social situations that they avoid socializing altogether. Or they may accept an invitation to get together but spend weeks or months worrying about the event beforehand. They worry about what others will think of them and fear embarrassment over making a mistake. This fear can be paralyzing. If they do socialize and make a minor gaffe, they worry excessively about what other people thought of it and ruminate about it for a long time afterward. They also may get so stressed and upset during a social event that they end up leaving early.

Sometimes people with social anxiety decline invitations altogether because they believe they can't handle the stress and anxiety of socializing. Because they avoid socializing, it makes it much harder to meet new people and make new friends.

EXAMPLE

Paloma has social anxiety. Her friends invite her out to a restaurant for another friend's birthday and she wants to go, but she has anxiety about eating in front of others. She worries that people will be judging how she chews and that they won't like her. Paloma worries for a month about whether she should go. She spends a lot of time figuring out how she can attend the birthday dinner but not eat or just pretend to eat. Paloma talks through what the dinner will be like with her husband. She feels like she has a good handle on all the possible situations that may come up. She attends the birthday dinner and orders an appetizer, but she gets too anxious to eat and ends up feeling so stressed that she leaves early.

Understanding signs and symptoms

There are several signs and symptoms that people with social anxiety disorder may exhibit. Some of these symptoms are similar to those of shyness:

>> A racing heartbeat

>> Shortness of breath

>> Feeling faint or like they'll pass out

>> Shaky hands

>> Feeling nauseous and like they're going to throw up or be sick

>> Sweating

>> Not being able to think — their mind goes blank

>> Feeling dizzy or lightheaded

Exploring coping strategies

If you have social anxiety, it's important to remember that it can be treated. Therapy, especially CBT and exposure therapy, are used to treat social anxiety disorder, and medication is often used in addition to therapy. (See the nearby sidebar for more on CBT and exposure therapy.)

DIFFERENT TYPES OF THERAPY

Cognitive behavioral therapy is a structured type of psychotherapy that helps people identify and reframe negative and unhelpful thinking patterns and behaviors so that they can regulate their emotions more effectively, improve their quality of life, and be able to cope with their problems in a healthier way. CBT is effective for depression, anxiety disorders, eating disorders, insomnia, and many other mental health conditions.

Exposure therapy is when you gradually confront your fears in a safe space, with the help of a therapist. Your therapist will have you create a *fear hierarchy* of the situations that cause you the most anxiety. At the bottom of the fear hierarchy are the situations that cause you the least anxiety, and at the top are the situations that cause you the most anxiety. Your therapist may have you start exposure therapy by imagining yourself in the situation you fear. When you're able to tolerate imagining the situation, the therapist will then help you gradually work your way up the fear hierarchy one step at a time, until you're able to handle more challenging exposures, while using relaxation techniques and other coping strategies.

Here are some ways that you can empower yourself to cope with social anxiety disorder on your own:

>> **Plan ahead.** Have an action plan in place for how you'll handle any anxiety-producing situations that come up. This may involve talking through the situation with a friend, family member, or therapist; anticipating what may come up; and troubleshooting how to handle it.

>> **Have a support person talk you through it.** If you have an empathetic and comforting spouse or partner or a family member who is able to coach you through your anxiety (for example, on the phone), this can help you remember your coping strategies and get through the anxiety-producing situation. See if you can call your support person to get help if you're feeling so anxious that you're starting to panic or if you want to leave a social situation. Eventually, you'll become confident enough about using your coping skills that you'll be able to coach *yourself* through stressful and anxiety-producing situations.

TIP

If you don't have anyone to coach you, write down your coping strategies on index cards and put them in your purse, bag, or pocket so you can refer to them when needed.

>> **Challenge negative thoughts.** One effective coping strategy for social anxiety is taking a close look at your automatic negative, anxiety-producing thoughts and asking yourself what the evidence is for these negative thoughts. For example, if you want to socialize but you think that everyone is going to be staring at the birthmark on your face and judging you for it, ask yourself what evidence you have to support the thought that people will dislike you because of your birthmark. Even if you were teased as a child about the birthmark, and this made you feel anxious, chances are, it'll be difficult to come up with evidence that other people *dislike* you because of it. Over time, you can learn to automatically ask yourself what the evidence is for your negative thoughts, which can help you talk yourself through the anxiety-producing situation.

>> **Engage in positive self-talk.** Another coping strategy for social anxiety is reframing your negative and critical self-talk into more realistic, balanced, and positive self-talk. For example, maybe the negative self-talk statement you've been saying to yourself is: "Everyone is going to remember that I forgot the host's name. I'm so stupid. No one will ever forget this." Reframe that negative self-talk to: "People aren't focused on me and that I forgot the host's name. They're preoccupied with their own stuff. They likely forgot all about my mistake a few minutes after. It's unlikely that anyone will remember this in a week."

>> **Engage in positive visualization exercises.** If you're feeling too anxious to go up to people and make small talk because you're worried about being judged or you're *catastrophizing* (thinking about worst-case scenarios), it can be helpful to do a visualization exercise before the social situation. Visualize yourself confidently going up to people and making small talk; visualize everything going smoothly and people liking you and responding well. Think about how it would look in your mind if everything worked out ideally, and practice visualizing that scene unfolding in a positive way in your mind. This can help you feel much more relaxed before going into a social situation.

>> **Do deep-breathing exercises.** Deep-breathing exercises are very helpful for anxiety. You've probably heard about deep breathing as a coping strategy in the past, but maybe you aren't convinced that it could be helpful for you. The reason why deep-breathing exercises are helpful is because they calm the nervous system when you're in a heightened state of anxiety. Taking a few calming breaths helps lower your stress and tension levels. It also helps slow your breathing down if you're hyperventilating, which can cause lightheadedness and dizziness. You can do deep breathing before or during a social situation to calm you. For example, if you get especially anxious and panicky before walking into a social situation, you can practice deep breathing in the car or outside the building to calm yourself before walking in.

TIP

There are tons of different deep-breathing exercises out there. One breathing exercise I really like that's easy to remember is called *box breathing*. To do it, you imagine a box shape, and breathe in for a count of four, hold for a count of four, breathe out for a count of four, and repeat. While you do this exercise, you can visualize tracing the sides of a box, or you can use your finger to trace the shape of a box. Keep doing box breathing until you feel yourself feeling calmer and less stressed. Another deep-breathing exercise is called 4-7-8 — inhale for the count of 4, hold for the count of 7, and exhale for the count of 8; then repeat until you feel calmer.

TIP

If you have a hard time remembering your coping skills, you may want to use an app for anxiety, which will walk you through different breathing, visualization, guided imagery, and relaxation exercises to help with anxiety symptoms. Some popular ones include Breathwrk (www.breathwrk.com), Calm (www.calm.com), Happify (www.happify.com), Headspace (www.headspace.com), and MoodMission (https://moodmission.com).

» **Engaging in mindfulness.** Mindfulness is one of the best coping skills for anxiety, and it's very popular now, with many books and apps dedicated to the practice. It means being in the present moment and allowing your thoughts to pass by without judgment, so you're not worrying about the future or ruminating about the past. The reason mindfulness is so helpful for anxiety is because you can't be worrying while simultaneously being focused on the present moment — your brain can't do those two things at once. Meditation is one type of mindfulness practice that many people find extremely helpful for reducing and managing their anxiety.

TIP

Just like the anxiety apps, there are also apps for mindfulness, which walk you through different mindfulness exercises. Calm, Headspace, Let's Meditate, Meditation Oasis, Mindfulness Coach, and Sattva are some popular ones.

TIP

One helpful mindfulness exercise that many people find very effective is called 5-4-3-2-1 (and it's very easy to remember). This exercise can be done anywhere and just involves sitting quietly and noticing your surroundings. In this exercise, you look around where you are and name five things you can see, four things you can feel, three things you can hear, two things you can smell, and one thing you can taste. You can do this exercise anywhere, and no one will notice that you're doing it. You can do it in the car or before you go into a social situation. If you need to take a break because you're panicking, you can do it outdoors or in another room. It grounds you in the present moment and focuses your attention on the present.

EXAMPLE

Cameron was at a party, and was starting to get overwhelmed and panicky at the idea of talking to new people. He thought about leaving, but then remembered his 5-4-3-2-1 exercise. Cameron went outside and found a quiet area. He picked up a pinecone and started to focus on the way its ridges felt in his hands. He sat under a tree and named five things he could see (the tree, the grass, a car nearby, a bird, and his watch), four things he could feel (his sweater, his ring, his wallet, and the grass underneath him), three things he could hear (crickets, an owl, and people's voices from the party), two things he could smell (the scent of flowers and the smell of beer), and one thing he could taste (his breath mint). After a few minutes, Cameron felt calmer and was ready to go back inside to the party.

IN THIS CHAPTER

» **Discovering how to be more friendly**

» **Learning how to be a warmer person**

» **Exploring how others feel when they're with you**

» **Expressing vulnerability**

» **Walking through how to initiate plans with others**

Chapter **9**

How to Be Friendlier

Have you ever wondered why some people have lots of friends and a full social life while others struggle to make even one friend? One of the variables that determines how easily you'll make friends is how friendly and approachable you are.

Think for a moment about a person you know who has a lot of friends. Why do you think people are drawn to them? What qualities make them so personable? Is it that they have an effortless sense of humor and connect with others in a light-hearted way? Do they have a natural charisma and make others feel important and valued? Do they chat with everyone they meet, and seem genuinely interested in people? Examining the qualities that make someone friendly and approachable can help you incorporate some of these qualities as well.

Learning how to be a friendlier and more approachable person is one of the most powerful tools in your friend-making toolbox, one that will open the door to a more fulfilling social life. Some people believe that being personable is completely innate, a certain quality that can't be taught. But it's actually a mix of innate characteristics and characteristics that can be learned and practiced, so there is plenty of opportunity to improve.

In this chapter, you find out how to increase your approachability. The first part of the chapter explores the traits you can cultivate to become more personable that are within your control, such as becoming more positive, showing warmth, and being more easygoing. In the second part of the chapter, I discuss ways that you can make others feel more liked, including giving compliments, being responsive, and showing appreciation.

Discovering the Importance of Being Friendlier

When you're trying to make new friends as an adult, being friendly and approachable are important qualities to cultivate. Not only do personable people make friends more easily, because others enjoy their company and want to be around them, but they also have a higher likelihood of succeeding at work and are often treated better throughout life.

MAKING A GOOD FIRST IMPRESSION

First impressions are formed fast: It's widely believed that people form an opinion of someone within seven seconds of meeting them! You want to make a good first impression in those seven seconds and show people that you're friendly and approachable. Otherwise, you may not get the chance to befriend them later.

Think about how can you present the most positive first impression. Remember back to the last time you met someone new: How did you decide whether you liked them? Was there anything they did in those first few minutes that especially made you like them or turned you off? Reflect on ways you can improve these qualities on your own.

To make a good first impression, focus on the following:

- Cultivating warmth
- Having a genuine smile
- Being neatly groomed
- Maintaining good hygiene
- Being enthusiastic
- Having an expressive voice and facial expressions
- Remembering names and using the person's name often
- A firm handshake

Helping to enhance your social life

When people like you, they want to be around you. They'll start inviting you to do things and want to call you a friend. When people aren't sure if they like you, they may not be as enthusiastic about starting a friendship, and the friendship may stall or take much longer to blossom.

Becoming a more friendly and approachable person means you're more likely to make friends and have a vibrant social life.

REMEMBER

The good news is that being friendlier and more approachable is within your reach because it's something you can work on and cultivate. Even adopting one or two of the tips discussed later in this chapter will likely make a positive change for you socially.

Helping you do better on the job

More personable people also do better at work. They tend to get higher performance reviews, get jobs more easily, and are promoted to leadership roles more frequently. Additionally, when you have friends at work, you enjoy your job more, feel a sense of community at work, and are more likely to get invitations to after-work social events. Interviewers often hire people that they like who they think will fit in well with the culture of the organization, even if the job applicant doesn't have the exact qualifications they're looking for.

EXAMPLE

Fred had worked at the same job for 20 years. He was well-respected at work and always got good performance reviews, but he wasn't well liked by the other employees. He often overheard his coworkers talking about getting together over the weekend or going to parties, but Fred was never invited to these social events. Fred was a friendly guy, so he was perplexed as to why he wasn't well liked at work. He had a feeling it was because, in his first few years on the job, he never accepted any of his coworkers' invitations to meet up for drinks or dinner after work. His coworkers never felt like they knew him, and they didn't include him because they thought Fred was aloof and not interested in being social. When it came time for a promotion, Fred was disappointed when he wasn't promoted. Fred was qualified for the position, but believed it was because he wasn't well liked by his boss and coworkers.

TIP

Start a new job on the right foot by being friendly with your new coworkers right away. If your coworkers ask you to join them for lunch or meet them for drinks, say yes. When you accept invitations, you come across as more personable. Show interest in your coworkers and try to get to know them. People are most responsive to getting to know new people the first few weeks or months at a new job, so make sure to work on being friendly those first few crucial months.

Helping you get treated better

Have you ever heard the famous expression, "You can catch more flies with honey than with vinegar?" Personable people tend to get treated better, whether it's by customer service reps, waiters, or doctors. If you find yourself in a dispute and you're polite, calm, friendly, lighthearted, complimentary, and empathetic with the other person, you're more likely to get the outcome you want.

Be polite and friendly with the receptionist when making a new appointment or checking in for your appointment. Be polite and chatty with the server taking your order. Be patient and understanding with customer service reps when trying to resolve a dispute. Service workers will often give better service or even special perks to people they like.

Cultivating More Approachable Traits

You can't control who likes you and who doesn't, but you can set yourself up for success by developing some of the traits that increase a person's approachability. Adding just one or two of these traits to your social skills repertoire will likely improve your ability to make friends.

Being positive and uplifting

People like being around happy and positive people. Positive people make others feel uplifted and inspired, and people want to be around positivity. People who are negative and complain all the time sap others' energy. Have you ever had the experience of telling a friend about something you're excited about, but instead of being enthusiastic and supportive, they say something negative or critical? That can really rain on your parade and make it less likely you'll share things with them in the future.

No one wants to be around someone who is negative most of the time, because that can be draining and drag them down. It's also frustrating when someone emotionally dumps on you or when your friends treat you like their therapist. Positive people have their negative moments, just like anyone else, but they know that there is a time and a place to share their negativity, and they do it sparingly. They may periodically make a negative comment about something, but they usually follow that up with how they're addressing or trying to resolve the issue, or follow it up with something positive. Be considerate of how others are feeling so you don't overwhelm them with negativity.

Here are three practical ways to increase your overall positivity and happiness:

>> **Find joy in everyday small things.** Focus on using all your senses to celebrate the little things that can bring you happiness, like the scent of a rose growing in your yard, the taste of warm coffee in the morning, or the feel of your cat's fur as she snuggles up against you.

>> **Create positive affirmations.** To further emphasize the importance of positivity, you can create several positive affirmations that you can repeat to yourself before a social situation. This is a way to give yourself a little pep talk and remind yourself of the importance of being positive around others. An example of a positive affirmation is: "If I'm positive and upbeat, that will draw others in."

>> **Do a daily gratitude exercise.** If you're more of a glass-half-empty kind of person and you find being positive a challenge, there is a therapeutic exercise called Three Good Things, which was created by positive psychologist Martin Seligman. In the Three Good Things exercise, at the end of the day you think of three positive things that happened that day, and write them down if possible. The reason this exercise makes people happier is because it encourages them to look for the good in their day.

If you're going to meet up with a friend or acquaintance, think about some of the positive things you noted in your Three Good Things exercise this week, and bring them up in conversation, which should help you cultivate a more positive frame of mind.

People view friendships as light and fun, and friends don't usually want to be your therapist. Be positive, and limit negative talk and complaining. You also don't want to emotionally dump on others or saddle them with your emotional baggage. If you find that your own problems and concerns are weighing you down and keeping you from being upbeat around others, consider finding a therapist. A weekly therapy appointment can be a safe space for you to unload your negativity. Many people find that when they have that weekly therapy session, they don't feel the need to vent their problems to friends and acquaintances, leaving room for more positivity in their interactions.

Exuding warmth

One quality that most personable people have in common is that they exude warmth. When you show warmth, you're friendly, kind, and expressive. Someone who's warm makes you feel good in their presence and shows you that they like and care about you.

TIP

Here are six ways that people demonstrate warmth:

>> **They're huggers.** A warm person may greet you with a big, friendly hug and exclaim, "I'm so happy to see you!," setting the tone for a positive interaction. A fist bump can communicate a similar sentiment.

How do you feel about hugging? Some people who aren't huggers are fine with receiving a hug but won't initiate them, which is perfectly okay. If you feel uncomfortable with that level of physical touch, but your friend is a hugger, you could do a half-hug or a fist bump instead, and you can always say: "I'm not a hugger, but I'm so happy to see you!" to avoid a hug. It's good to figure out how you feel about hugs before you go into a social situation.

>> **They focus on you.** When they interact with you, a warm person gives you all their attention, has excellent eye contact, listens more than they talk, asks questions to show interest, and shows enthusiasm in the conversation.

>> **They're expressive.** A warm person smiles a lot. They have an expressive voice and facial expressions, which further shows interest. They use different vocal intonations to communicate their emotions.

>> **They make you feel good about yourself.** A warm person may compliment you during your interaction, which makes you feel good, or they may bring up something you mentioned last time, to follow up or ask how it went. They have a caring vibe.

>> **They put you at ease.** A warm person has a lighthearted manner. They joke around, make small talk, and have a kind tone.

>> **They end on a positive note.** When they say goodbye, a warm person tells you how nice it was to spend time with you, and they may ask to schedule another get-together soon. They may give you another hug goodbye.

Someone who lacks warmth, on the other hand, may come across as serious, aloof, grumpy, or unfriendly. When they see you, they may mumble an unenthusiastic "Hi" and avoid eye contact. They don't really give you their full attention, and they look all around the room when talking to you, making you feel like they don't want to be there. When they say goodbye to you, they may just give an indifferent "See ya" and walk away. They make you feel like you really don't matter to them, and that they couldn't care less about being with you.

When you first meet someone, it's important to start your interaction warmly. This will set the stage for the rest of your conversation to go well. Smile, make good eye contact, have a firm handshake if applicable, and greet them warmly. Here's a good opener that shows warmth: "Hi, Taylor! it's so great to see you! How have you been? I've been thinking of you and wondering how you're doing."

During your conversation, make sure to do some of these actions to further show warmth:

>> Compliment them.

>> Ask questions to show interest.

>> Listen more than you talk.

>> Maintain good eye contact.

>> Avoid distractions. (Put away your phone.)

>> Be lighthearted and have an easy laugh.

>> Let them know how much you enjoyed talking to them.

>> Show interest in meeting up again.

TIP

Warm people smile a lot, and they have genuine smiles. You may have heard the expression that a "smile is contagious." When you smile at someone, they're likely to smile back, which spreads a positive feeling.

TECHNICAL
STUFF

NOT ALL SMILES ARE THE SAME

Did you know that there are different types of smiles? The *Duchenne smile* is considered to be the authentic smile and a sign of genuine happiness. This type of smile is controlled by the limbic system and reaches the eyes, causing the edges of your eyes to crinkle.

A *fake smile*, which does not represent genuine happiness, relies on a different area of the brain, the motor cortex. With a fake smile, you're making yourself smile on command and only smiling with the mouth, not the eyes. A fake smile can seem inauthentic and turn people off or make them think you're being insincere.

Some people find it hard to smile, either because they're chronically unhappy or because they're more serious or reserved. If you have difficulty smiling, try practicing your smile in the mirror to notice the differences between an authentic Duchenne smile and an inauthentic smile. To help you feel happy enough for an authentic smile in a social situation, think of a time or situation that made you smile or brought extreme happiness.

NOTORIOUS RBF

What can you do if you have the common affliction called *resting bitch face* (RBF), which means that your natural neutral expression makes you look constantly deep in thought, mad, dissatisfied, grumpy, or cold? If you have RBF, it's because the corners of your mouth are naturally downturned, which makes for a chronically serious look. People with RBF get annoyed when they're told to "smile more" or constantly asked, "What's wrong?" or "Are you upset?" The problem with having RBF is that you may think you look perfectly fine and happy, but to the outside world you look angry instead. It's hard to be considered a warm person, even if you feel that way on the inside, when your expression always looks angry.

If you have RBF, don't despair! There are things you can do to overcompensate.

Here are three tried-and-true tips for looking more approachable:

- **Perfect the art of the neutral expression.** You can practice having a more neutral look on your face or a slight smile, to look more approachable. Think of the *Mona Lisa* — her slight smile is all you need. (You can skip the Renaissance garb.)

- **Be more expressive.** You can try to add more expressiveness to your face and voice to counteract your natural serious expression.

- **Experiment with makeup.** You can use makeup tricks to make it appear that the corners of your mouth are elevated. There are different strategies involving lip liner that you can learn about online. One to start with is a tutorial by famed makeup artist Lisa Eldridge — check it out at https://youtu.be/EHOqJLHZqD8.

Looking put together and having good hygiene

Personable people look reasonably put together and have good personal hygiene.

For better or worse, people judge others by their appearance. If you're sloppy or disheveled, you're more likely to be disliked or overlooked than someone who has taken the time to look put together. Someone who looks polished and put together gives the impression that they care about themselves and take care of themselves, both of which are personable traits. People are drawn to people who take care of themselves and seem to have it all together.

REMEMBER

You don't have to look like a fashion model to look polished, but your clothes should be clean and unwrinkled, fit well, and be free of holes or tears. Having a basic "uniform" that you wear every day like jeans and a brightly colored sweater, can help you feel put together with minimal effort.

Someone who has poor personal hygiene is more likely to be disliked, because no one wants to smell body odor or bad breath. Good hygiene includes having fresh breath, no body odor, trimmed nails, and tidy hair.

Showing expressiveness

Approachable people are usually expressive — you can see their emotions on their face or hear their emotions in their voice, as opposed to someone whose demeanor is flat. When someone has a flat affect, their face and body language don't show their emotions very readily, so you don't know what they're thinking or feeling. People tend to feel wary and distrustful of someone who isn't very expressive. If you're more reserved and you don't show much facial expression, focus on being expressive with your voice and hands. Avoid having a monotone or flat-sounding voice, but instead show enthusiasm with vocal inflection.

Your social energy also plays into expressiveness. People who are charismatic are usually very likable — they're outgoing, animated, playful, and confident in social settings. They have a good energy about them and their vibe draws people in. People who are more passive and just sit there or who don't talk and don't engage have a weaker social energy about them, and people are less likely to be drawn to them.

TIP

If you tend to be more passive and want to become more personable, focus on being more animated in social settings and use your voice and facial expressions to show your emotions.

Having a sense of humor

Another important trait that many personable people share is having a sense of humor. You don't have to constantly crack jokes — not everyone has the gift of a stand-up comic — but you can work on not taking yourself too seriously and being generally more lighthearted. Sometimes people who are seen as too serious or uptight have a harder time making friends, because many people prefer to hang out with others who are more playful and fun-loving.

You don't have to be a comedian, but to be more personable, try to work on being more entertaining and playful. Laughing together is one of the most often mentioned activities that people like to do with friends. People love other people who make them laugh. Being able to poke fun at yourself occasionally and find the humor in a serious situation are important qualities in your quest to make new friends. At a minimum, try to laugh at others' jokes heartily if you can.

HOW IMPROV CAN HELP YOU MAKE FRIENDS

Some people who are working on making more friends and improving their self-confidence take improv classes, which many communities offer. *Improv* is short for *improvisation* and refers to comedy that is created on the spot (so, without a script).

Anyone can sign up to take an improv class, and you don't have to have any acting experience. Improv classes can help you become more lighthearted, more playful, and less uptight. When you're up on stage performing in front of strangers, you build your self-confidence. The experience can also help you become more spontaneous and more in touch with your goofy side.

One of the most famous improv theater companies is called The Second City (www. secondcity.com); they have locations in Chicago, New York, and Toronto. The Second City offers improv classes that anyone can take, both in person and online.

LAUGHING YOUR WAY TO NEW FRIENDSHIPS

Laughing easily is another way to be more personable. A 2005 study by Stephen Reysen in the journal *Social Behavior and Personality: An International Journal,* used his own scale, called the Reysen Likability Scale, to find out how likable test subjects were perceived who read a paragraph in three different ways: with genuine laughter, with no laughter, or with fake laughter. The study results showed that people who read the paragraph while laughing were the most likable. The takeaway here is that laughing more often could make you be seen as a more likable person.

People who have an easy laugh are seen as more jovial and less uptight. If you have difficulty laughing because you're a more serious type, try imagining a funny scene in your mind (perhaps from a movie) that you can call on anytime you want to laugh more spontaneously at other people's jokes. When it's time to laugh, recall that scene, and laughing may come more easily.

Being easygoing and flexible

Being easygoing and flexible, a go-with-the-flow type of person, is another trait that many personable people share. People like others who are easy to be with. If you're too rigid or exacting when it comes to making plans, that can be a turnoff. Some people are so particular about making plans that it ends up taking dozens of emails or texts to plan a simple get-together.

Personable people are generally agreeable and easygoing and are willing to compromise. They're also understanding about rescheduling plans as long as it doesn't happen too often.

EXAMPLE

Emily wanted to make plans with Debbie. Emily suggested going out for dinner and a movie. "Sounds fun! You name the place," Debbie said. "I'm up for anything." Emily chose an Italian restaurant. "I chose the restaurant, so you choose the movie," she said to Debbie. Both Emily and Debbie are flexible and easygoing.

EXAMPLE

Contrast this with Anna's lack of flexibility. The next week when Emily wanted to make plans with Anna, she also suggested going out for dinner and a movie. "How about coffee instead of dinner, and mini golf instead of the movie?" Anna suggested. "Okay," Emily said. "Now that I think about it, I'm really busy this weekend, so how about we just meet for coffee near my house?" Anna said. Anna is more particular, and she makes it harder to make plans. Anna probably has a harder time making and keeping friends than Emily and Debbie do.

Being humble

Being humble and not braggy are important traits of personable people. There is a difference between being proud of something and wanting to share it with others versus trying to one-up someone or wanting to elicit a reaction of envy. Someone who is humble will not post their new car or large purchase on social media, and they won't even mention it at all, whereas a braggy person would make it a point to post about these purchases on social media and tell you all about it. A humble person may talk about their upcoming vacation but not discuss that it was expensive or talk about the type of hotels they stayed in, whereas a braggart will name-drop hotels and let you know that they flew first class.

People appreciate humble people, and humble people are usually well liked.

Being a people person

Another quality that makes someone personable is being a *people person* (the type of person who is naturally chatty, talks to anyone and everyone, and loves being in social settings). When you think of someone who is the quintessential people person you may think of the friendly neighbor who walks every day in your neighborhood and chats with everyone they see. Or, you may think of your local grocery store cashier who makes it a point to chat with every customer and greets their regulars by name. You may think of an acquaintance who you go to a bar with and, at the end of the night, they seem to know everyone's life stories.

Someone who is a people person has a friendly vibe, is willing to talk to anyone, and enjoys getting to know others. They'll talk and laugh with random people in line, store clerks, and people at the next table at a restaurant, and in five minutes they seem to learn everything about them. You'll often hear them say, "I'll talk to anyone." People like them because they're open, friendly, and gregarious. Their chattiness puts people at ease and makes them open up.

TIP

If you want to be more of a people person, you can start small. Try having a short, friendly conversation with one or two random people per week. These may be neighbors you come across while walking your dog, the server who is waiting on you at a restaurant, or another parent you see in the school pickup line. Focus on what it feels like to get to know the other person and be curious about their experience.

Being supportive and caring

Being supportive and caring is an important friendship trait. This means showing support for others' dreams and goals, asking how you can help, showing interest, and being supportive when someone is feeling down or having a challenging time. For instance, if your friend is sick or just had surgery, you could be supportive by doing any of the following:

>> Checking in with them to see how they're doing

>> Asking how their surgery went

>> Bringing by a meal or flowers

>> Asking how you can help lighten their load

For example, a supportive and caring person may say, "I'm so sorry to hear that you broke your ankle, Bonnie. How are you doing now? Can I take out your trash this week so you can rest?"

Being a good listener, validating what the other person is saying, and asking questions to show interest is another way to be supportive. If your friend is excited about a new business idea, being supportive means asking questions, being positive about the idea, and showing interest and enthusiasm. Not being support-ive would involve being critical of the idea, saying it won't work, or telling them all the reasons why they shouldn't be pursuing it.

TIP

Try to match their enthusiasm with your enthusiasm. If you respond with an unenthusiastic "That's great" when they tell you about their new book deal, you won't be seen as a supportive friend.

Showing vulnerability

Showing vulnerability is one of the most important friendship traits you can cul-tivate. Vulnerability means letting down your guard and sharing your flaws, chal-lenges, and heartaches at an appropriate time with someone. You don't want to be vulnerable with everyone, and you also don't want to be too vulnerable too soon. But being vulnerable at the right time and in the right dose, does a lot to deepen a friendship.

In today's world of social media, many people try to curate an image of perfection, where nothing is ever wrong in their lives. Being vulnerable helps to break that myth and shows the other person that you're authentic, with real challenges. Peo-ple connect more with real people who have flaws than they do with someone who portrays themselves as never faltering. When you express vulnerability, other people can relate to you better and it brings you closer.

People value others who are willing to be honest about their challenges and short-comings, because we all have them. People who never show vulnerability seem wooden and show less humanity. They make it seem like they have it all together, all the time, which can feel off-putting or inauthentic. Plus, never showing vul-nerability can make it seem like someone is holding you at arm's length, never really letting you into their inner world. When someone does show vulnerability, then the other person shares their challenges as well, and the two become closer.

EXPLORE

As an exercise, think about a way to be vulnerable with a current friend or acquain-tance. If you haven't yet shown vulnerability, choose something minor to show vulnerability about at first. For example, sharing that you're struggling with pro-crastination in your job would be a good example of a minor vulnerability to share. See how they react. If the other person reacts with empathy and it seems to bring the relationship closer, then later on you can gradually share something more personal. An example of showing inappropriate vulnerability would be sharing with an acquaintance that you're estranged from your parents. You'd want to wait until you're closer friends to share something that personal.

Making Other People Feel Liked

One of the best ways to be more personable is to make others feel liked. Researchers have shown that we tend to like people who we think like us; this concept is called the *reciprocity of liking.* There are many ways you can show others that you like them. These include making others feel good when they're around you, being responsive, being interactive on social media, checking in on others, reaching out and extending invitations, and being interested in others' lives.

Making people feel good when they're around you

The poet Maya Angelou once said, "I've learned that people will forget what you said, people will forget what you did, but people will never forget how you made them feel."

This powerful quote is a reminder that what's most important is how we make others feel about themselves. Do others feel positively about themselves when they're with you? If so, you don't need to worry too much about stumbling over your words, saying the wrong thing occasionally, or forgetting someone's name. Conversely, if you make someone feel badly about themselves when they're with you, whether by showing disinterest, ignoring them, or rejecting them, they'll remember and avoid you in the future. The takeaway is to try to make others feel important and valued.

In order to be a more likable person, strive to make others feel good about themselves, feel cared about, and feel interesting and worthwhile. Here are some ways you can do this:

>> Giving people your full attention

>> Asking follow-up questions

>> Being happy to see them

>> Being supportive and caring

>> Being enthusiastic

>> Showing up for them in times of need

>> Making them feel important and valued

>> Showing respect

>> Letting them know you enjoyed spending time with them

>> Asking for advice or recommendations

>> Making them feel comfortable or putting them at ease

TIP

Before you socialize, create a positive affirmation for how you want the people you interact with to feel after spending time with you. Repeat this affirmation to yourself multiple times before and during the event to remind yourself how you want others to feel. In order to create your affirmation, reflect on how you would like to feel (or already do feel) after talking to a supportive friend. An example could be: "I make others feel heard, valued, inspired, and cared for."

EXPLORE

As an exercise, think about how you feel when you spend time with different friends and acquaintances. Is there anyone who makes you feel really good about yourself? Is there anyone who makes you feel badly? What is the other person doing or saying to make you feel good or bad? Do you feel like the best version of yourself when you're with them, or do you feel inhibited in some way? Use the insights you gleaned in this exercise to inform how you'd like others to feel when they're with you.

Checking in on people

These days, with everyone being so busy, it seems like few people take the time to check in on their friends. But checking in on friends is a small but important way to make others feel liked. Everyone wants to be thought of, and all it takes is a quick text message, email or voicemail to let someone know that you're thinking of them. You can say, "Hi, how's your week going? Thinking of you." This simple gesture can make someone's day so much brighter.

Besides a general check-in about how their day, week, or month is going, you can also check in with friends about how an important job interview went, how it went with a doctor's appointment they were anxious about, or how their vacation was. Checking in is a powerful yet simple gesture to show how much you care, and it will make the other person feel liked and valued.

TIP

When you're first getting to know someone and you've just exchanged contact information, try not to overwhelm them with check-ins. At first, consider sending them a check-in message once a month. Then, as you get to be better friends and are texting or emailing more often, you can check in more frequently. There are no official guidelines on this; just go slow and see what feels right. You don't want to be overeager, but you do want to show interest in your new friend.

Being responsive

Being responsive is another way to show others that you like them. When you're responsive, you answer texts and emails in a timely fashion, and if a friend asks something of you, you make it a priority. When you take a long time to answer or respond, or it takes you a long time to get around to doing something for a friend, it gives the impression that the other person isn't a priority to you, and they may think you don't like them.

Think about how quickly you prefer someone to respond to you, and try to do the same for others. There are no cut-and-dried rules for what being ideally responsive looks like, but a good benchmark is to try to respond to people's emails or texts within a day.

Connecting on social media

When someone sends you a friend request on social media, or you friend someone else, take that opportunity to show them that you're interested in them. Being active and engaged with their social media can make it clear that you like the other person and want to get to know them better. Liking their photos or leaving supportive comments on their posts goes a long way toward making them feel valued and appreciated. Think about how good it makes you feel when others comment on or like your posts, and try to do that for other people. Being engaged with someone's social media can strengthen your bond.

There are no guidelines for how engaged you need to be on someone's social media, but try to like or comment on their posts every so often (it doesn't need to be every day). Just keep in mind that the more often you engage, the more supportive you'll appear.

Showing interest in them

Have you ever noticed what it feels like when someone isn't giving you their full attention? Maybe you're trying to talk to them and they're looking all around the room, or maybe they keep checking their phone during your conversation. These actions make it clear that they'd rather be talking to someone else or they'd rather be somewhere else.

Part of making others feel liked is showing interest and giving them your full attention. This is a skill you can practice at first by making small talk with random strangers and giving them your full attention. As you do this, notice what it's like for you when you give others your full attention and when you receive others' full attention. Be curious about others and be open to learning about them.

TIP

Take a look at the following suggestions for how to show interest in others:

>> **Ask questions.** Ask questions to learn more about the other person. Common questions to ask someone you've just met include where they're from, how long they've been in the area, how their summer/holiday/weekend was, what they've been up to lately, and what they like to do in their free time. Balance asking questions with answering them yourself, to make the conversation flow better. For example, "How long have you lived in Wilmington? I've been here for eight years already."

>> **Follow up.** If someone mentions they're about to go on vacation, take note, and the next time you see them, ask how their trip was. Or if they mention they're going to their grandmother's ninetieth birthday party, ask how it was when you see them next. Remembering important events and milestones shows the other person that you were actively listening and took the time to remember an important detail. This type of attention to detail will endear you to others.

>> **Practice active listening.** Active listening means focusing on the other person, nodding your head to encourage them to keep talking, asking questions when appropriate, and making supportive comments like, "That sounds really interesting! I'd love to hear more."

>> **Remember and use names.** People love to hear the sound of their own name, so make sure to learn and remember names and use them often during your conversation.

>> **Give the other person your full attention.** Put away your cell phone, avoid looking around the room, and try not to let your mind wander. Focus your attention on what the other person is saying, and reflect what they're saying back to them from time to time.

Being happy to see them

When you see someone you know, and you're happy to see them, show them! You can show them by giving them a hug, or if you're not a hugger, by being enthusiastic with your voice and greetings. "Hi, Shelley! It's so great to see you!" goes a long way toward making someone feel liked and valued. People will remember if you greet them with enthusiasm, because so many people interact in a lackluster way.

Similarly, after your conversation, make it clear that you enjoyed your chat by saying how nice it was to talk with them. "It was so great talking with you, Phil. Enjoy the rest of the conference, and I hope to see you again soon" will help them remember you as a kind and friendly person.

Initiating plans

Reaching out, making the first move, and initiating plans with others are all great ways to show someone that you like them. These days it seems like everyone waits for the other person to make the first move. The result is that no one ends up doing anything and that first get-together doesn't happen (and a friendship never forms). But you can break that cycle by being the one to initiate plans with others. Making the first move shows the other person that you like them and want to get to know them better.

It takes courage to initiate plans, however, because many people fear rejection. There's always the risk that if you reach out, the other person will say no. Keep in mind, though, that rejection is a universal experience, and there are always more people out there to try to befriend. So, don't let the fear of rejection hold you back from reaching out to others. Giving yourself a little pep talk before reaching out to someone can help build your confidence.

TIP

Take a look at the following strategies for initiating plans with others:

>> **Choose something easy.** When you first initiate plans, choose something low-key, like coffee or a walk. These types of events are low stress and not as intimidating or formal as lunch or dinner at a restaurant. People tend to prefer more casual get-togethers, especially at first when you don't know them, and coffee or a walk can easily fit into someone's schedule and is shorter in duration, which can be more appealing than a two-hour restaurant meal.

>> **Don't invite them to your home right away.** Remember to save an in-home get-together like a game night for people you know well. In-home get-togethers are most appropriate (and safer) after you've gotten to know someone a while. Trust your gut and take things slow before giving out your address.

>> **Make your plans specific.** When you initiate plans with someone, make sure to specify a date and time, or several dates and times to choose from, instead of saying, "We should get together sometime." Requests like these are too general and often don't end up happening, because it's too much work for the other person to narrow down a date and get the ball rolling. In order to set yourself up for success, have some specific date and time options ready for the other person. For example, "Let's get together for coffee. Are you free Tuesday around 10 a.m. or Thursday after 2 p.m.? If those days and times don't work, let's look into next week."

Showing up for them

Showing up for friends during their time of need shows them that you like them. When you show up for someone, you communicate that you care about them and value what's important to them. Showing up can take many forms: You may help someone look for their lost pet, bring a meal if someone is having surgery, attend their art gallery opening, or offer to pick up their child from the bus stop if they're running late. Find out what's important to your friend or any upcoming milestones in their life and figure out how you can show up for them. Showing up helps build your sense of community, too. If you show up for them, hopefully they'll show up for you when you need it.

TIP

When you're first getting to know someone, look for little ways to show up for them while you're building your friendship. It can be as simple as letting them know you're going to the grocery store and asking if they need anything when they're sick, or offering to carpool to the upcoming soccer game.

Giving compliments

Another powerful yet simple way to make others feel liked is to give them compliments. It's so rare for most people to hear a compliment that people will think of you positively when you give them. Giving a genuine compliment makes the other person feel appreciated and lets them know that you value them. Giving compliments also shows the other person that you've noticed one of their positive qualities, traits, or actions and you're giving them positive feedback, which shows that you're trying to get to know them.

TIP

The types of compliments that work best are genuine, authentic ones about a personal characteristic or trait. Avoid complimenting others about personal appearance because that can come across as being flirtatious or superficial. For example, you may say, "Charlene, you did such a great job coordinating that bake sale! You're always so organized. That was the best bake sale I've ever been to. Great job!"

Try to vary how often you compliment someone. Try not to compliment them every time you see them, because that can start to feel insincere and fawning. Complimenting someone once every few times you see them would be a good frequency.

Showing appreciation

Showing appreciation for others also demonstrates that you like them. You can show appreciation by thanking someone for meeting up and telling them how much you enjoyed it or by letting them know how much you appreciate them as a friend. Appreciation is something that people don't hear enough of, so someone who shows appreciation toward others will definitely stand out in a good way.

Sometimes people feel shy about letting others know that they like them. If you like someone, let them know! There are many ways to let them know that you'd like to be friends, such as "I can't believe we have so much in common! It's been so great getting to know you," or "I really enjoy spending time with you. I think we're going to be great friends," or "I look forward to getting to know you better." Sometimes people don't realize you want to be friends until you explicitly tell them.

Did you know that in the United States there is a National Friendship Day? It's the first Sunday in August. Sending your friends a text, email, or card saying you're thinking of them and appreciate them as a friend would be a thoughtful gesture on this special day.

Chapter **10**

Making Deeper Connections with People

Congratulations! You've made a friend, which is no small feat! Now, it's time to think about deepening that connection. Many people seek closer friendships in order to have a friend or two who really "get" them and know them inside and out. Deep friendships make life more fulfilling and meaningful because you have someone to share many of life's important moments with. If a closer friendship is your goal, then it's important to work on connecting at a deeper level which can include being vulnerable, having deep and meaningful conversations, and letting them get to know the real you.

Some people find it difficult to form deeper connections with others. They may be great at forming superficial friendships and have a few casual friends, acquaintances, or activity partners they can hang out with from time to time. For some people, that's enough. But others aren't satisfied with only surface friendships and want closer, deeper connections, but they don't know how to make them.

There can be several reasons to explain why it's been hard for you to form deeper connections: Maybe you aren't meeting people you have enough things in common with, maybe you haven't yet initiated more meaningful conversation, maybe you haven't demonstrated vulnerability, or maybe you haven't yet set the stage for forming closer connections, so the relationships stay superficial. This chapter helps you diagnose your problem areas so you can course-correct and be well on your way to deeper, more satisfying friendships.

In this chapter, I cover everything you need to know about how to connect with friends on a deeper level. In order to deepen your connections, you need to be vulnerable, share more deeply about yourself, and connect reciprocally. This chapter starts by helping you diagnose your challenges with connection, so you can better understand where you're having difficulties. Then it walks you through the "main ingredients" of closer connections. Next, it discusses the importance of vulnerability and how to be more vulnerable with your friends. Finally, it shows you how to engage in deeper and more meaningful conversations.

Diagnosing Your Connection Challenges

So you'd like a friend you can connect deeply with and be your authentic self with, but you're frustrated and confused about why you can't seem to find these kind of friendships. You might feel like you have some acquaintances and casual friends, and you're doing all the right things to become closer with them, but you wonder why others have close friendships and you can never move beyond surface ones. You might also feel envious when you go out to a restaurant or bar and see big groups of people talking, laughing, and seemingly having a great time whereas you've never had fun like that with the people you know. You might have a case of FOMO (fear of missing out) and wonder, "Why can't I ever seem to make close friendships like I see everyone else having?"

REMEMBER

The truth is that many people have difficulty forming deeper connections. I hear this all the time in the therapy office. They may have plenty of acquaintances such as a gym buddy, walking partner, or folks they hang out at bars with, but they're dissatisfied with these more superficial friendships and lack of meaningful conversation and don't know how to turn these casual friendships into something deeper. They want a close friend or best friend but are chronically stuck with more surface-level friendships. They may feel like they're missing out on an important life experience if they don't have any close friends.

TIP

If deeper friendship is your goal, but something keeps getting in the way of forming these closer connections, the first step is to do some self-reflection. This step is especially important if you find that you're unable to connect more deeply in all of your friendships, versus just one or two. When you have more clarity and insight about what's getting in the way, you can course-correct and chart a new path forward.

Engaging in self-reflection

The first step in your quest to form deeper friendships is to take an honest look at yourself and your friendships in the form of self-reflection.

While you self-reflect, it's important to find a space where you can focus on doing your inner work.

TIP

It can be helpful to do this kind of self-reflection while you sit quietly in a room by yourself with a piece of paper to make notes on, while engaging in a repetitive task like cleaning, or while talking a walk in nature where you can fully clear your mind.

TIP

If you have difficulty with looking inward on your own, you may want to explore with a spouse/partner, close family member, or therapist the question of why you've had difficulty forming deeper friendships to get some feedback from different angles and perspectives. You can ask your support person the following questions:

>> Why do they think you're having difficulty forming deeper relationships?

>> What have they noticed you doing or not doing when you're with friends that could be getting in the way of a deeper friendship?

>> Is there anything significant they've noticed that you could be doing better?

>> What advice do they have for you about making closer friendships?

>> Have they ever experienced similar challenges? If so, can their experiences help you make different choices?

EXPLORE

Turning back to your own self-reflection, make a list on paper about what you think may be getting in the way of your forming deeper friendships. Think about your last few attempts at making closer friends — what you tried and what didn't work out. What is your gut feeling about what got in the way? Often our gut feelings are right on target. Your gut feeling may be saying something like: "I'm too shy and hard to get to know, and that's why people don't want a closer relationship with me" or "I don't have much in common with people I meet, so it's hard to get into deeper conversations." Go with your gut.

Here are some common reasons people have difficulty forming closer friendships. Do any of these ring true for you?

>> They aren't putting in the necessary time and effort to nurture a closer friendship.

>> They shy away from deep and meaningful discussion and prefer to keep things more casual and surface-level.

>> They move frequently and haven't been in one place long enough to form close-knit friendships.

>> They have trust issues and don't want to get too close to people out of fear of getting hurt.

>> People see them as someone they don't feel at ease with or who they can't be themselves with.

>> They haven't found anyone who has the vibe they're looking for. They just aren't clicking with anyone.

>> They haven't found anyone who sees them as having close friend potential.

>> They don't have much in common with the people they meet.

>> People aren't matching the effort they put into relationships.

Determining what's in and out of your control

Some of the reasons why you're having difficulty making closer friendships are in your control, and some are out of your control. For the reasons that are within your control, you can make the decision to take some positive action now so things can change in a positive direction for you.

For instance, if the reason that you don't have close friendships is because you haven't been putting in the necessary time and effort to nurture them (Professor Jeffrey Hall's 2018 research showed that it takes approximately 200 or more hours to turn a friend into a best friend), you can make the decision now to start making the time. You can do this by setting aside a few hours a week to meet up regularly with a friend for coffee or lunch, set reminders to check in with friends weekly, and make sure to carve out time for a friend in need. Or, you may decide that you're not willing to take any positive action to improve the situation, in which case you may need to accept having more surface-level friendships, for now at least.

For the reasons that are out of your control, such as your acquaintances being too busy to put effort into your friendships, you can do one of the following to cope with the situation:

>> Reframe your negative thoughts on the situation.

>> Accept the situation as it is.

>> Do what you can to take an action step in the right direction.

For example, if people aren't matching the effort you put into relationships, you can do one of the following:

>> Reframe your negative thoughts about the situation into something more neutral (for example, going from "No one has time for me" to "This is a busy season of life for many people").

>> Accept the situation as it is, even if it's not what you would choose or want.

>> Take a small action step to improve the situation by looking for people who have more free time to spend with you, such as newcomers to your area who are eager to make friends.

Exploring compatibility

Meeting people who are compatible with you is the first step to building deeper friendships. Some people have plenty of acquaintances and situational friendships, but notice that when the environments or situations that brought them together go away, those friendships fade. For example, maybe you made a good friend at work, but when you changed jobs, you never heard from them again. Or maybe you made some good parent friends at your child's school, but when your child changed schools, those friendships faded out. Part of the reason for these situations is that what connected the two of you was mainly the temporary situation you shared, and not a greater compatibility that would've made the friendship long-lasting.

The first step to forming deeper and longer-lasting connections with others is to make friends who have close friend potential. This means that you have a lot in common and lots to talk about, share important values, want to put the same level of energy into the friendship, and feel supported.

TIP

One way to tell if there is close friend potential is feeling a click when you first meet them. When you click with someone, it tells you that you have friendship chemistry. When you have friendship chemistry, it may feel like you've known them forever, and you find that you have lots in common and endless things to talk about.

After you've determined they have friend potential, you can work toward a deeper connection with the strategies described in this chapter.

EXPLORE

If you're seeking close, deep friendships, it's important that you and the other person are compatible. Think about the friends and acquaintances you already have. Do you feel that you're compatible with all of them, or are you just friends because you were brought together in the same situation (like you work in the same office)? Who of your friends are you most compatible with and why? If you don't feel that you're compatible with any of your current friends, this is probably part of why you're not forming close relationships, and it's time to explore new ways to find people to connect with who you have more in common with. (Check out Chapter 5 for more on how to join new groups.)

Knowing when you've connected deeply

It's helpful to know when you've connected deeply with someone. There are several ways to know:

>> **You feel like they know you really well.** They can predict what you'll think or do in certain situations, and they know important facts about you, like your favorite restaurant, how you met your spouse/partner, or your favorite vacation spots. "I knew you were going to say that" is something a close friend might say.

>> **You feel comfortable with them and feel like you can talk about almost anything, at any time.** You regularly have deep conversations.

>> **They regularly invite you places.** They're investing as much energy into the friendship as you are.

>> **You can be vulnerable with them and know that they'll be supportive.**

>> **They have your back, and you feel supported.**

>> **They remember your birthday and other important milestones.** You feel valued and cared for.

TIP

People who have close friendships usually just have a few best buds. They may have lots of acquaintances and a bunch of casual friends, but just one or two close friends. That's because it takes lots of time and energy to cultivate and nurture these close bonds.

EXPLORE

Think about the last person you felt a deep connection with. How did you meet them? Was there a turning point when you started to feel a close connection with them?

Understanding the Ingredients of Deeper Connections

Some people believe that deep connections "just happen" and there's not much you can do to facilitate the process. However, nurturing deeper connections with other people is actually something that is tangible and achievable. In order to have deeper connections with people, you need to have a few of these "ingredients" in your friendship: spending time together, having an intense experience that bonds you, showing your true colors, showing up for others, being open, paying attention to others, and having fun together. The following sections explore each of these ingredients in more detail.

Spending lots of time together

In order to have a deep connection with a friend, you first need to spend lots of time together.

If you have acquaintances and casual friends that you've made in one setting (like the gym) and you want to deepen those friendships, take the friendship out of that setting and into a new one. For example, if you have an acquaintance whom you chat with at yoga classes, invite them for coffee after yoga to get to know them better. Then you can find out if you have other things in common besides your love of yoga poses to bond you. Over time, if you continue to spend time together outside of yoga class, the stage is set for a closer relationship to form. Having new experiences together and making memories all helps the friendship grow closer.

TIP

If you tend to default to coffee, walks, or lunch, think of other creative ways you can spend time with your friend. Going to a museum, taking a hike, or going to a fair or festival are other ways to spend time together.

Put yourself out there, invite people to do things over and over again, and follow up. Yes, it's a lot of work and a large time investment. But the more you spend time with someone, the more likely you are to form a deeper friendship as you two get to know each other better.

REMEMBER

Creating close bonds with a new friend takes a lot of time. If you've only met with someone for coffee twice and you expect to be best buds, your expectations aren't realistic. You'll both have to invest equal amounts of energy into the friendship over many months and years to achieve that super-close connection. If you're willing to put in the work and be patient, it's likely you can make a new close friend over time.

Don't be discouraged if it's taking a really long time to form close friendships. Back in your childhood, teen years, and college years, you were spending lots of time in close quarters with your friends, so friendships formed quickly. As an adult, you're probably only seeing your friends once or twice a month for a few hours at a time, so it's going to take much longer to get that same level of close friendship. Your new friend may have lots of other close friends they've known for years or decades already, and they may be focusing more on those friendships for now. Think about it this way: If you had very limited free time and had a free Saturday night, would you choose to spend it with friends you've known for decades or a brand-new casual friend you just met a month ago? You'd probably choose to spend your precious free time with people you know and value deeply rather than with an unknown newbie.

Having an intense experience that bonds you

One way that some people form close friendships quickly is by having an intense experience that bonds them together. For example, medical residents who are in the same residency class often form super-close friendships because they're all in a pressure-cooker environment for several years, trying to survive as they learn to become doctors. Being in the military together is another example of an intense experience that often creates strong, lifelong bonds. Working together in any stressful environment is another example where you'd likely become close friends with your coworkers.

REMEMBER

Not everyone has this kind of intense experience in their adult life, but there are other ways you could experience something similar where the camaraderie is high and you're working closely with or supporting others. People who volunteer together on a time-consuming committee to help an organization reach a goal may become close, as may people who are in a cancer or divorce support group together.

Showing your true colors

Deep friendship is formed from authentic connection. You want to show your true colors and be your authentic self when getting to know someone, so they know and like the real you. People usually want to click or feel chemistry with someone in order to invest more deeply in the friendship.

If you feel reserved and inhibited around others and your true self can't show through, it's less likely that someone will feel that spark with you. If this is a concern, think about why. Is self-consciousness getting in the way? Do you feel shy and awkward around others? Turn to Chapter 8 for more on how to cope with shyness and social anxiety.

REMEMBER

Sometimes it's the person you're with who makes you feel reserved and inhibited. Maybe you don't like how you feel around that person or you don't like how that person makes you feel. If that's the case, reevaluate if this person will really be a good close friend match for you. Close friends should bring out the best in each other and make each other feel good. When you're with a close friend, you should be able to be your authentic self without shame, including the goofy and silly parts.

REMEMBER

If you feel self-conscious around others, it can help to remind yourself that no one is scrutinizing you because they're too busy worrying about themselves and their own issues. This can help balance out any negative self-talk you may have.

Showing up for others

Another way to nurture a deeper friendship is to consistently show up for your friend when they need you. You can show up for them in a variety of ways — by bringing them a meal if they're sick, offering to help if they just had surgery, or being a shoulder to cry on if they're having a tough time. When people know you're there for them, it demonstrates your commitment to the friendship, and they're more likely to connect deeply with you.

TIP

Showing up for others can also take the form of supporting your friend not just in their time of need, but in their accomplishments and dreams as well. For example, if they're selling their art at a festival, you can show up to support them, or if they're performing in community theater, you can show up to watch the show. Think of different caring ways you can be supportive of your friend, and when they realize you're there for them, a deeper connection will usually take root.

Being open

In order to have deeper relationships, you need to be open. People find it easier to connect with someone who shares easily about themselves than they do with someone who's more guarded. Someone who is more guarded and keeps people at a distance doesn't let other people in, so it's harder to get to know them well.

REMEMBER

In a friendship, if one person is open and vulnerable and the other is more guarded, it can lead to an uneven, uncomfortable feeling in a friendship. The relationship likely won't grow closer because one person is left sharing openly about their life and the other person is more of a closed book, which can frustrate the person who is doing the sharing. The one who isn't sharing can come across as inauthentic or putting up a false front, and the friendship can feel superficial.

People usually feel safe opening up after the other person does. People who are guarded tend to ask a lot of questions about the other person's life instead of revealing much about themselves.

To ensure that you're being open in your friendships, you can practice self-disclosure in a gradual, appropriate way. The goal is to open up and share more of yourself over time; you don't want to emotionally dump on someone or share your deepest, darkest secrets right away. The more you open up, the closer your friend will likely feel to you. As you learn to trust the other person, gradually peel away the layers to get to deeper topics. That way, no one feels overwhelmed and you don't share too much, too soon.

EXPLORE

Think about how much you're willing to share about your personal life. Some people are willing to share a lot, and others share very little. If you're not willing to share much about your personal life, it'll be harder for people to get to know you.

Paying attention to others

Many people yearn for others to pay attention to them. They want to feel heard, validated, valued, and appreciated. When you make someone feel valued, it's more likely your relationship will grow closer. There are many ways you can do this: Listen closely, follow up on what your friend says, point out positive qualities you notice about them, praise them for their accomplishments, check in with them regularly, follow up about important things in their life, and make them feel special.

TIP

Being thoughtful is a very good way to show others you're paying attention. Remember their important details, and bring them up later, such as remembering their birthday or asking about how an important job interview went. Show that you're paying attention to what they share with you.

Having fun together

Many people are looking for a fun, upbeat friend they can have a good time with. Having a good time with each other and making each other laugh are important qualities for many people to want a deeper relationship. People are drawn to those who are positive and upbeat versus people who are more negative and complain often, which brings people down.

TIP

People who laugh easily usually make friends quickly because they put the other person at ease and seem like they're having a good time. Frequent laughter can bring your friendship closer.

Being Vulnerable in Friendships to Form Deeper Connections

One essential ingredient to deepening friendships that many people don't think about is showing vulnerability. This means expressing your fears, insecurities, flaws, and challenges in an appropriate way to reveal your fully authentic self. The reason that vulnerability is important is that it helps others see us as fully human, flaws and all. It chips away at the idea that we're perfect all the time and makes us more relatable to others.

REMEMBER

Being vulnerable helps people feel closer to you. Someone who doesn't ever show vulnerability can be hard to relate to or seems to portray their life as 100 percent perfect. This can make people less likely to feel comfortable sharing deeply with them because they fear being judged for being less than perfect.

Being vulnerable builds trust

When you're vulnerable with your friend, it builds trust. This is because when one person shares something and confides in the other, then the other friend also feels comfortable sharing what *they're* insecure about. When your friend responds with empathy and validates your feelings, it builds trust.

Some people struggle with vulnerability because they worry about being judged if they reveal something that shows weakness or flaws. Others worry that their friend will break their confidence, or use what they said against them later. However, when your friend responds with empathy and care, it helps you feel secure and willing to reveal more next time.

Think back to your childhood when it was fun to share secrets with your friends. Sharing a secret was something that bonded you together, because you knew they were the only one who knew your big secret. If they told someone, you would know they weren't trustworthy and you would be cautious about telling them any secrets in the future. If they kept your secret, it made you feel known and validated that they knew something important about you.

Being vulnerable helps you to feel supported by your friends. When you reveal something that you have fears about or that makes you feel insecure, and you're supported, your relationship with your friend grows closer.

WARNING

Some people find it easier to get vulnerable while drinking. The alcohol loosens them up and allows them to speak their true feelings. Be careful, though — you don't want to reveal anything *too* vulnerable while you're drunk, because you may regret it later.

Sharing something small

If you're feeling anxious about being vulnerable, or if you've really never done it before in a friendship, think of a way to share a small vulnerability in a light-hearted way. This can make the disclosure more casual and less intimidating.

TIP

Share something *slightly* vulnerable (like a 2 on a scale of 1 to 10 scale, with 10 being something significantly vulnerable). You could share something about being overwhelmed with work or household responsibilities, which is a relatively safe topic to start with. Let them know what you're looking for — are you looking for advice or just general support? If they respond favorably and with empathy and validation, or if they share their own vulnerability, then you may feel comfortable sharing something more vulnerable another time. If they ignore what you shared, invalidate what you shared, or change the subject, then you'll know to be more cautious when being vulnerable with them next time.

EXAMPLE

Here's an example of sharing something small:

"Hey, Kamal. How are you doing?"

"I'm all right, I guess. I've had a rough week because my wife was sick over the weekend and I got really behind on all the chores. The laundry is piling up, the dishes haven't been washed, my kitchen floor has spilled spaghetti sauce all over it that I didn't have a chance to clean, and I haven't been to the grocery store in a week. I just haven't had the energy to tackle it all, and it's bringing me down."

"I'm sorry, that sounds really hard. You sound really overwhelmed this week. I'm happy to lend an ear anytime you need to talk. Or if you want me to come by and help you get started with all the cleaning, I'm happy to do that on Saturday."

When you ask someone how they are, follow up on their responses or read between the lines to determine how they're feeling.

Being vulnerable is a good way to move into a more meaningful level of conversation. Share something personal about yourself or your experience and see where that takes you. Most likely, the other person will open up, too, and it will increase your closeness.

EXAMPLE

Here's another example:

Tony: "I'm one year out from retirement, and I'm still having difficulty figuring out what to do with all my free time. I tried volunteering, but I haven't found anything that appeals to me, and I've already read all the books on my reading list and play pickleball a few times a week. I'm feeling a bit lost, and I'm not sure what my next steps are."

Steven: "I felt the same way when I first retired — you're not alone. I was depressed for a few years because I didn't know what to do with my free time. Then I decided to start working again part-time, and that really helped a lot."

Notice in this example that Tony is expressing a little vulnerability, and it really opens up the conversation. Then Steven can show empathy, validate what his friend is going through, and share his own related experiences. Save anything too weighty (like family estrangement, serious medical conditions, a divorce) for when you've gotten to know your friend better.

Here are several other ways to show vulnerability:

>> Be sad in front of your friend and share why you're sad. If tears come, let them.

>> Reveal a personal flaw.

>> Reveal an insecurity about your parenting or family relationships.

>> Show your friends affection. This shows vulnerability because you're putting it out there how you genuinely feel about them, and they may not respond the way you'd hoped.

Being able to confide in each other

Being someone's confidante shows that you've reached a deeper level of friendship, and it allows your relationship to grow closer. Being able to confide in someone is one of the benefits of having a friend. A friend should listen nonjudgmentally and be supportive when you confide in them.

WARNING

There is a line between confiding in someone and emotional dumping. *Emotional dumping* is confiding a large number of distressing issues all at once, or unleashing an overwhelming amount of emotional turmoil at the same time, *and* expecting your friend to have the emotional bandwidth to deal with it all. Before you share, ask yourself if you would feel overwhelmed if someone shared that with you. Also, make sure to be respectful of your friend's time and don't confide major things too often or all at once. Let your friend share with you in between. If you do inadvertently emotionally dump on a friend and they gradually get less and less responsive, don't engage with you, or recommend you see a therapist, take that as a sign that they're overwhelmed and not willing to be emotionally dumped on again. Respect their boundaries. If you feel the need to emotionally dump on your friends, try to find a therapist instead, or consider journaling your feelings to help you process them more effectively.

Moving from Small Talk to Deeper Conversations

One important way to deepen your connection to others is to have deeper and more meaningful conversations. Small talk is important and necessary, and it has its time and place. It helps you to break the ice and get to know someone better when you first meet them.

But in order to further develop your relationships, you need to transition at some point from small talk to deeper conversations.

Understanding the differences

Small talk is surface-level conversation about light topics such as the weather, current events, the environment or the setting you're both in and things you both like to do. You can make small talk with anyone: strangers, people you've only met once or twice, or good friends.

In contrast, deeper conversations are usually saved for those you've gotten to know better, who you would consider friends. You wouldn't typically want to try to have a deep conversation with someone you've just met because it would be jarring and unexpected, and would likely make the other person feel awkward (though there are exceptions).

Deeper conversation focuses on thoughts, feelings, important experiences, fears and worries, relationships, and your personal life, among other topics. It allows you to share more fully about your life and who you are and get to know someone on a deeper level. Deeper conversations also usually feel more meaningful and memorable than small talk.

There are several benefits of deeper conversation. Deeper conversation allows you to:

>> Get to know someone by understanding more about how they think and feel.

>> Discover mutual interests as you discuss hobbies and passions.

>> Get to know their values, thoughts, and opinions.

>> Dig deeper to find commonalities and differences.

>> Learn more about their insecurities and fears.

>> Learn about their hopes, dreams, and goals.

>> Learn about their childhood experiences and how they were raised, which can sometimes explain some of their current thoughts and behaviors.

>> Learn about challenges they're facing and how they're overcoming them.

Deeper conversation enables you to connect on a deeper level and get to know who the other person really is.

Recognizing the challenges

Not everyone enjoys deep, meaningful conversation. Some people are uncomfortable sharing deeply about themselves or talking about feelings and want to keep their friendships light and airy. If you try to take the conversation deeper, and the other person balks multiple times and just wants to stay more surface-level with you, you can either accept the relationship for what it is or find a new friend who is interested in deeper conversation.

REMEMBER

Some people are uncomfortable with deep conversations because they feel awkward or feel they aren't good at contributing. As a result, they don't say much and take a more passive role in conversations. This can lead to others thinking they're disinterested, aloof, or too reserved, and people may leave them out of conversation. If you want to get more comfortable with participating in deeper conversations, try contributing to conversations in small ways while you build up your self-confidence.

Preparing for deep conversation

Many people like the idea of having deep and meaningful conversations in theory but struggle with conversation and don't really know what to talk about. If this describes you, there are several strategies that can help:

>> **Read widely — books, newspapers, the news, and magazines.** Reading will help you keep on top of different subjects so you'll be able to contribute to conversations, and it'll give you fodder to start deep conversations with. It will also help you seem more worldly and interesting as a conversation partner. If you read widely, it's likely that when a topic comes up, you'll be able to mention an interesting tidbit from a book you're reading that relates or enhances the discussion.

For example, if the conversation topic is about kids' schools and you're reading a book about education, you could mention a fact or statistic in the book you're reading that relates to the conversation, and the other person will then comment on it, which may take the conversation to a deeper level.

>> **Stay on top of current events.** Current events make great deep conversation starters. From there, you can learn more about someone's values and beliefs. You can stay on top of current events easily by reading the newspaper, watching the news, or listening to talk radio.

>> **Be curious about the other person and their experiences.** Try not to be judgmental. Instead, stay open-minded.

>> **Make sure the conversation topic you're initiating is interesting to the other person.** You can determine whether the other person is interested by paying attention to social cues that indicate boredom (like looking around the room, fidgeting, sighing, and so on).

Moving things along with conversation starters

Going from small talk or more surface-level conversation to deeper conversation often happens organically, but there are also things you can do to move things along.

Deep conversation starters are a great way to guide your conversation into deeper waters. Deep conversation starters are open-ended, so they invite a more lengthy, involved answer. This is in contrast to asking your friend a question that can be answered with a simple "yes" or "no." These types of questions are fine, too, but they won't do as much to help you deepen your conversation or learn more about your friend.

REMEMBER

Open-ended questions that ask what, where, why, or how are ideal. However, you don't want your time with your friend to feel like an interview. You might sprinkle one or two of these questions into your conversation when they come up naturally, but you don't want your entire conversation to consist of you asking open-ended questions and your friend answering them. Here are some examples of open-ended questions:

>> What was the highlight of your summer?

>> Where do you feel most at home?

>> How did your move go?

>> What were the best parts of your childhood?

>> How did you know your spouse/partner was the one for you?

>> What have been the best moments of the past few years for you?

>> What is your biggest accomplishment?

>> What has it been like meeting new people in this area?

TIP

How will you know if you're actually having a deep conversation with someone? You'll know because it's satisfying and it feels like you've gotten to know a new aspect of them. You'll come away feeling like the time was meaningful and well spent, and that you now know more about them.

Deeper conversations can be brief or last a long time. They can last ten minutes or several hours.

EXPLORE

Do some self-reflection about the last time you had a deep, meaningful conversation with someone. Who were you with and what were you doing? What did you learn about the other person?

Being a good listener

In order to successfully have a deep conversation with your friend, it's important to also be a good listener. Here are several ways to be a good listener:

>> **Put your phone away.** Or, at the very least, turn it over so you aren't tempted to keep glancing at it during your conversation.

>> **Make good eye contact to show that you're listening.**

>> **Reflect the person's comments back to them periodically to show that you're listening.** You can do this in a natural way by saying something like: "It sounds like you've had a tough time adjusting to retirement — you've tried a bunch of different volunteer roles, but it doesn't seem like you've found the right fit yet."

>> **Avoid excessive fidgeting or looking around the room, which can communicate boredom.**

>> **Be expressive with your face or voice to show that you're interested in what the other person is saying.**

>> **If you're bored, try to change the subject.** If you can't change the subject, try to think of interesting questions to ask the person to jazz up the conversation.

>> **Face your whole body toward the person who's talking to show that you're paying attention.**

Chapter **11**

Turning Acquaintances into Friends

O ne of the most challenging but important stages in the friendship journey is turning an acquaintance into a friend. This is a stage that everyone has to go through in order to emerge on the other side with a bona fide friendship. However, many adults are rusty on how to make the leap from acquaintance to friend. As a result, they end up getting stuck in the acquaintance stage long-term, which can be frustrating and disappointing.

This chapter helps you avoid this same fate by showing you everything you need to know to navigate the transition from acquaintance to friend. First, I help you recognize when you've made an acquaintance and how to identify the signs that there is potential for an actual friendship. Then I cover how to determine if there's a spark between the two of you, and what to do if there is no spark. I also explain how to slowly ease into a friendship so you don't do too much, too soon, which can be detrimental to a budding friendship. Finally, I fill you in on the specific strategies you can take to successfully go from acquaintance to friend.

Recognizing When You Have an Acquaintance

Before you can transform an acquaintance into a friend, you first need to know if the person you're interested in is already an acquaintance. In general, there are four stages of friendship: acquaintance, casual friend, close friend, and best friend. Sometimes it's hard to tell if someone is an acquaintance or has already crossed the line over to casual friend.

TIP

Here are some ways to know if you have an acquaintance in your life who's just waiting to be turned into a casual friend:

>> You know their name and some basic information about them.

>> You're friendly with them and, when you see them, your interactions are pleasant.

>> You see them primarily at group events, classes, teams, or functions.

>> You may have met up once or twice for a casual, low-key activity like coffee or a walk.

>> You make small talk and have pleasant conversation with them, but you don't have deep conversations yet, and you don't tell each other your problems or secrets. You haven't gotten to the point where you share personal information with each other.

>> They don't yet know important facts and details about you, like your birthday, how you and your spouse met, or where you grew up.

>> You may text them for logistical reasons, like to coordinate a get-together, but you don't text just to say hi or to ask about their day. You only text when needed for informational purposes, not to exchange friendly banter.

>> You haven't yet been to each other's homes.

Determining If There's Friend Potential

Not all acquaintances are meant to turn into friends. Some acquaintances just stay acquaintances, and that's perfectly okay. When you have an acquaintance, it's important to decide if you have enough in common and like this person enough to put in the work to turn them into a casual friend. Sometimes the answer is no.

When you want to make more friends, it can be helpful to ponder whether there's potential with this acquaintance for a friendship.

TIP

Ask yourself the following questions to determine whether this is a relationship you'd like to see deepen:

>> Does it seem like the two of you have enough things in common so that you have lots to talk about?

>> When you've talked with them, has the conversation flowed smoothly or has it been more awkward?

>> Do they fill up your cup or drain it?

>> Do the two of you have personalities that mesh well together?

>> Do you feel a spark or platonic chemistry with them?

>> Do they have traits or qualities that appeal to you? If so, what are they?

>> Have they shown signs of wanting to be your friend, like inviting you to do something or texting you just because?

>> Do you feel good about yourself around them?

>> Do the two of you have a good time together and laugh together?

If you've answered yes to three or more of these questions, it's likely that there's a good potential for a friendship.

EXPLORE

Reflect on whether you have any acquaintances right now that may have the potential to turn into friends. What do you like most about these acquaintances? How can you test the waters to see if they would be interested in a closer friendship?

REMEMBER

All friends once started out as acquaintances. You have to go through the steps of turning an acquaintance into a friend in order to progress to the prize, which is true, close friendship.

Deciding if there's a spark

One of the most important determinations of whether there's going to be a friendship is feeling a platonic spark. It's hard to describe what it feels like to experience a spark or chemistry, but you know it when you feel it. Similar to dating, when you feel a platonic spark with someone, you feel a certain magnetism and you're drawn to them and want to spend more time with them. When two people feel a spark, it's more likely they'll become friends because there's a feeling of compatibility and feelings of comfort and ease around each other. The relationship usually then progresses in an organic way without feeling forced or awkward.

TIP

You know you have a spark with someone if the conversation flows freely, you have multiple things in common, you feel like you could talk with them for hours, and your time together seems to go by very quickly. When good chemistry is there, you feel like you've known them a long time, the two of you laugh easily together, and you just feel comfortable and at home with them. You also may have a gut feeling that this person is going to be a very good friend.

EXPLORE

Think about the last time you felt a platonic spark with someone. How did you meet them? Was it at a group, in a class, through work, or in some other way? What qualities appealed to you most about them? Did the two of you become friends? How can you meet other people you feel the same way about?

Troubleshooting when there's no spark

Sometimes you meet someone you'd really like to be friends with, because you admire them or you share certain things in common, but there's no spark or chemistry. Ideally, there'd be a mutual spark, but if there's no platonic spark for one party, can a friendship still blossom? The answer is yes, but it will take longer.

Just as in romantic relationships, chemistry and mutual positive feelings can build over time as you get to know each other and share new experiences.

First impressions are formed quickly. When two people first meet, one person may have a preconceived judgment about the other person that they later realize is wrong (for example, they may assume someone who is very serious wouldn't be a fun friend). Over time, they can correct their assumptions as they get to know the other person better, and the chemistry can start to build.

When there's no spark, but you want this particular friendship, you may need to make peace with the fact that the person you're trying to befriend may feel luke-warm about you. Because many adults are so busy and have limited free time, if someone doesn't feel a strong connection right away, they may not be enthusiastic about putting in the work required to nurture a new friendship. They may do the bare minimum or do nothing at all to advance the friendship, and it may become one-sided. You'll need to be okay with working harder and putting more energy into the friendship.

WARNING

One complaint I hear a lot as a therapist is when people who don't feel a spark in their initial relationship then try to force the relationship and it turns into a one-sided friendship. Then they become upset and resentful. They want the friendship to work more than the other person does. The person who wants the friendship ends up feeling resentful because they're putting in all the effort while the other person does little to nothing. It's important to remember that when you start to feel a friendship has become one-sided, it's better to pull back a little, put less energy into it, and see if the friendship will grow and develop organically. If this doesn't happen, it may make more sense to move on and keep looking for people who you *do* feel a mutual spark with.

TIP

If you find that you're not feeling chemistry with *anyone* you meet, it's time to do some self-reflection and adjust your approach to meeting new people. Consider looking to join groups where you share a mutual hobby or interest with the other group members, take a class on a topic that interests you, or join a religious congregation. You're more likely to find a friendship match that way.

Planting the Seeds of Friendship

Now that you have an acquaintance in mind that you'd like to befriend, it's important to get into action mode. There are multiple strategies to turn acquaintances into friends. You may be champing at the bit to make a friend right away, but remember to be patient: Nurturing a closer connection takes time. Try to do at least a few of the following strategies for best effect.

Inviting them out

The most important step to turning an acquaintance into a friend is going out on friend dates so you can get to know each other. It's through spending time together and getting to know each other better (and eventually growing closer) that you'll make real friends. Even though it can be nerve-wracking, put yourself out there and invite them to do something with you. Most likely, they'll be thrilled with the invitation!

TIP

Many people are hesitant to make the first move, but there's a very easy way to do this: If you met them in a group or class, you can invite them to get coffee or lunch right after an upcoming group or class. This is an easy and efficient way to schedule a get-together because they'll most likely be available and it doesn't involve challenging logistics to plan. Spending time with someone in a new setting, other than the one you met them in is the best way to start off a new friendship. For example, if you met them in a Zumba class, invite them out for a smoothie after class. Something short that's an hour or less is a very unintimidating and manageable way to get to know someone. In this way, you'll start spending time together and getting to know each other.

Spending quality time together is an important factor in making a new friend. Research by Professor Jeffrey Hall in the *Journal of Social and Personal Relationships* shows that it takes 40 to 60 hours of time together to go from acquaintance to casual friend. Think about all those hours you'll need to rack up in order to become casual friends — that's a lot of coffee dates! If you see your acquaintance only once a month for an hour, it may take *years* to become friends. Try to make time to see your acquaintance frequently.

REMEMBER

Make sure when you invite someone out that you get very specific. Make sure to propose an actual date and time for your meetup. Just saying, "We should meet up sometime" is too vague and usually results in no one actually making set plans. Instead, inviting them to meet up for a specific activity on a specific date and time, such as lunch at noon next Friday, is more effective. This makes it more likely that they'll commit.

TIP

When you invite your acquaintance out the first few times, keep the get-togethers short and sweet. In these early months of getting to know each other, an hour-long walk is preferable to a three-hour dinner where it's harder to wrap things up if one of you is feeling uncomfortable or you run out of things to talk about. Other ideas for shorter get-togethers include getting coffee, going for ice cream, getting drinks, or doing an exercise class together. If there's an active activity involved, even better — that can make some people feel more comfortable, because there's something else to focus on besides staring at each other from across a table. Brainstorm other ideas that are an hour or less in duration. After you've gotten to know each other more and know you have a lot to talk about, you can expand your get-togethers to longer events.

Showing that you're into them

It's important to show your acquaintance in little ways that you like them and are interested in them. People tend to like others who like them. Think about how much it makes your day brighter when someone shows you that they like and value you. Give signs that you like them and are interested in getting to know them:

>> Compliment them.

>> Point out the things you have in common.

>> Show interest in their lives.

>> Remember important tidbits they mention to bring up later. For example, if they mention that their tenth wedding anniversary is coming up this July, remember the date and give them a card or wish them a happy anniversary.

>> Find something small your friend would like while you're out and about, and get it for them.

>> Send them a text with an article or meme you saw that reminds you of them.

>> Offer to bring them a coffee if you're meeting up for a walk.

BEYOND COFFEE: CREATIVE IDEAS FOR YOUR NEXT FRIEND DATE

So, you're ready to take the next step and invite your new friend to do something, but your mind is drawing a blank. Sometimes it's easy to get stuck in a rotation of coffee and lunch dates and it can be hard to come up with more creative ideas. Never fear. Here are ten activities you can do with a friend:

- Going on a botanical garden walk
- Taking a yoga or exercise class
- Attending a paint-and-sip event
- Visiting a museum
- Going to a festival or fair
- Attending a local event like a book signing
- Attending a theater or ballet performance
- Taking a class together
- Going to an amusement park
- Attending a sporting event

Thoughtful gestures like these help turn someone into a friend.

TIP

Another thoughtful gesture you can try is to text them just because you're thinking of them. Let them know you were thinking about them and wanted to reach out and say hi. This lets them know that you think about them from time to time and will make them feel special.

Asking for a favor

Another strategy to turn an acquaintance into a friend is to ask your new acquaintance for a small favor. A 2016 study in the *Journal of Social Psychology* showed that asking someone to do you a favor makes them like you more. It's flattering to be the one someone is asking for a favor, whether that's asking someone to drive you to the airport before a trip or to pick up your child from day camp if you're stuck in traffic. So, go ahead and ask an acquaintance for a small favor, and chances are, it will strengthen your friendship.

Inviting them into your home

When you feel comfortable enough with your acquaintance and you've met with them a few times in a public place, consider inviting them to your home for a meal or coffee. Author Jeanne Martinet, in her book *Life is Friends: A Complete Guide to the Lost Art of Connecting in Person* (Stewart, Tabori & Chang), explores how inviting someone to your home is one of the best ways to become better friends, because inviting someone into your personal space and showing them how you live is something that will bring the two of you closer.

Think about the last time someone invited you to their home for a meal or just to hang out. It was probably flattering to be asked, because it doesn't happen that often these days. Martinet explains that many people find entertaining at home to be a hassle, so they meet up with friends at restaurants, bars, or other venues instead.

Inviting someone to your home shows that you like them and want to invite them in for a more intimate gathering than you get when you meet up with someone for dinner in a crowded restaurant, where it's hard to hear and there's time pressure to finish your meal. At an in-home gathering, you can linger as long as you want and entertain at a more leisurely pace.

Acting like they're already your friend

You've probably heard the phrase, "Fake it 'til you make it." This adage is really on point when it comes to turning an acquaintance into a friend. Acting as if you like someone and they're already your friend makes you come across more warmly toward them, which in turn makes it more likely that the two of you will actually become friends. In a 2009 study published in *Personality and Social Psychology Bulletin*, researchers called this the *acceptance prophecy*. So, make sure to assume your acquaintance likes you, even if you internally struggle with low self-confidence. Even if you're scared of rejection, assume that the other person likes you and wants to be your friend. You'll give off a warmer vibe, which in turn can make this actually happen.

Being vulnerable and authentic

One way to get closer to an acquaintance is to be vulnerable with them in a small way. Nothing too deep or earth-shattering at first, but sharing a minor vulnerability that you would feel comfortable sharing with someone you don't know that well can bring the two of you closer. An example may be that you're feeling stressed at work and thinking about changing jobs, or that you're feeling overwhelmed balancing work and parenthood. When you're authentic with someone and show the good, as well as the messy realities of your life, you'll grow closer.

Save the really big vulnerabilities for when you've gotten to know them better.

Being a good listener

Being a good listener is a rare skill but one that is much valued when you're trying to make new friends. Being a good listener and learning more about your acquaintance helps you get to know them better. Practice *reflective listening*, where you paraphrase what they said and reflect the person's words and their tone of voice back to them. Reflective listening helps strengthen your connection.

Make sure to encourage them to talk by nodding your head and making small positive comments. You can also ask open-ended questions, which shows that you're being a good listener.

Being there when they need help

A great way to go from acquaintance to friend is to be there for them. If you notice an opportunity to offer help, do it. People value others who are helpful. If they're going through something challenging or just having a rough time, offer to hang out and let them vent about it. When they see that you're a nonjudgmental, empathetic person who cares about them and is happy to be there to listen or to lend a hand, the two of you will become closer.

Noticing the Shift

When you first meet someone, you go from stranger to acquaintance level pretty quickly, after just a few minutes of pleasant conversation. However, the shift from acquaintance to friend takes much longer and can be more subtle. Sometimes people aren't even sure if their acquaintance has morphed into an actual friend.

There are several details to notice that indicate there's been a shift, and that signal the relationship is naturally transitioning from that of acquaintances to casual friends. There's not a cut-and-dried moment when someone becomes a friend. It's more of a subjective feeling that you've become closer than just acquaintances and you've reached a deeper level in your relationship.

Some of the signs to look out for include the following:

>> They text you just to say hi or see how your week is going.

>> You feel like the two of you have good chemistry. When you're together, things seem effortless and flow organically. There's little or no awkwardness and the conversation doesn't feel forced.

>> They seem to be putting the same amount of energy into the relationship as you are.

>> They've asked you for a small favor, which builds trust and likability.

>> You start to see each other regularly.

>> They're interested in your life and ask questions to get to know you.

>> When they're around you, they seem happy — they're smiling and laughing a lot, and they seem to be having fun. The two of you have a good time together.

>> They pay attention and remember your important life details, like your spouse's and children's names, where you grew up, and where you moved from. They listen closely when you talk, and they follow up on things you say.

>> They initiate get-togethers with you and want to spend time with you. They invite you to do things with them.

>> You feel like they care about you. They show that they care in different ways with small gestures.

>> They're considerate of your feelings and treat you with respect.

>> They're supportive and cheer you on.

Troubleshooting Friend-Making Challenges

Sometimes things don't go as planned, and you run into a few challenges as you try to turn an acquaintance into a friend. One challenge is that, despite your best efforts, you can't seem to make any progress in your relationship, and the two of you are perpetually stuck in the acquaintance stage.

It can help to do some self-reflection to try to figure out why you may be having difficulty with this step in the friendship-making process. If after doing some introspection and reading this chapter, you still find that you're stuck, consider talking with a therapist to help you further identify and process why your friendships aren't progressing the way you'd like.

Being perpetually stuck in the acquaintance stage

Some people have a hard time moving beyond the acquaintance stage. They have lots of acquaintances but no actual friends. They long for deeper relationships, but all their friendships are surface-level. This problem can be frustrating, especially if you keep putting in the effort to make meaningful friendships, but it never seems to work out.

There may be several reasons behind this issue:

>> **You never feel a spark with anyone.** Chemistry is an important part of friendships, just as it is with romantic relationships. Some people you'll feel a spark with right away, and other people you'll just feel lukewarm about. But if you never feel a spark with anyone, consider whether you're meeting enough people or enough different kinds of people. You may need to join more groups in order to meet more people, so you increase the chances of feeling a spark with someone.

>> **You feel a spark with other people, but they don't feel a spark with you.** This issue is a common one I hear a lot about in the therapy office. Clients tell me that they feel a spark with others and want to pursue a friendship, but the other person never seems to be interested. Then they seem to end up in one-sided friendships where the other person is lukewarm about them and doesn't reach out or put in any effort. If this sounds like a problem you're having, reconsider where and how you're meeting new people. You may need to find others who have more in common with you, so you share more interests and values in common. Think about different groups or clubs where you could meet these kinds of people, and then join those groups. Also, consider whether you're doing something off-putting that is preventing others from fully connecting with you.

>> **You're too "extra."** Some people are so eager to make new friends that they come on too strong and scare others away. This can involve extending too many invitations in too short a time, or focusing on one person too much instead of having a variety of friends. People then keep their distance from you because they feel smothered. There's a fine line between putting yourself out there and being too aggressive with initiating plans. To correct for this, space out your invitations so that you're only inviting someone to do something once a month at first and try to make a variety of friends so you don't become too dependent on any one person.

>> **You're too quiet, reserved, or serious.** People tend to like others who are positive and fun-loving, and who have a lively energy about them. If you tend to be a quieter, more serious type, try to loosen up more and have fun when

you're with people you'd like to befriend. You can do this by smiling more often, laughing more often, and being more chatty.

TIP

People who are quick to laugh tend to make friends more easily. If you have a hard time laughing easily, have a funny scene from a movie you like in mind before you go to a social gathering. Think about this scene when it's socially appropriate to laugh, and this may help you laugh more easily.

Try to come across as more friendly, too. If you think you come off as too quiet, try to be more spontaneous and share what's on your mind more often. What comes out of your mouth doesn't have to sound perfect. Try to be more conversational with others.

» **You're too low energy.** Lower-energy people tend to not be liked as much as higher-energy people, who come across as friendly, exuberant, and open. If you think low energy is a problem for you and that it's impacting your friendships, as a first step, try to be more expressive with your facial expressions and voice. Also think of someone you know who you would consider higher energy and figure out what qualities and characteristics they have that you can also emulate.

» **You're intimidating to others.** Do you have a career or hobbies that come across as intimidating to others? Or do you come across as intimidating in other ways, such as by having model looks or an impeccable vocabulary? If so, this may be a cause of your friendship challenges. You shouldn't try to change yourself, but if you think this may be why you're not making friends, consider downplaying whatever it is that may be off-putting to others while you're trying to get to know new people. When people get to know you and like you, then you can showcase your authentic self more fully. For example, if you're a neurosurgeon trying to make new friends, that could make others feel intimidated, so consider not bringing up your career until others ask about it and then focus more on the similarities you share with them.

» **You're trying to make friends with people who already have enough friends and full social calendars.** Some people's dance cards are full, and they're not looking to make new friends, so you get stuck in the acquaintance stage. Sometimes the problem is that you're not finding the people who are actually open to new friends. Try looking for ways to meet people who are more open to making new friends, like newcomers' groups. Newcomers are usually very open to making new friends, because they don't know many people yet. Two good ways to find newcomers' groups is through Meetup (www.meetup.com) or on Facebook (www.facebook.com).

Identifying the pitfalls of trying to befriend any random person

Some people, especially those who have few or no friends, just want to become friends with someone, anyone. They're so starved for friendship that any random person will do, even if there's no spark and they have nothing in common.

This is one of the biggest friendship mistakes you can make, however, and it may be one reason why you've found it challenging to make good friends. Don't just try to befriend any random person — be more selective in who you try to be friends with.

The problem with befriending any random person is that you'll have a very weak foundation, and the friendship probably won't last because you won't have much to talk about or much in common. Being more selective in who you want to befriend is more effective.

TIP

The best way to become more selective in who you befriend is to join a few groups and get to know people over time in a casual way through the group, before trying to invite them out or turn them into a friend.

EXAMPLE

For example, Dominique wants to make new friends and decides to attend a dinner club for women in their thirties. At her first meeting, she chats for a few minutes with Nicole, who seems nice. She immediately invites Nicole out for lunch. Nicole accepts, and the lunch goes okay, but the two of them really don't have anything in common other than being in the dinner club. Dominique doesn't feel a spark, but she's thrilled to find someone who could be a potential friend. She follows up with Nicole the same week to set another lunch date but never hears back. Dominique feels sad and confused about why she continually strikes out with friendships.

What do you think Dominique could have done differently to guarantee a more successful outcome? Taking things slower and chatting with Nicole over several group meetings to see if they have anything in common first before inviting her out would've been a better approach. That way, maybe Dominique would've realized that she and Nicole don't have much in common, and she wouldn't have asked her to go to lunch — she could've moved on to someone else she had more in common with.

Handling fear of rejection

When you're trying to transition from acquaintance to friend, some people worry excessively about rejection, and it limits how effectively they interact with others. Getting hung up on rejection is common, but it's important to realize that it's a normal part of the friend-making process, and although it temporarily stings, it's important to develop a thicker skin when making friends.

TIP

Fear of rejection doesn't need to stop you from taking the initiative and reaching out to people. You can handle rejection more effectively by reframing your thinking about it. Instead of feeling like rejection would be the most terrible thing ever if it were to happen, you can reframe your thinking in a more realistic way: If someone rejects you, it hurts, but it's not the worst thing in the world. When thinking about rejection, ask yourself if rejection by an acquaintance is going to matter in a few months or a year. If not, try to let it go and move on.

If you tend to worry that the other person doesn't like you, and feel like you're always being rejected, ask yourself what the evidence is for your thoughts. Can you point to something specific the other person said or did that proves they don't like you? Can you identify specific instances when you were actually rejected? If not, then you can surmise that they most likely do like you.

REMEMBER

Just as Dr. Julie Smith said in *Why Has Nobody Told Me This Before?* (HarperOne), "Thoughts are not facts." Just because you *think* the other person doesn't like you or you *think* that you're being rejected doesn't make it true. Remind yourself that your thought is just a thought, not a fact.

Taking Things Slowly

It's important to take things slowly when you're trying to transition from acquaintance to friend. You don't want to do too much too soon because that can scare the other person away.

TIP

Here are a few ideas for how to take things slowly, so the other person feels comfortable:

>> **Avoid coming across as too eager.** Avoid texting an acquaintance or new friend multiple times per day (unless you're setting up a get-together). Avoid inviting them to do something as soon as your last get-together ends. You want to give them a little space and breathing room in between your get-togethers.

>> **Space out your invitations.** When you're just starting to transition from acquaintance to friend, try not to overwhelm them with invitations. Inviting them to do something once a month is plenty at first.

>> **If you've initiated with them the past three to four get-togethers, take a step back and see if they take the reins and invite you for the**

next one. If a few months go by and they don't invite you to do something, you'll need to evaluate whether they're really interested in a friendship. Friendships don't have to involve bean-counting, but they should be more or less reciprocal.

» **Try not to ask too many questions in one sitting.** This can come across as an interrogation. Instead, ask a question, and then after they answer, answer the question yourself and share more information about yourself. You want to come off as interested in the other person, but your get-togethers shouldn't feel like an interview.

» **Keep things short and casual at first.** Invite your acquaintance out for coffee, a walk, or a drink on a weekday. Save dinner or a weekend get-together for after you've known them for a while.

Building Courage and Self-Confidence

In order to transition from acquaintance to friend, you need to have the courage to put yourself out there and take a social risk. There are many ways you can build your self-confidence in small steps. Try inviting one acquaintance who you like the best to do something casual and easy, like taking a walk, and see how that goes. If it goes well, that will improve your self-confidence to invite them out again. Starting small and taking small social risks over time is one of the best ways to build your self-confidence.

TIP

Here are other ways to build your self-confidence as you turn acquaintances into friends:

» **Practice small talk with strangers.** Go to a grocery store or bookstore, and make some cheery small talk while standing in line. When you practice doing this often enough, it will improve your self-confidence over time so you're more confident talking to new people.

» **Meet up with an old friend or someone on your social media friends/ followers list for coffee or a walk.** A successful get-together will build your self-confidence and will help you invite an acquaintance to do something later.

» **Work on becoming an interesting, well-rounded person if you worry about not having anything to talk about with others.** To accomplish this, read the news daily, read a variety of books, or read a magazine that you wouldn't normally pick up. Try new experiences in your local area, like new restaurants or going to festivals or fairs. All of these pursuits will help you have new and interesting things to talk about.

>> **Work on changing your negative self-talk.** If you find that you routinely have negative self-talk, such as "No one likes me," find a positive affirmation you can say to yourself instead, such as, "I am a worthwhile person who will make a great friend. I haven't made friends yet, but I'm working on it."

>> **When you worry about being rejected, ask yourself, "What's the worst that can happen if I put myself out there and get rejected?"** Chances are, it's really not the end of the world, and you'll be able to handle it just fine.

Identifying When You've Made a Friend

It's finally happened: You believe you've successfully turned an acquaintance into a friend. But how will you actually *know* that you've made it into bona fide friend territory? Here are signs to look for that indicate you've successfully made a new friend:

>> Your friend texts you regularly just to say hi.

>> You feel more comfortable around your friend and begin to share more and more about yourself.

>> You like how you feel when you're with them. You can be your authentic self.

>> You feel that you can confide in them, and they won't betray your confidences.

>> You can ask them for a small favor and start to feel like they're part of your social support network. If you're in a bind, you know they would help you out.

>> They respond promptly to your messages. You feel like you're a priority.

>> They put the same amount of energy as you do into your friendship. They invite you to do things. You feel like you have equal investment in the friendship.

>> They make time for you. You feel like they make the time to spend time with you, even if they have a busy schedule.

Turning Online Friends into Real Friends

Many people make friends online through social media, discussion forums, or chat groups. Making an online friend satisfies many people's need for conversation and companionship. It's also easier to make an online friend than a real-life friend, because there are more opportunities to do so. There are thousands of chat rooms, discussion forums, and groups to join online to meet people. And people online are usually very friendly and open to chatting and connecting.

Many people find having an online friend extremely satisfying, but it can feel limiting to only interact with your virtual friend via online messaging. If you want to deepen your relationship, you can turn an online friend into a real friend. Here are some tips to make this happen:

>> **Decide what your goal is for having an online friend.** Do you want a friend with whom you share an interest in common and can talk about the interest with? Do you want a friend you talk to every day? Do you want a friend you can confide in? Clarifying your friendship goals is the first step.

>> **Interact with your online friend regularly.** Regular interaction leads to getting to know them better, which leads to a real friendship. You can message your online friend weekly or several times a week. Figure out what feels right given the circumstances. Eventually, with regular interaction, a deeper relationship will likely form.

>> **Take the relationship offline.** Exchange cell-phone numbers or email addresses. You can email, text, or call your online friend. Or do video chats, which give you some of the same vibe as meeting in person.

>> **Make sure the relationship has give-and-take, and that you're both putting in roughly equal energy.** Avoid emotionally dumping on your friend. Make sure that if you confide in them that you're also giving them the opportunity to confide in you.

>> **Deepen the relationship in the same way you would with an in-person friend.** Gradually share more and more about yourself. Don't overwhelm the person right away with too many personal details or secrets. Gradually reveal a little more about yourself over time.

>> **If you're both interested and after you've gotten to know them, consider meeting in person if it's feasible.** Depending on the distance, this may or may not be realistic, though you can always make arrangements to visit if finances allow. Some people want to keep their online friends 100 percent online, which is fine, too. Meeting up in person is better, but you can still have a meaningful friendship with a fully online friend.

3
Keeping Your Friendships Going

Sometimes the hardest part of a new friendship is keeping it going. In this part, you learn all the tips and tricks for how to maintain a friendship, from being a good friend to reaching out to others. You also learn about the importance of building community and how to build a community that will serve as your support system for years to come.

Chapter **12**

Reaching Out to People

B y now you've done the hardest part: You've mustered up the courage to put yourself out there, you've gone to a social event or met someone online, and you've found a person you'd like to get to know better. The next step on your journey toward a beautiful friendship is to reach out to your new pal and invite them to get together.

Though it sounds easy, reaching out to others can be quite a stressful feat. You may not be sure when or how to initiate a get-together, and you may worry about your friend saying no.

In the past, you may have heard someone say, "Let's get together sometime," but then neither party made a move, and the get-together never ended up happening. Someone has to reach out first, and that someone may as well be you! Reaching out to others can be nerve-wracking, but this chapter will improve your self-confidence and lower your stress levels about making that initial ask.

In this chapter, I walk you through everything you need to know about reaching out to others, initiating get-togethers, and dealing with rejection.

Staying in Touch with Your New Friend

The time is right — you're at a social gathering, you've met someone new, and you've felt a connection. The person you've been having a great conversation with seems like they'd make a perfect friend for you.

You're feeling hopeful, and you want to take things to the next level. There's only one thing holding you back: You need to ask for their contact information. In theory, asking someone for their digits sounds easy, but it can actually be quite nerve-wracking in practice.

By psyching yourself up and giving yourself a pep talk, you'll become a pro about staying in touch with new people.

Determining the right time to exchange contact information

The first step in initiating contact with your new pal is determining the right time to exchange contact information. This can be tricky to maneuver — on the one hand, you want to be proactive and reach out, but on the other hand, you don't want to look too eager and scare them off.

The best way to approach this dilemma is to take a close look at the social setting and circumstances where you met, because that will determine how quickly you need to act.

When you meet a new person, it's helpful to have more than one chance at conversation before asking for their contact information so you can determine if the other person seems like they could be a good potential friend for you. Sometimes it's hard to determine this after one short meet and greet at a social event. If it turns out that they're really not a good match and you have nothing in common, you may not want to take the next step to invite them out.

The social setting you met them in will determine how likely it is that you'll run into them again. Let's say you meet someone at a book club and you have one getting-to-know-you conversation that goes really well. You can hold off on asking for their contact information (so you can get to know them better) because it's likely you'll see that person again at a future group meeting. On the other hand, if you're at a one-time business networking event and you have a great conversation with someone, it's possible you won't run into that person again, so *now* would be an ideal time to ask for their contact information.

To determine whether you need to act now, figure out the likelihood of running into that person again. This will let you know whether you should ask for their contact information now, or if you can wait until next time when you've gotten to know them a bit better. There are no hard-and-fast rules about this — just feel it out and go with your gut.

Psyching yourself up for the big ask

You've decided that the time is right and you're ready to make the first move. It's go time!

Before you ask for their contact information, you may need to psych yourself up first. You may be feeling anxious or excited (or both), which is completely normal. Putting yourself out there can be stressful! Butterflies in the stomach, sweaty palms, muscle tension, facial flushing, a racing heart, and fast breathing are all signs that you're feeling anxious about the task in front of you.

You can power through the anxiety, however, by using a few helpful coping strategies:

>> **Give yourself a pep talk.** Say something positive to yourself to muster up the motivation to make the first move, such as: "I'm going to reach out and initiate an awesome get-together. The worst they can say is no, and I can handle that."

>> **Put things in perspective.** If they do say no, what's the worst that can happen? You may be upset or disappointed, but you'll probably get over it quickly and be able to move on. Another way to think about it is if they decline, will it still really bother you in a month, three months, or a year? If not, it's probably not worth stressing about.

>> **Deep breathing.** Deep breathing is a good coping strategy for anxiety. One of my favorite deep-breathing exercises is called *box breathing*. In box breathing, you breathe in for the count of four, hold your inhale for the count of four, and breathe out through your mouth for the count of four, then hold your exhale for the count of four. Imagine slowly tracing the sides of a box for each step of the exercise. Then repeat until you're feeling calmer.

>> **Remember the times you've initiated before and it's worked out.** Have you taken the initiative with a new pal before, and it's worked out? If so, recall those experiences and focus on them to remind yourself that you've succeeded in this before.

Asking for their digits in person

When you're feeling ready to make a move, there are a few different ways you can phrase your request. At the end of your conversation, when the time feels right, you can ask for their contact information. Read through the following examples and see if they resonate; if not, feel free to adapt them in whatever way suits your style best:

>> "It's been so nice chatting with you. I'd love to keep in touch! We should swap numbers! Here's my cell."

>> "It was so fun getting to know you! We should grab coffee sometime!" If they seem interested, you could then say, "Cool, let's exchange numbers!"

>> "It was so nice meeting you. We have so much in common! Let me give you my email so we can stay in touch!"

>> "It was great meeting you. We should meet up sometime. Can I get your number so I can text the next time I'm in the area?"

Practice a few different ways of asking for contact information so when the time comes to actually do it, the words will flow smoothly.

Asking for their digits electronically

If you've met someone online, either in a discussion group or through social media, things can be a little more casual because you already have one way to contact them. If you want to contact them in another way, like if you've been chatting through Reddit and now you want to text them, there are a few ways to phrase it. You might say something like, "It's been great chatting on Reddit. Here's my number if you ever want to text." Or you could say, "Hey, if you ever want to chat on the phone, here's my number." When you say this, it gives the other person an out. If they're interested, they'll give you theirs. If they don't give you their number, you can conclude that they want to keep things online only, which is perfectly fine.

Choosing what contact info to give

When meeting someone new, people generally give one of four types of contact information:

>> Cell-phone number

>> Email

>> Social media *handle* (username)

>> Paper or electronic business card

Which type of contact information you provide is a matter of personal preference and the context in which you've met. If you want to err on the side of caution, provide your email address. If you feel more comfortable with the person, then providing your cell number is fine.

The setting can also dictate what seems most appropriate. If you meet someone at a business networking event, a business card or LinkedIn handle may make the most sense. If you met a fellow parent at a preschool event, handing out a business card would seem too formal; instead, giving them your cell number or email address gives off a more friendly and casual vibe.

TIP

If you want to be really high-tech, you can create a digital business card through an app called Blinq (`https://blinq.me`). The nice thing about this method is that you don't have to remember to bring your actual business cards to an event. The other person just scans the QR code on your phone, and your info is downloaded into their contacts, which they can save for future reference. Super easy and quick!

WARNING

Never give anyone you don't know well your home address, because that's a safety concern. Focus on meeting at a public place like a restaurant, bookstore, or mall the first few times you meet up with someone, until you get to know them well. Then, when you're comfortable, you could consider inviting them to your home if you want. An exception could be if you meet a friend of a good friend at a gathering, and decide to invite them to your home. In this case, you may feel comfortable doing so, because you both share a mutual friend (assuming you value your friend's judgment).

Responding to the "we should get together sometime" phrase

Sometimes you meet someone, you have a nice chat, and you seem to have some good friend chemistry going. Then they say: "It was great meeting you. We should get together sometime." This can throw some people off. Is this an actual intent to get together or just a friendly pleasantry?

This phrase can be interpreted in a couple different ways. It can mean that

>> **The person really does want to meet up later but doesn't want to commit to anything right now.** In this case, it invites a vague opportunity to connect in the future.

>> **The person wants to put the ball in your court.** They like you, but they're not sure how you feel, so they don't want to invite you to something too soon and risk being rejected. Instead, they want to put it on you to make the next move.

It's important to note that people rarely say "We should get together sometime" without actually meaning it. But they might respond, "Yes, for sure!" when they don't actually want to follow through. This can get really confusing because they may *seem* enthusiastic about meeting up, but they just don't want to hurt the other person's feelings. If they responded what they really felt — "I'm actually not interested in meeting up with you" — that could come across as too direct, insulting, or hurtful, so instead they imply that they'd like to meet up when they really don't.

TIP

What should you do if someone responds enthusiastically to you when you suggest meeting up, but you're not sure if they really mean it? There are a few ways to handle it. One response is to try to get them to commit right away. You can say, "Great! Let's get something on the calendar before we forget," and then proceed to pull out your planner or your phone so you can figure out a date that works on the spot. The other person may become very uncomfortable if you do this, because they actually don't want to get together. In that case, they may avoid committing to anything and instead hem and haw about being really busy in the next few months. Or they may be ecstatic that you're taking charge and getting the ball rolling and are ready to commit on the spot. It could go either way!

Alternatively, you can say, "Great, I'll reach out soon with a few possible dates, and we can go from there" or "I'd love to get something on the calendar. What days tend to work best for you?" That will get the conversation rolling and give them a chance to either show enthusiasm for the idea or back out gracefully.

Reaching Out to Your New Friend

Now that you have their contact information, who reaches out first? If you both have each other's contact information, you may wonder if you should make the first move or if your pal should. Sometimes people wait, assuming that the other person *should* make the first move, and then nothing ever ends up happening. Has this ever happened to you? In therapy, people of all ages often complain that they're always the one reaching out, and they're tired of being the one to initiate. They want someone else to take the initiative and be the one to reach out to *them*. (Turn to Chapter 15 for more on this subject.)

If you decide to wait until your new friend reaches out, it may take a while, and your budding friendship may lose momentum. If you reach out first, on the other hand, you may be able to start spending quality time sooner with your new pal.

Knowing when to reach out

It can be hard to figure out how much time needs to go by before it's okay to reach out and invite your new pal to do something. You may want to reach out right away after you get their contact information, but is this a good idea? The danger is that doing so may come across as too eager, which can be a turnoff to some people.

TIP

You may want to wait a bit before reaching out. Consider giving it a few days or a week before reaching out first.

Keeping things casual

When you do reach out, keep the tone light and friendly. Have an idea already in mind of what kind of get-together you'd like to suggest. Coffee, drinks, or a walk is a good option for your first meetup because people prefer casual, short get-togethers when they're first getting to know someone. Lunch or dinner can feel too formal or intimidating, and they last a lot longer, so save those ideas for when you've gotten to know them better. A new friend may feel like it's too much, too soon to meet up for dinner on a Saturday night versus a Tuesday afternoon coffee break, which can fit more easily into people's schedules.

Next, give them a few options of days and times for meeting up. It's more efficient if you propose a coffee get-together and then suggest a few days and times that work for you versus saying "How about coffee?" and leaving the details up to them. Make it easy for the other person to say yes to your idea.

EXAMPLE

Here are some examples:

>> It was so nice getting to know you last week at the church potluck. Would you like to meet up for coffee next week? Tuesday or Thursday afternoon works for me. Would either of these work for you?

>> It's been great getting to know you in the hiking group. You want to go for smoothies after next week's hike?

>> It was awesome meeting you at last week's networking breakfast. I'd love to hear more about your new business idea! Would you like to meet for coffee sometime next week to chat more? I'm free Thursday and Friday around noon. Either of those work for you?

WARNING

Make sure to meet in a public place for your first few get-togethers, until you get to know someone. Definitely don't invite them to your house right away — you don't want to give out your address until you feel really comfortable with someone. Coffee shops, restaurants, bookstores, and shopping malls are all good places to meet up.

Being willing to compromise

If you've suggested a get-together that doesn't work for your new pal, be willing to compromise. If they express interest in the idea, but the days and times you suggested don't work for them, suggest a few alternatives or ask them what works for their schedule. Or, if the specific outing idea doesn't appeal to them or isn't convenient, have some backup ideas ready.

REMEMBER

People want to be friends with others who are easygoing and flexible. If you have an "it's my way or the highway" attitude, your new pal won't want to stick around very long. (See Chapter 9 for more ways to develop an accommodating attitude.)

Making sure your hangout goes smoothly

TIP

There are a few ways to make sure your get-together goes smoothly:

>> **Exchange cell numbers beforehand.** Having each other's numbers will make communicating on the day of much easier.

>> **Be on time.** No one wants to sit around twiddling their thumbs at a coffee shop while you meander in 40 minutes late. If you *are* running late, be sure to text them and let them know when you'll be there.

>> **Let them know when you arrive.** You can text them that you're parking or walking up to the meeting point so they know you're on the way. If it's a big place, let them know where you're sitting so they don't have to wander around looking for you.

REMEMBER

When your pal arrives, greet them warmly (see Chapter 9 for more information on showing warmth). Have some ideas on what you want to talk about (see Chapter 7 for ideas on how to make small talk with new people). Show interest, ask questions, and try to have an easygoing, lighthearted vibe. Compliment them or ask for their advice on something. The two of you will be friends in no time!

Scheduling another get-together

If your first get-together went well, you'll probably want to keep the fun going. You can either take the initiative to schedule another get-together or sit back and see if your friend takes the reins. If you do schedule another hangout, wait a week or two before initiating plans. That gives your friend a chance to miss you and gives you more time to have enough things to talk about next time.

Dealing with no response

Sometimes people go radio silent when you invite them to do something. This can feel very hurtful and can also be confusing. How should you handle it if you reach out to your new pal and get no response?

Some people get very upset when they get no response. It can feel rude and dismissive, and they wonder why they can't just get an answer one way or the other.

People don't respond to invitations for a few reasons:

>> **They don't want to say no, so they think that by ignoring your request it comes across as a kinder response.** So, in essence, no response *is* a response, but it's a response that they're not interested. This can feel hurtful and can negatively impact your self-confidence if it keeps happening.

>> **They didn't get the message.** It may help to send a follow-up inquiry, just in case. Emails *can* get stuck in spam, and texts *sometimes* don't go through.

>> **They're interested, but they were busy doing something else the moment they saw your invite, and they forgot all about it a few minutes later.** They *meant* to get back to you but never did. Not responding was an innocent mistake, but it can still feel hurtful if you never find out what's going on.

TIP

You may decide that if you don't get a response, you'll follow up once. If you still don't get a response, you may decide to move on and let them make the next move.

Coping with rejection

TIP

Putting yourself out there and inviting someone to do something takes bravery and courage. If the other person says no, it can feel crushing. Some people have a huge fear of rejection. If this describes you, keep the following tips about coping with rejection in mind:

>> **Consider how much this rejection will affect you down the road.** Think about how this rejection will affect your life in a week, a month, or six months

from now. Remind yourself that the rejection may sting a lot now, but you can tolerate and work through it, and it likely won't bother you very much in a few weeks or months. Turn your efforts instead to getting to know new people, instead of rehashing the rejection.

>> **Process the rejection.** Talk about the rejection and how it made you feel with a close friend, family member, or therapist. If you don't have any of these, writing about the rejection in a journal can help you more effectively process it.

>> **Work on acceptance.** Accept the rejection for what it is, without trying to deny it. Pretending the rejection didn't happen or being in disbelief doesn't help you process it and move forward. Even though it's unfortunate that it happened, remind yourself that you've coped with rejection in the past and managed to work through it.

>> **Focus on other friendships.** Remind yourself that there are people in your social network who like you and value you, and remind yourself to focus on them, as well as other new people.

>> **Reframe the rejection as a learning experience.** Even the most painful rejections provide the opportunity to learn something or do something differently and grow. What did you learn from this experience that can benefit your future relationships?

REMEMBER Don't let the fear of rejection get in your way! If you do, you may be missing out on potential beautiful friendships.

HOW YOUR BRAIN TREATS REJECTION

The reason why social rejection can feel so acutely painful is because it activates the same areas of the brain that are responsible for physical pain. In a 2003 study published in *Science,* researchers did an experiment where they had volunteers play a virtual ball-tossing game inside a functional magnetic resonance imaging (fMRI) scanner. They noted which areas of the subjects' brains lit up in response to feeling excluded. They found that an area of the brain called the *anterior cingulate cortex* lit up in these volunteers — and that's the same brain area that is activated when you experience physical pain. One takeaway from this study is that when you're excluded, it can feel like an intolerable pain, very similar to a physical wound, because the same area of the brain is activated when you're rejected as when you're in physical pain.

A few years later, researchers decided to study this phenomenon further in a 2010 study published in *Psychological Science*. The researchers wanted to see if taking acetaminophen (an ingredient in Tylenol) or a placebo during the three-week study would help volunteers feel less socially rejected in their day-to-day encounters, because the areas of the brain that experience social rejection are the same ones that experience physical pain. Interestingly, they found that the volunteers who took acetaminophen daily reported that they had less social pain than the volunteers who took a placebo, because it was working on the same areas of the brain that registered social rejection and physical pain. This was also confirmed by the results of the fMRI scanner, which showed that the acetaminophen was working to reduce the activity in brain regions responsible for physical pain, including the anterior cingulate cortex.

Of course, you shouldn't take acetaminophen in order to prevent or treat social rejection (at least not without your doctor's approval). The point is that if you feel hurt when you're rejected, there's a very good reason for that based on brain anatomy.

Following Up with Your Friend

You've reached out and met up. Now what? Before your next get-together, should you keep talking by text or email or just wait until you see them again in person? This is up to you! You could keep the conversation going by following up with them. You may want to check in now and again to say hi and see how their week is going, send them a funny meme, or start a back-and-forth text conversation.

Or you may decide to leave the ball in their court for now, in order to see if they reach out to you. Then, after some time has passed, you can decide if you want to invite them to do something again.

Determining how often to meet up

It's up to you and your friend how often you'd like to meet up. It all depends on several factors, including: the nature of the friendship, how close you live to each other, and how busy your schedules are.

If you're both retired and you have a lot of free time, you may want to meet up often, perhaps weekly. If you're a busy working professional with young kids, you may only have time to see your friend a few times a year.

Try to let things play out organically instead of asking them directly about how often they expect to get together. Read between the lines to get a sense of your friend's schedule and preferences. For example, one way to go about it is to ask your friend to meet up again in a week, and if they say, "Oh, my schedule is crazy right now! Are you free next month instead?" then you've just found out that they aren't going to be interested in super frequent get-togethers.

You may have some friends that you'd love to see more often, but they have too much going on to make that happen. Ideally, you'll be okay with that, and you'll meet up with them when both your schedules align. In the meantime, focus your efforts on getting together with multiple friends so you don't over-rely on any one person.

Handling a lack of reciprocity

In a perfect world, your friend would reciprocate your invitations roughly half the time. You invite them and then they invite you — lather, rinse, repeat. However, some people are busy, some don't have good manners, some don't believe in reciprocity . . . and sometimes relationships start to feel one-sided. Only you can decide if a lack of reciprocation is a deal-breaker or something you can live with.

Turn to Chapter 15 for more on handling a lack of reciprocity and one-sided friendships.

Chapter **13**

Being a Good Friend

You've come so far on your friendship journey. You put in the time, and you've been able to make a new friend. Now the challenge becomes keeping and nourishing that friendship long-term, which you can accomplish by being a good friend.

Have you ever heard the famous saying by Ralph Waldo Emerson: "The only way to have a friend is to be one"? Being a good friend includes putting in the time and effort to spend quality time with your pal, being considerate and thoughtful, showing support, and maintaining good communication and boundaries.

This chapter starts out by discussing why it's so hard for many adults to be a good friend, with so many commitments vying for their time and energy. Then it explores how childhood experiences with friendship role models impact adult friendships. Next, it explains the most important qualities of being a good friend and delves into how to communicate more effectively with your friends. This chapter also covers the importance of setting healthy boundaries with friends, which are vital to communicating your needs and preferences. Just as good fences make good neighbors, good boundaries make good friendships.

Understanding the Challenges to Being a Good Friend

Some people are able to make new friends, but then struggle with keeping the friendships going. Being a good friend takes a lot of time and energy, and that's part of why it's so hard for adults to nourish new friendships. Here are the main reasons some adults find it difficult to be a good friend:

>> **They're stretched too thin.** Because they're pulled in so many different directions with work, family, and household responsibilities, many people don't have the time, energy, bandwidth, or desire to put in the work required to be a good friend. This is especially the case with new friendships, which require the most work (as opposed to long-standing friendships). As a result, some adults' friendships fizzle out and never progress to the level of close friends. Many adults have a lot of superficial friendships or people they meet up with as activity partners, but few close friends.

Some adults find it hard to justify putting in all that time and effort on a new friendship when their free time is so limited. Some people are focused on their health and medical issues, eldercare responsibilities, or financial concerns, and they just don't have the bandwidth to do what it takes to be a good friend.

>> **They want to avoid drama.** Another reason why some adults find it hard to be a good friend is that they don't want to risk getting involved in friendship drama, so they keep things surface-level to avoid getting sucked in. Some people have been betrayed by friends in the past, so they're wary to trust, out of fear of being betrayed again.

>> **They're afraid the person will move away and they will have put all that time into someone who won't be around long-term.** When you meet someone new, you may wonder if it's really worth putting in all that time if the friend is just going to move away someday. And there's some truthfulness to this fear. People do come and go in and out of our lives all the time, and some geographic areas are more transient than others. But most people don't worry about wasting their time with romantic relationships and are willing to date and get to know someone new in the hopes of finding a romantic partner. However, some adults are less willing to risk it when it comes to platonic friendships.

EXPLORE

Think about any friendships you've made in the past few years that fizzled early on. Was part of the reason that either you or your friend didn't put in the required effort to maintain the friendship? If you've noticed in the past that you could do more to be a better friend, make sure to do that now, by putting into practice some of the suggestions in this chapter so your next friendship will be sure to flourish.

REMEMBER

If you don't put in the time, you can't reap the rewards of a deep and meaningful friendship. Making good friends can take years of consistent effort. If you put in the time and keep showing up, over the months and years you'll form close friendships. Most people feel that the effort is worth it because good friends are hard to find and friendships have so many benefits.

EXPLORE

Do some self-reflection about a friend you've had in the past or have currently, who does a great job at being a good friend. What qualities do they do well that you'd like to emulate? What qualities do they not do well that you want to do a better job with? For instance, is your friend always upbeat and cheerful, with a positive vibe? Or are they always late (which shows a lack of respect for your time)? Someone you know who demonstrates the qualities of being a good friend can serve as a friendship mentor for you.

Considering Who You Tend to Gravitate Toward

Part of being a good friend is making sure you're giving and getting the kind of friendship you need. For example, if you're looking to make a close friend, make sure you're doing the kinds of things to maintain close friendships, like checking in regularly with your friend and doing thoughtful gestures. If you're not getting the kinds of friendship you want, take a look at the types of people you tend to gravitate toward. This can help you discover why your friendships aren't meeting your needs fully. Maybe you're looking for friendships with the wrong type of people.

Some people tend to gravitate toward extroverted types who are the life of the party and have tons of friends. These people, because they're so likable and have so many friends, tend to be stretched thin friendship-wise. Their social calendars are packed to the brim, and they may not be able to put the amount of energy into the friendship that you'd like. As a result, you may feel chronically upset and resentful that your friend isn't putting the time and energy into the friendship that you are.

TIP

A solution may be to instead look for people who have fewer friends and are less outgoing. This could be newcomers to the area or people who are more introverted and have smaller social circles. Friends with these qualities will probably have more time and energy to spend on your friendship, which may make for a better relationship.

Exploring Your Earliest Friendship Role Models

Parents and other close family members are our earliest role models for how to be a good friend. Think back to your childhood and whether your parents or other caregivers had friends. If you saw your parents have friends, invite people over, take meals to friends who were sick, and support their friends, chances are, observing these activities helped you develop good friendship-making skills. When you grow up with good friendship role models, you learn how to be a good friend in part by observing your parents (even if they didn't specifically teach you any friendship skills).

A child who helps their mom or dad put together a care package for a friend or pick flowers for the bouquet they're taking to a sick friend, or who sees their parents carving out time from their busy schedules to go out with friends, learns a lot about the importance of friendship and how to be there for pals.

Being included in these important friendship activities with their parents teaches kids how to be a good friend. If you had good friendship role models growing up, you may have gained some of the following skills and insights:

- The importance of supporting friends in good times and bad
- When and how to support a sick friend (for example, how to take a friend a meal or care package or start a meal train)
- How to entertain friends and be a good host
- How to be a good guest
- The give-and-take of friendships
- How to resolve conflict in friendships
- The importance of making time for friends
- How and why friendships are an important and enriching part of life

If your parents didn't have any friends while you were growing up, you may have missed out on some important life skills for how to be a good friend because you didn't have positive friendship role models in your formative years. You may have been a late bloomer friendship-wise. Maybe you struggled with friendships in childhood. Kids who don't see their parents valuing friendships may also be less likely to value friendships of their own.

As most kids do, you may have eventually learned how to make friends from everyday social situations at school and in your neighborhood, camp, or after-school activities, or even from books and movies. School teaches important friendship skills like sharing, taking turns, conflict resolution, and how to be inclusive.

But even if you feel that you missed out on having good friendship role models in your parents, the good news is that friendship skills can be learned at any age.

TIP

If you didn't have a good friendship role model growing up, you can still find one now. A friendship role model can be a friend you admire, a neighbor who has good friendship skills, a coworker who is socially savvy, or anyone else you know who seems to have a lot of close friendships and seems to understand how to be a good friend. Study the traits and characteristics these people have and see if you can incorporate some of them into your own friendship-skills repertoire. (Check out Chapter 17 for more on friendship mentors.)

EXPLORE

Do some self-reflection on whether you had good friendship role models while you were growing up. If your parents had friends, how involved were you in the activities they did with their friends (for example, dinner parties or card-game nights). Do you think your parents' friendships had any influence on how you make friends as an adult or your own friendship skills? If your parents didn't have friends when you were growing up, how do you think this lack of role models influenced your own friend-making journey?

Embodying the Qualities of a Good Friend

Some adults could use a refresher on how to be a good friend. Many adults invite a friend out for a drink or watch sports with a friend, but they often don't put in any more effort than the occasional get-together. They don't really know when or how to be a good listener, support a friend during a hard time, or make thoughtful gestures toward their friend. Just like a garden, relationships require feeding, watering, and constant tending.

Think back to childhood and what being a good friend meant back then. Sharing, taking turns, asking your friend to play, being kind, not bullying, and being a good listener are all ways that we teach kids to be a good friend. Many of these friendship qualities are still important for adult friendships.

EXPLORE

As a self-reflection activity, take out a piece of paper and ponder your thoughts about the most important qualities of a good friend. Think about friends you've had in the past and the type of friend you'd like to have now. One way to think about friendship qualities is the way a real estate agent would: What are your "must-haves," "nice-to-haves," and "do not want" when it comes to friendship? After you've written down these qualities, it'll be easier to figure out where you can find friends that have them.

REMEMBER

It's up to you to be the type of friend for others that you wish you had. Take the time to spread positive energy to your friends, whether that's sending them regular texts to say hi and see how they're doing, taking the initiative to plan activities, or making thoughtful gestures. Don't expect that everyone will reciprocate your efforts, but some hopefully will. Eventually, if you keep doing these things enough, people will respond, and you'll find your kindred spirits.

Being a good friend as an adult includes being kind, thoughtful, considerate, inclusive, understanding, and supportive, as well as taking the initiative. In the following sections, I walk you through what being a good friend involves.

Being supportive

A good friend is supportive, both in good and bad times. A supportive friend is encouraging and positive about their friend's goals, dreams, and wishes. This includes cheering your friend on and celebrating their accomplishments when something good happens. In good times, you can be supportive by:

>> **Asking about or mentioning their accomplishment when you see them:** For example, ask how their novel writing is going or about the new album they just released. A supportive friend knows how important their friend's goals and dreams are to them and shows interest by inquiring about them.

>> **Showing up to their important events:** For example, if your friend is participating in an open-mic night, running a 10K, or performing in a play at the local community theater, show up to offer support.

>> **Asking to hear more about their ideas, goals, and plans:** For example, if your friend is starting a new business, ask thoughtful questions about their business ideas. If your friend is trying to get in shape, ask about their fitness goals.

>> **Extending a thoughtful gesture for them to celebrate their wins.** For example, if your friend earns their graduate degree, order them a cake that says "Congratulations" and share it together. Or if your friend just got a big promotion, take them out to dinner to celebrate.

>> **Offering to help out with some aspect of their dreams:** For example, help post flyers for their new business or write a review for their newly published memoir.

>> **Working on your goals together to show support and accountability:** For example, if you both want to lose weight, check in with each other about your weight loss goals frequently and be accountability partners for each other. Or if you're both working on your New Year's resolutions, check in with each other regularly about how they're going and motivate each other to stick with them.

A friend is also supportive when their pal is down on their luck. There are many ways you can support a friend in bad times:

>> **Be there for them.** Ask how you can help. You can say, "I'd really like to be there for you. What would be most helpful for you right now?" or "How can I help?" Alternatively, if you're really good friends, you can just step in and offer to do something during their time of need that you know they would find helpful, like walking their dog, picking their kids up from school, or mowing their lawn.

>> **Sit with them and just be a supportive presence.** Especially during illness or while they're grieving, just being there can be comforting and sometimes all someone needs.

>> **Let them vent.** Being a good listener and listening without judgment or jumping in to giving advice can mean so much. Sometimes all a person needs is a shoulder to cry on and to feel heard.

>> **Help out if they're sick.** Bringing a meal, setting up a meal train, driving them to medical appointments, and setting up a GoFundMe (www.gofundme.com) if needed are all good ways to show support.

Initiating get-togethers

Reaching out, making the first move, and initiating get-togethers are all part of being a good friend. After you've made a new friend, you need to spend lots of time together so you can get to know each other better.

Instead of waiting for your friend to make the first move, you can be the one to organize a get-together and make it happen. Friendships don't always have to be 50/50 — people go through busy periods — but both friends should put in roughly equal energy most of the time. Make sure that you're putting in regular effort to nurture your friendship.

Being a good listener

Another way to be a good friend is to be a good listener. This means listening closely to your friend and allowing them to vent without judgment and without giving advice. Sit with them and listen until they're finished talking. If you'd like to give advice but you aren't sure if it would be welcomed, you can ask, "Would you like me to just listen, or would you like me to give advice?"

TIP

Many people could use some help with their listening skills, because they tend to interrupt, monopolize conversations with their own ramblings, or not give space for their friend to share what's on their mind. Here are some tried-and-true ways to be a good listener:

>> **Ask questions to show interest and follow up on particular things your friend mentions.** If your friend mentions an upcoming vacation, make sure to ask how it was when they come back.

>> **Give your friend your whole attention when listening.** Even if you're bored, avoid zoning out and do what it takes to bring your attention back to focusing. Ask questions to show that you're listening.

>> **Don't interrupt.** Interrupting is rude and frustrating for the other person. If you do interrupt, make sure to apologize.

>> **Don't talk over your friend.** Wait for your friend to finish speaking before you start talking.

>> **Try not to monopolize the conversation.** Each person should get roughly equal time to talk.

Being nonjudgmental

It's important for friends to be nonjudgmental. Being nonjudgmental means not judging your friend for having a different perspective, taking a different action, or having different behaviors or beliefs than you do. Being nonjudgmental means keeping an open and curious mind. In order to be nonjudgmental, try to take the time to understand their motivations and perspectives. Having empathy helps you to be nonjudgmental, because it allows you to put yourself in your friend's shoes to help understand where they're coming from.

REMEMBER

Accept your friend for who they are, without judging them, just as you'd like them to accept you. Remember that no one will be the perfect friend — we're all different and we all have different priorities and perspectives. Instead of focusing on your friend's flaws, focus on their strengths.

Making time for your friend

Another important way to be a good friend is to make time for them. This means carving out regular friend time in your schedule to get together.

Some people want new friends but believe they're too busy to spend time with friends. They make excuses that they're too "crazy-busy" to meet up, but making time for friends is a choice. Even the busiest people can fit in a coffee date once in a while. People can make the time if they really want to.

If you want new friends, it's important to make seeing them a priority. Decide how often you'd like to see your friend, and then carve out the time. You can treat it like an appointment and block out time in your calendar for your friend get-togethers.

New friendships need regular feeding and watering; otherwise, the relationship never really has a chance to blossom. If you haven't seen your friend in a while, check in with them and see if you can schedule a get-together soon.

How often should friends get together? There are no hard-and-fast rules about this. In general, it would be ideal to see your friend at least monthly in the beginning when you're first building a friendship, so that you spend enough time together to become better friends. Research by Jeffrey Hall in the *Journal of Social and Personal Relationships* found that it takes around 200 hours of together time before someone becomes a best friend. Most people can fit a monthly coffee date, walk, or lunch date into their busy schedules, to start racking up those hours. Some people find multitasking makes it easier to fit in friend dates — if you walk with your friend, you get to socialize while you're exercising.

Showing interest

Showing interest is an important part of being a good friend. You can show interest by doing things like asking them questions about their hobbies, passions, hopes, and dreams; following up on important things they said; learning about their interests (and even getting involved in them); and attending their important events.

Here are several other ways to show interest in your friends:

>> **Keep up with what's going on in your friend's life.** Text, email, or call them to see how their week is going. Contact them just to say hi. If you haven't heard from them in a while, reach out and check in.

>> **Find out what your friend's interests are and learn a little about them.** Ask questions about them to show interest. Find out if you can join them in one of their interests or watch if they're playing a sport or are in a performance.

>> **Interact with them on social media (if you're both on it).** Like and comment on their posts as a way to connect with them.

>> **Find out the books they like to read and ask questions about them.**

>> **Try to attune to what they're feeling.** If you notice that one day they don't seem like themselves, ask if they're doing okay or if they're feeling upset about something and want to talk. Let them know you're there for them.

>> **Learn the names of the important people in your friend's life, including family members, pets, and other close friends.**

Making them feel valued

An important part of being a good friend is making your friend feel valued. When you make your friend feel valued, it shows them how important they are to you. You can do this in several ways:

>> **Respond promptly to messages and texts.** Responding promptly shows your friend that they're important to you. You don't have to respond instantaneously, but do respond in a timely fashion. There are no cut-and-dried rules about this, but responding within 24 hours is ideal.

TIP

It can be helpful to ask your friend what their communication preferences are, and let them know your communication preferences as well. If they prefer texting and you're not a texter, let them know so they know that your responses by text may be delayed.

>> **Reach out to them by text, email, or phone to say hi and let them know that you're thinking of them.** You can send them a quick text saying something like, "Hi! Thinking of you! How's your week going?" People greatly appreciate when others check in with them. Many people complain that their friends never check in just to say hi and see how they're doing, and they wish their friends were more communicative. Be the person who does check in.

TIP

If checking in with friends is hard for you to remember, write a note in your calendar to check in on your pal every so often.

>> **Compliment them on their strengths or things you genuinely appreciate about them.** If you notice something they do well, comment on it. Everyone likes to feel appreciated and valued. If you feel your friend is an excellent

activity organizer or trip planner, or if you think they manage to juggle work and home life well, let them know! This will help them feel valued.

>> **If they help you with something, show appreciation.** Let them know how much their help meant to you and find a way to help them when you can.

>> **Offer to help them.** If you know your friend is struggling with something, or if you can think of something that would make their life easier in a specific way, offer to help them without being asked. This could involve offering to take them to a medical appointment, offering to watch their pets or plants when they're on vacation, or offering to pick up food for them if they're home sick.

Avoiding being clingy and needy

Part of being a good friend is giving your friends some space and avoiding being too clingy or needy. It's important to remember that it's healthy to have several friends so that you spend time with more than one person. To avoid being clingy and needy, try to make more friends/activity partners, so you don't rely on any one person too much, or try to fill your free time with more meaningful and purposeful activities, like volunteering or joining social groups.

If you recognize that you're being too clingy, try to give your friend some space. Signs that you're being too clingy include calling or texting them multiple times a day for no specific reason, inviting them to do things with you constantly, and keeping tabs on what they're doing and being upset when they do things with other people. You may notice your friend distancing themselves or being less responsive in order to get some more space.

Showing up for them

A friend shows up for their pal in good times and bad. Showing up for your friend means helping them when you can, attending their important milestones and events, being a supportive presence, and being there when they need you, with or without being asked.

If your friend is participating in a special event, like a theater performance or tennis match, showing up for them means attending the event and cheering them on. If their child is participating in an important milestone, it means showing up to show support for the family. If your friend is going through a tough time, like a serious illness or a death in the family, you can show up for them by taking them to appointments, bringing by meals, or just sitting with them in solidarity during hard times.

For a good friend, you can go beyond asking "What can I do?" and just find things that you know they would appreciate and do them. Showing up for them can also mean dropping everything to be there for them if there's a crisis. It's a comforting and warm feeling to know that your friends are willing to show up for you.

Being considerate

A good friend is also considerate of their friend's feelings. You can show consideration for your friends in several different ways:

>> **Ask how they're doing and make sure they get enough time to share their thoughts and feelings.**

>> **Take into account their preferences.** Ask what they'd like to do when you meet up and try to compromise instead of unilaterally making the decision. If your friend is vegetarian and you're going out for dinner, find a restaurant that has a good selection of vegetarian dishes so your friend feels included.

>> **Downplay sensitive subjects.** Don't flaunt things that might make your friend feel bad. For example, if you were invited to a party at a mutual friend's house and your friend wasn't invited, don't talk about how great the party was. Or, if your friend is going through a bad breakup, don't go on and on about the amazing date you had with your significant other.

Avoiding emotional dumping

A good friend doesn't use their friend as their therapist. Some people *trauma dump* on their friends, which means unloading all their emotional baggage on their friend and expecting them to listen and sort out all the pieces. This can overwhelm someone and make them feel resentful and used. This isn't fair to your friend, and it isn't something a good friend does. Instead, a good friend relies on their spouse/partner or therapist to help them process difficult feelings.

Being honest

Being a good friend also means being honest with your friends. A good friend lets you know in a kind and respectful way what they think. Many people value others who "tell it like it is." A good friend will be honest when they notice something concerning and help you to work through the situation. If they notice that you're about to make a fool of yourself, or they notice something that's not quite right, they'll let you know in order to save you embarrassment.

Being respectful of their time

Being respectful of your friend's time is another way to be a good friend. Being respectful of their time can take many forms. It can involve being mindful of your friend's other commitments when you're talking on the phone with them and not keeping them too long.

Another way to be respectful of your friend's time is to be punctual. It's important to be on time for get-togethers and not leave someone sitting and waiting for more than a few minutes.

TIP

If you're going to be late, make sure to call or text them to let them know. It's frustrating when someone is 15 to 20 minutes late and doesn't try to contact you to let you know. Being late shows a disrespect for your friend's time. If you tend to run late, set a timer for 30 minutes before you need to leave to meet someone so you can get ready earlier. But try not to make lateness a habit — it can be annoying to your friends.

Being loyal

Being loyal is another quality of a good friend. Loyalty means being there for your friend and standing up for them and always being on your friend's side. Having a loyal friend is comforting, because it helps people feel supported and less alone in the world. A loyal friend will always look out for your best interests and won't betray you.

Being thoughtful

Another way to be a good friend involves being thoughtful and regularly making thoughtful gestures. This can involve sending them a text or email just to say hello and let them know that you're thinking of them, remembering their birthday, and acknowledging their important dates and milestones. If you go on vacation, picking up a small souvenir to let them know you were thinking of them is another thoughtful gesture. Thoughtful gestures let your friend know that they're valued and appreciated.

TIP

If you tend to drop the ball when it comes to thoughtful gestures because they slip your mind, a helpful strategy is to note them down on your calendar. If your friend mentions an important date or event coming up for them (a job interview, a birthday, their child's birthday, or a vacation), make a note for yourself in your calendar so that you can acknowledge it. Your note could say "Text Taylor about job interview," and then you'll remember to do it. These little gestures add up to show that you're a thoughtful friend.

Being inclusive

A good friend is inclusive rather than exclusive — they'll try to include you whenever possible and invite you to all the events and activities they host. If they're planning to do something with another friend, they'll try to include you, too. They also won't talk about or plan activities or events with others right in front of you, which can lead to hurt feelings.

Being inclusive also applies to group settings. If you're talking in a group of several people, being inclusive means including everyone in the discussion and making sure people who aren't participating feel included. Try to talk with everyone equally if possible in a group setting. Only talking with one other person and ignoring everyone else is inconsiderate.

Being a good conversationalist

Another aspect of being a good friend involves making good conversation. You don't have to be a dazzling conversationalist, but having things to talk about and having good conversation skills is important. Luckily, these skills can be learned, improved on, and practiced.

If thinking of new topics of conversation is difficult for you, consider inviting a friend to do activities where the conversation can ebb and flow naturally, such as playing sports, going to a fair or festival, going fishing, or taking a hike. When you engage in these activities, the conversation can focus on the things you're doing and seeing, as opposed to just getting together for coffee, which may be more challenging for someone who struggles to make conversation. Also, check out Chapter 10 for more tips on making conversation.

To become a better conversationalist, before meeting up with your friend, you can write out a few notes about what you've been up to and questions to ask them.

Keeping a New Friendship Going

In order to be a good friend, you need to do your share of keeping the friendship going. This includes reaching out, initiating plans, and staying in touch. Many people struggle to keep a new friendship going, mainly because it takes a lot of time and energy. The following sections offer a few steps you can take to keep your blossoming friendship moving forward smoothly.

Taking the initiative to plan get-togethers

Being a good friend means reaching out to your friend to make plans, which lets them know that you're thinking about them and value them. It can be hard to take the lead and be an initiator, but it's an important friendship skill to master.

Many people worry that they don't have the time to plan or get together with their friends very often. They believe that, between work, family obligations, and household tasks, their free time is very limited. But if you want to, you can make the time, even with an extremely busy schedule.

REMEMBER

Some people struggle with figuring out what they can invite their friend to do, but it doesn't have to be so difficult. You can keep things causal and invite your friend to join you in something that you're already planning to do, which keeps the stakes low and helps you worry less about rejection. As an example, you can say, "Hey, I'm planning to check out this new movie on Sunday. Would you like to join me?"

Alternatively, you can make a list of the activities you think your friend would enjoy, and figure out which ones also appeal to you. Then choose one that would appeal to both of you and invite your friend to join. Other ideas for regular friend dates include:

>> **Taking a class together:** A weekly exercise class, art class, language class, or yoga class can be a great way to spend time together and learn something new.

>> **Committing to a weekly exercise routine together:** Suggest that you meet one morning per week for a walk in a park. This helps you get exercise and social time in, and also helps solidify the friendship, especially if it's a newer friend.

>> **Doing errands together:** Meet up once or twice a month to shop at a big-box store, mall, or grocery store together.

>> **Volunteering together for a cause you both believe in:** Commit to volunteering once or twice a month. You can help an important organization and get some friend time in, too.

Putting yourself out there

Part of being a good friend is putting yourself out there, over and over. Reaching out to your new friend and inviting them to do things is how your relationship grows closer. Some people shy away from the idea of reaching out to others. They may be shy, feel self-conscious about being forward, worry about coming across as too needy, or fear rejection. If these issues are getting in the way of your reaching out to others, consider talking it through with your spouse/family member, or a therapist so you can process your feelings, work through them, and create an action plan.

Knowing What to Do When Your Friendship Feels One-Sided

Relationships start to feel one-sided when both friends are putting unequal amounts of energy and effort into a friendship. One-sided friendships often lead to resentment and disappointment, when one person feels they're putting in all the work and the other person isn't doing as much. Part of being a good friend is taking care to reciprocate your friend's invitations when you can, so that the friendship feels more balanced.

To avoid your friendship feeling one-sided, try to match energies with the other person. That means you invest your time and energy into the friendship at the same level your friend does. To make sure the friendship feels roughly equal, one friend should not be putting in the lion's share of the effort while the other friend barely puts in any effort at all. If your friend reaches out to invite you to something, try to reach out the next time. You shouldn't keep score, but your friendship will feel lopsided if your friend invites you out ten times and you've only invited them once.

If you're the one always doing the inviting, and you notice that your friend rarely, if ever, reciprocates, you may decide to pull back a bit from the friendship if it bothers you. Or you may decide that being the initiator doesn't bother you at all, and if that's the case, just keep on inviting. You may conclude that you're just more proactive than your friends are, and as long as they keep accepting your invitations and showing up, it shows that they enjoy spending time with you, and you'll keep inviting them. You can also think about whether your friends invest in other ways — maybe they don't reach out to invite you to do things, but perhaps they bring flowers when you invite them over to your home for dinner, drop everything to help you out in an emergency, treat you occasionally when you invite them out for dinner, or pick up your favorite chocolates from the grocery store while they're out shopping. If your friends do thoughtful gestures or show up for you in other ways, you may conclude that they *are* investing in your friendship in a way that feels meaningful for you, even if they're not inviting you to do anything.

REMEMBER

People struggle to reciprocate for a variety of reasons. One reason is because of inertia — they just don't have the motivation to invite people to do things. Others don't reciprocate because they don't have time or they're financially strapped. Others are bogged down with worry about their own personal problems and don't have the bandwidth to think about reaching out to friends. They may be preoccupied with work or childcare responsibilities, have a health issue, or are overwhelmed in their own life and don't have the energy to reach out. They may not prioritize friendships the same way you do, or they may be satisfied with infrequent get-togethers.

The fact that you're reaching out regularly shows that you have a healthy lifestyle balance and are competent enough to handle all your adult responsibilities and initiate in friendships as well.

REMEMBER

Everyone goes through busy or rough patches now and again, and it's important to be patient with your friend through those, even if it means they're not able to reciprocate as much as they used to. Hopefully, after their stressful period has passed, they'll be able to fully invest in the friendship once again.

Interacting on Social Media

Some people who are active on social media expect that a good friend will also be interactive with them on it. They may feel that interacting with friends on social media shows that you value them, appreciate what they post, and are supportive. When a friend doesn't like or comment on their posts, they get upset and worry this means their friend really isn't into them.

TIP

Different people use social media in different ways, so it can become a problem when you assume that the way you use social media is the same way your friend uses it. For example, if your new friend expects you to interact with them on social media every day and you don't like or comment on their posts very often, they may think you don't like them. This can become a tricky situation and can lead to misunderstandings and hurt feelings. If you're not very active on social media it can help to mention that to a new friend, so they know not to expect constant interaction. If you're not on social media at all, you can also mention this to your new friend early on.

Another problem arises when people get envious because of posts on social media or their feelings get hurt because of behavior on social media. For example, if you're always posting about parties or get-togethers they weren't invited to, it can cause them to feel left out.

When your post involves your social life, think about how others might react to your update. Will they feel neutral or happy about what you post, or will they be jealous? Ask yourself, "Am I posting this because I genuinely want to share this aspect of my life, or am I posting to show off a bit?" If it's the latter, it can help to dig a little deeper. Do you routinely feel the need to prove to others on social media what an amazing social life you have, when you actually feel a bit insecure deep down? If so, it may be worth doing some more introspection, either on your own via journaling or with a therapist, about why this is. When you feel more secure with yourself and your friendships, your need to frequently broadcast your social life on social media may decrease.

Determining when to become friends or followers on social media

These days, many people send a friend request right after becoming acquaintances with someone. Sometimes they do this because they want to have as many friends/followers as possible; other times they do this because social media is a convenient way to stay in touch with people. Others like to add people because they use social media messaging to keep in touch with friends.

There are no cut-and-dried rules about when you should become friends on social media. Feel things out and do what feels right. If you worry about appearing too eager, you can always wait until you become better friends. The benefit of that is that you'll have more time to get to know the person and decide if you actually do want to add them on social media.

Some people don't send anyone friend requests because they fear rejection. If you're wondering why your new friend hasn't tried to add you on social media, that could be why.

Interacting with your friend's posts

Supporting your friend on social media can involve interacting with their posts in a positive way. You can choose to like most or all of your friend's posts and comment on many of their posts. When your friend leaves a positive comment on your post, it feels very gratifying. Only you can decide how much interaction is the right amount.

Keep in mind that your friend's feelings may be hurt if they notice you interacting with other mutual friends' posts but you rarely, if ever, interact with theirs.

Responding to declined friend requests

Friend requests are a tricky subject and easily lead to hurt feelings. This can happen when you send someone a friend request and they decline or ignore it. Or it can happen when someone (like your boss or a neighbor) sends you a friend request and you don't want to be social media friends with them. What's the best way to handle these situations?

REMEMBER

If you send someone a friend request and you never hear back, it can be easy to jump to worst-case scenarios, like the person really doesn't like you. However, before you do that, ask yourself what evidence you have that your friend doesn't like you? Could there be any alternative explanations for their lack of response to your friend request? Maybe your friend only wants close friends or family on their friends list, or maybe they never saw the request in the first place. Many people don't check their friend requests very often or aren't active on social media even though they have accounts.

TIP

If your friend ignored your friend request, and you're feeling perplexed or hurt about it, consider letting it go. If you ask your friend whether they received your friend request, you may put them in an awkward position about having to explain why they chose not to accept the request. It may be better to choose to not sweat the small stuff and try to let it go, even if you feel hurt. Try not to let it bother you, especially if your friend seems great in other ways.

If someone sends you a friend request who you don't want to be social media friends with, you can just ignore the request. Just pretend you didn't see it if it ever comes up in conversation, to avoid hurting their feelings.

Improving Communication with Friends

One aspect of being a good friend is being a good communicator. When you have good communication with your friends, you limit the chances of misunderstandings, conflict, drama, and hurt feelings because you're communicating clearly and effectively. Improving communication can vastly improve all your relationships.

TIP

Here are several ways to improve communication with your friends:

>> **When a problem comes up, decide if you want to directly address it with your friend or let it go.** Try not to let problems fester.

>> **If a big problem comes up, try not to address it via text or email.** A phone call, video call, or in-person conversation is much better for addressing a

complicated issue because tone of voice and emotion aren't conveyed very well in writing. You don't want to end up having a heated argument over text!

>> **Make sure to think before you speak (or text).** Try not to say things impulsively, especially when you're angry. When you start to feel angry, take a short break to pause and think before speaking. This decreases the chances that you'll say something you regret.

>> **Use *I* statements as opposed to *you* statements.** *I* statements put the focus on how the speaker thinks and feels. *You* statements blame the other person and put the other person on the defensive. *I* statements start off with expressing how you feel and open up the conversation, whereas *you* statements tend to shut it down quickly. For example, saying "I feel hurt because I've invited you out the last ten times, and you haven't really reciprocated" is likely to get a better response than "You're a bad friend because you never invite me anywhere!" Check out Chapter 15 for an in-depth discussion of *I* statements.

TIP

When you put the emphasis on how *you* feel instead of on how the other person *makes* you feel, it helps the other person not feel blamed and put on the spot. You can also soften your message, which helps convey a caring and concerned vibe, as opposed to an accusatory vibe, like this: "It feels like lately I've been the one doing all the initiating — I asked you out for coffee last week, and a few weeks before I invited you to the movies, and before that I invited you to that baseball game. I love that you're always up for the things I invite you to, but I'm starting to feel hurt that you haven't invited me anywhere in a while." If you gently remind your friend of all the things you've invited them to, they may respond with, "Oh, wow, you're right!"

Setting Healthy Boundaries with Friends

Setting healthy boundaries and respecting your friend's boundaries are part of being a good friend. Setting a boundary lets your friend know what you are and aren't willing to do and accept. The purpose of setting a boundary is to ensure that your needs and wishes are respected and to ensure you only do things you're comfortable with.

TIP

You can set a boundary around anything, from when you're available to talk on the phone to topics of conversation that you don't want to discuss. You can set a boundary in order to more effectively communicate your needs and to let others know what's acceptable to you.

Clearly communicate your boundaries as things come up — and stick to them. If a friend disrespects your boundaries, it's important to respectfully call them out on it every time; otherwise, they can steamroll right over you, and you'll be left feeling frustrated and upset.

Understanding when to set boundaries

You can set boundaries around anything, but especially consider it for areas where you've encountered problems in the past with feeling pressured to go outside your comfort zone. For example, if a friend keeps pressuring you to try something you're not comfortable with, it's time to set a clear boundary — for example, "I've told you a few times now that I'm afraid of heights and I don't want to go bungee jumping with you. Please don't ask me again — you know how I feel."

When a friend disrespects your boundaries, it's important to call them out on it when it happens so they know they violated your boundary. Let them know why it bothered you and what you want to see instead. If it happens repeatedly, let them know that you're upset that this keeps happening and give a consequence if it happens again.

EXAMPLE

For example, Clare reserves weekends to spend time with her family. Her new friend Vernice always wants to meet up with Clare on the weekends. The first time Vernice invited her to a Saturday night dinner, Clare gently explained that weekends are family time because she barely sees them during the week. The next week, Vernice invited Clare for Sunday brunch. Clare held firm with her boundary and again calmly explained to Vernice that her weekends are reserved for family time. Vernice asked a few more times for weekend get-togethers, but Clare stayed true to her boundary. Soon Vernice stopped asking about weekends and only invited Clare for weeknight get-togethers. Clare stood firm to her boundary, and Vernice eventually respected it.

EXPLORE

Think about a time when a friend disrespected one of your boundaries. What was the boundary and how did the fact that your friend disrespected it make you feel? Did you try to uphold your boundary? If so, how did you do that?

Saying no respectfully

Sometimes it can be hard to say no to a friend. Always try to be kind and respectful, but firm, when telling a friend no. Think about how you would prefer to be said no to. Make sure when you say no that you explain why you're saying no, which can help your friend understand better and decrease the possibility of conflict or pushback.

Being a good friend means saying no respectfully when the situation calls for it so that you don't become a pushover and you honor your own boundaries.

Saying no respectfully also means being considerate of your friend's feelings and understanding how some people are especially sensitive to hearing no. Think about how you can communicate no in a kind and gentle, but firm way. If a friend invites you to do something and you can't make it, instead of saying, "No, that doesn't work for me" (which can come across as harsh), you could say, "I'm so sorry, but I'm busy that day. How about we meet up the next weekend instead?" The latter has a much softer, gentler tone to it.

Chapter 14

Creating a Sense of Community

Many people believe it's important to build a sense of community for themselves and feel like they belong. These days, many people struggle with not having a social support network. Moving far away from your hometown and family and settling in a place where you don't know anyone for job opportunities, higher education, or personal fulfillment is very common. However, moving to an unfamiliar place can make it challenging to build a strong sense of community and can lead to loneliness and feeling like you don't belong.

The good news is that there are many ways to create a sense of community, from joining groups or getting involved in causes you're passionate about to finding your niche in your neighborhood to making friends who are like family. Many people experience a sense of community by cheering for their favorite sports team in a packed stadium and feeling camaraderie with other fans or by volunteering with a community organization and feeling a sense of purpose with the organization's mission.

I begin this chapter by explaining what it means to have a sense of community. Then I discuss how to build a sense of community. I also walk you through how to create a family of choice and find people who are looking to make friends who are like family. Finally, I help you identify when you've finally built the community you were looking for.

Understanding the Concept of Community

Think about the last time you felt a sense of community. Maybe it was when you lived in your hometown and were surrounded by people you grew up with and who knew your entire family. Maybe it was when you were rooting for your city's sports team and felt the electricity of the cheering crowd. Or it may have been when you were at your last high school or college reunion, feeling a sense of connection and camaraderie with fellow alumni. However you felt a sense of community, it was most likely a positive feeling that stayed with you for a long time afterward. Feeling like we're a part of something larger than ourselves makes us feel a sense of connectedness and belonging.

Having a strong sense of community is also about having a robust support network. When you've built a close community, you feel that you have people who value and care about you, feel a part of something larger, and feel like you have backup support if needed. You feel comforted knowing you can rely on people who care about and value you, people you can ask for favors, and people who support you. It's about people who have your back, people who will bring you a meal, and people you can count on in an emergency.

When you don't have any community, you tend to feel isolated and alone, like no one cares about you. It's a sad feeling.

REMEMBER

Having a community behind you is a comforting feeling — it's a feeling of belonging and security. When you have a strong sense of community, you feel at home. You've got people to bounce ideas off of, to give you feedback, and to consult on various things. It can make you feel stronger and more supported than if you were going through life alone.

EXPLORE

Would you describe yourself as having a strong sense of community now? How connected do you feel to your community and neighborhood? Do you feel connected or disconnected? Do some self-reflection about what is contributing to your feeling connected or disconnected. Can you think of any action steps you can take to feel more connected?

When you walk in the door of your own home, you know that you're in a welcoming place and have a feeling of relief and belonging because you can relax and just be your authentic self. It's a similar vibe when you feel like you belong in your community. There are people and places in your community that welcome you and make you feel at home. When you don't feel a sense of belonging or community, you often feel a sense of unease and a sad feeling like there's nowhere you really fit in.

Exploring how community enriches our lives

Community enriches our lives in many ways. It helps us feel like we have a strong social network filled with friends and supporters who care about us and look out for us. Here are several other ways that having community enriches people's lives:

» They have people to cheer them on.

» They have emergency backup or a safety net.

» They feel cared for during tough times.

» They have a sense of belonging.

» They have pride in their local community.

» They feel inspired to give back or pay it forward.

» They have a support network.

» They have a reason to stay in their current geographical area.

» They're less lonely.

» They can cope more effectively with anxiety or depression.

» Their emotional and physical well-being are enhanced.

THE IMPORTANCE OF COMMUNITY FOR NEW PARENTS

It's especially important for new parents to create a sense of community for their young family. New parents often feel stressed, overwhelmed, and alone while caring for their young children. Having a strong sense of community helps them feel like they have a support network, emergency backup, and parenting mentors they can turn to.

New parents can find community by:

- Joining social groups for new parents
- Meeting other parents through parent-and-me classes, preschool, or after-school activities
- Starting their own group for new parents
- Inviting other parents and their kids for playdates
- Creating a local support network who can help each other out with childcare

Identifying what it feels like to lack community

Some people don't have a social support network and lack community, even despite their best efforts. They may not fully understand how to build community, or maybe they've tried to make friends in the past, but nothing has worked.

Feeling like you don't belong or don't fit in anywhere can cause you to feel depressed or anxious. It can be painful to feel like everyone else has found their people except you, while you always feel like an outsider. These feelings of a lack of belonging can actually start in childhood and last well into adulthood, or they can begin in adulthood.

Many people who lack community feel lonely or existentially alone. They may feel like no one cares about them or wouldn't miss them if they moved. People who don't have a support network may feel all alone in the world.

If you lack community, you may experience some of the following:

>> Your social calendar is empty most of the time, because people aren't inviting you to events and activities.

>> You don't reach out or text anyone for a month, and no one checks in on you to see how you're doing.

>> You feel socially invisible; no one thinks of you.

>> You feel like you could pack up and move, and no one would notice.

>> You go on vacation and don't miss anyone back home.

>> You've lived in your town or city for years or even decades, but it still doesn't feel like home.

>> If you're getting married, you consider eloping because you have no one to invite to your wedding.

>> When you're pregnant, no one offers to throw a baby shower for you.

>> You don't feel like you belong anywhere.

>> You spend birthdays and other milestone occasions alone because you don't have anyone to celebrate with.

>> You feel like everyone else has found their "people," but you're always searching and alone.

>> You feel anxious about something bad happening to you, like getting sick or having an emergency situation, because you have no backup help.

>> You have no one to list on emergency contact forms for yourself or your children, so you ask a random neighbor or coworker if they're willing to serve in this role. You feel ashamed that you don't have anyone closer to ask.

>> You don't have anyone to be your children's godparents or guardians. If something were to happen to you, you'd have a tough time figuring out who to name as guardian.

>> No one shows up for you, in good times or in bad.

THE IMPORTANCE OF COMMUNITY FOR OLDER ADULTS

Many older adults live far from their families. Some live alone as *solo-agers* (older adults who are living alone without the support of a spouse/partner or children). It's especially important for seniors who are solo-agers to have a strong support network, because they're making all their own life decisions independently without the benefit of feedback or support from a spouse/partner or adult children. Having a strong sense of community gives them people to ask for advice if needed and helps them feel supported if they were to need a ride from a medical procedure or a check-in after surgery. It's vital that older adults feel like they have a safety net.

Older adults can build their social support network by:

- Joining a senior center, attending programs, and making new friends

- Joining a local village through the village movement (www.vtvnetwork.org), where members help other members age in place

- Participating in organizations that serve older adults

- Joining support groups for physical and mental health conditions

- Taking lifelong learning classes designed for seniors and meeting new people

- Asking for help from neighbors when needed

- Finding a home health-care company they trust that they can use if needed

- Building relationships with trusted professionals like geriatric care managers, daily money managers, attorneys, home health aides, personal care assistants, and housekeepers

Dominique feels alone all the time. She moved to her city ten years ago but has yet to make any close friends or feel like she has a community. She tried making friends through work and through neighbors, but no one seemed interested. Dominique spends every holiday alone, despite letting people know she has nowhere to go for the holidays and hoping they'll invite her. Her social calendar is always empty. She can't remember the last time she had any plans that she didn't make herself. Dominique decides to start volunteering at an animal shelter and meets other people whose passion is also helping homeless animals. Over time, Dominique starts making friends and starts to feel like she's building community. Some of these people eventually invite Dominique to spend holidays with them.

The solution to feeling a lack of community is to put in extra effort to build community. You can do this in a variety of ways, which I explore in the next section.

Exploring How to Build Community

In order to build community, you need to get to know people. Having a network of acquaintances and friends is the bedrock of building a strong sense of community. Getting to know people one-by-one in the areas you frequent most will help you start to build community.

Starting with your neighborhood

Many people start by building community right where they live, within their own neighborhood. The best ways to do this are to get to know your neighbors by being outside as much as possible. Take walks in the neighborhood and make small talk with the people you see. Spend more time in your yard doing yard work, and make conversation with passersby. (If you have a dog, this makes things easier, because dogs are great conversation starters!) When you get to know your neighbors a little, do nice things for them from time to time — bring them holiday treats, offer to take their trash out or water their garden while they're on vacation, and look out for them. Soon, you'll start to have the beginnings of a sense of community.

If your neighborhood has large yards and the houses are far apart, it can be harder to get to know your neighbors. Try to compensate for this by being outside more often or taking more walks in the neighborhood and enthusiastically greeting the neighbors you do see. If you choose a regular time to walk outside, you'll start seeing the same people every day, especially dog walkers. When you're out walking, start learning people's names and greeting their dogs. Be friendly and make small talk. If your neighborhood doesn't have any community amenities like a pool, clubhouse, or common area, which are great gathering spots to meet neighbors, try to be outside more whenever you can.

If you live in a rural area, where the houses are far apart, look for ways to get involved in your town. Attend town meetings that are open to residents, volunteer at the local library, get involved in a local adult sports league, or become a regular at the local watering hole.

TIP

If you have kids, the bus stop can be a great place to get to know your neighbors. Wait with your kids at the bus stop to chat with other neighbors. This can be a great way to start forming connections! Here are some other ideas for getting to know your neighbors:

>> Serve on your neighborhood homeowners association (HOA), if you have one.

>> Join or start a social committee to help create neighborhood social events where you can meet other neighbors.

>> When a new neighbor moves in, take them a welcome treat and card with your contact information. Introduce yourself and welcome them to the neighborhood.

>> If your neighborhood doesn't have a Facebook page (www.facebook.com), Nextdoor site (www.nextdoor.com), or newsletter, consider creating one. If your neighborhood does have these, consider trying to make some connections with neighbors this way. For instance, if someone posts a question on Facebook or Nextdoor, you can provide helpful answers.

>> If your neighborhood has gathering spots, hang out at the neighborhood pool, clubhouse, tennis courts, or common area and make small talk with your neighbors.

>> Attend as many neighborhood social events as you can.

>> If you see something in your neighborhood that needs attending to, organize a team of neighbors to take care of it, like fixing up the neighborhood entrance sign or planting flowers in a community area.

>> Drop off small treats for your neighbors at holiday time.

>> Be outside doing yard work on weekends or early evenings when more people are out and about so you can get to know your neighbors.

>> Help start some new neighborhood traditions, especially around holidays. Halloween parties, Easter Egg hunts, garden tours, and potluck dinners are good ideas.

Building community at work

Another way to find and build community is at your workplace. Because you see your coworkers daily and spend lots of time together at work, getting to know them and forming strong bonds is easier.

TIP

Here are some ways to build community in your workplace:

» Invite a coworker out for lunch or coffee during the workday.

» Put a bowl of candy or a conversation piece (like an interesting plant or terrarium) on your desk to encourage coworkers to stop by.

» Start a new tradition in your workplace, like bringing in baked goods on Fridays.

» Start an exercise or volunteering program at your office to get to know people.

» Get to know coworkers and offer to help them out if needed. Be generous.

» If a coworker has a medical emergency or has a major surgery, start a meal train for them in the office.

» Help plan baby showers, last-day-of-work gatherings, or retirement parties for coworkers.

» If a coworker whom you like changes jobs, keep in touch!

Considering your congregation

Another good place to build community is at your place of worship. Religious congregations are set up to foster and nurture community, whether you're attending services, staying after services for a community meal, or celebrating holidays with your fellow congregants. You'll have a lot to talk about with fellow congregants, because you all have the same religion in common. Even if you're not religious, many people join congregations for the community aspect.

TIP

Here are other ideas for building community in your place of worship:

» Join committees at your congregation, so you can meet new people and work together on projects.

» Stay later to socialize after services.

» Join a group with a social focus, like a Bible study, sisterhood or brotherhood, ministry, or book club. If your congregation doesn't offer a group that would help you meet new people, consider starting one!

» Let your religious leader know that you're interested in meeting new people and building community, and see if they have any advice for ways to do this at your congregation.

>> Send your kids to Sunday school, Hebrew school, or the equivalent in your faith. You'll meet other parents through your kids' involvement in the program.

>> Teach Sunday school, religious school, lead youth groups, or help out in other ways with kids' programs in your faith.

>> Attend congregation events and celebrations throughout the year.

>> Find out if your congregation offers small groups where congregants get to know each other and celebrate holidays together.

>> Offer to volunteer at your congregation, perhaps in the library or in the front office.

Exploring "third places"

Third places, a concept developed by sociologist Ray Oldenburg in *The Great Good Place*, are places in the community outside of your home and work, where you can meet others and start to build community, like community centers, coffee shops, bars, gyms, bookstores, libraries, and anywhere else that people gather and socialize. At third places, you can become a regular and get to know people.

Do you remember the TV show *Cheers?* The theme song described the bar as a place "where everybody knows your name." Having a place, whether it's a bar or a coffee shop, where you're welcomed and valued feels good, and that's also the idea behind third places.

Imagine having a neighborhood coffee shop where you enjoy the ambience, where the barista remembers exactly how you like your drink, where you can sit at your favorite table with your laptop and do some work while the same regulars who always come at that time seek you out, chat with you, and remember important details that you've mentioned. If you do this regularly for several months, the coffee shop will start to feel like a home away from home and "your spot." This is how you start to build a sense of belonging.

REMEMBER

When you have a third place that's "your" spot, you've found somewhere you can go, hang out, feel like you know the staff and clientele there, and feel that you belong.

TIP

Here are some tips for building community at third places:

>> To find your third place, check out different community centers, restaurants, coffee shops, bookstores, or gyms around your area. Try to find at least one

that feels like a welcoming, comfortable spot. Then go there several times within a month and see if it feels like a good hangout spot for you. If not, keep looking.

>> After you've found a third place you like, go there around the same time every day. Over time, you'll start seeing the same people and be able to make small talk. Soon they'll get to know you.

>> Have something that's a conversation piece with you, like a laptop adorned with stickers or an interesting book. This conversation piece will draw people over to chat.

>> Get to know the staff and let them know that you're looking to meet more people. They may have suggestions from the regulars they know.

Seeing the same people regularly

One of the best ways to build community is to see the same people regularly. You can do this by joining a group with a social focus and attending meetings regularly, walking in your neighborhood around the same time every day to socialize with other walkers and dog walkers, and going to the same grocery stores, community centers, and gyms at consistent times to interact with the same people.

For example, if you go to your local gym every day at 8 a.m., you'll see the same regulars who come at that time every morning, and they'll get used to seeing you. Soon just *seeing* these regulars will help you feel like you're building community.

Here are some other ways to see the same people regularly:

>> Join a sports team like a community softball or frisbee team.

>> Volunteer at a local organization every Monday morning.

>> Go to your local diner for breakfast every Friday.

>> Chat with the cashiers at your local grocery store.

>> Go out for an evening walk in your neighborhood every day.

>> Take an in-person class at a local community center.

Starting your own group

Another way to build community is to start your own social or hobby/interest group. If you've been looking for groups in your local area and you haven't been able to find what you're looking for, or if you can't find groups that meet at the times you need, consider starting your own group.

Starting your own group is easier than you think! You can start your own group on Meetup (www.meetup.com) or through Facebook groups, or as a subgroup of another group you're already a part of. For example, if you're already in a local women's group, you could start a weekly craft group as a subgroup — that way you already have potential group members who might be interested.

Here are the benefits of starting your own group to build community:

>> You have full control over the group's focus, as well as when the group meets, so you know you'll be able to attend all the meetings.

>> You have full control over the activities your group does, including incorporating getting-to-know-you activities like icebreakers.

>> Everyone will be new to the group at the same time so it's easier to make new friends (as opposed to jumping into an existing group that's been around for years).

Here are several creative ideas of groups you could start depending on your interests:

>> Arts-and-crafts group

>> Bowling group

>> Writers group

>> Bird-watching group

>> Networking group for your career field

>> Rock-climbing group

>> Weekly social breakfast group

EXAMPLE

Sasha wants to join a running group, but she needs one that meets on the weekend because she works full-time. She can't find a weekend running group, so Sasha decides to start her own. She creates a group, and soon, lots of people are finding out about it. She schedules group meetings on the days and times that work for her schedule. Soon she meets other people who love getting together to run on Saturday mornings. After a few group meetings, Sasha feels like she's starting to find her people.

Using the internet

Another great way to build community is by using the internet. The internet is the ultimate people connector, because you can join online groups, start online groups, make online friends, and feel a part of different online communities. This is especially helpful if you live in a small town and your options to join in-person groups are more limited. (See Chapter 11 about how to turn online friends into real friends.)

Here are some other ways you can use the internet to build your community:

>> Take online classes.

>> Join your high school or college alumni group.

>> Join a support group.

>> Participate in discussion forums.

>> Find friends through friend apps like Bumble BFF (https://bumble.com/bff).

Participating in community events

Participating in community events is another great way to meet people in your local area, foster a sense of local pride, and start building your community:

>> **Choose a sports team to be "your" team.** Go to team games, wear team colors, learn facts and stats about the team, host team watch parties or happy hours, or go to bars and hang out with others who are rooting for the team. You'll gain a sense of belonging being around other enthusiastic fans.

>> **Attend holiday events, fairs, festivals, or other events specific to your community.** This can help foster a sense of hometown pride, which can help you feel a stronger sense of community.

>> **Participate in neighborhood or community cleanup efforts.** This will also help facilitate a sense of civic pride.

>> **Look on Eventbrite (www.eventbrite.com) for local events that interest you.** While you're there, chat with others at the event and try to make some connections.

>> **Volunteer or join a cause you believe in.** Joining a cause you believe in can be another good way to build community. Whether it's volunteering for a nonprofit that helps seniors, helping out at an animal shelter, or helping kids in need, volunteering your time to your community is a positive thing to do.

Inviting other people over

Another good way to build community is to invite other people to your home (after you've gotten to know them and feel comfortable). An easy and relatively low-effort way for people to turn acquaintances into friends and build community is by hosting potlucks. They invite a random assortment of coworkers, neighbors, and other acquaintances to their potlucks and host them several times a year, which builds a sense of continuity. Hosting a casual gathering can help you feel like you're building community and making new friends.

TIP

Here are other creative ideas of regular events you can host at your home (when you've gotten to know the potential participants):

>> **Book clubs:** Host a book club meeting at your house. You can even start your own book club.

>> **Cooking club:** Host a cooking club meeting. You can all cook together or make your own dishes at home to bring that everyone can try.

>> **Neighbors:** Invite neighbors over for happy hour, brunch, or just coffee and conversation.

>> **Parents from your kids' school:** If you have kids, get to know their friends' parents and invite them over to hang out during a playdate, or just to stop by for coffee and conversation.

>> **Friendsgiving:** Host a yearly Friendsgiving and invite acquaintances and friends who don't have Thanksgiving plans. Over time, this can become a special tradition.

Creating a Family of Choice

Family plays a big role in many people's sense of community. Some people are lucky to have a large, loving group of local family nearby who can be there for them and be a large part of their community. They always know they can spend holidays and other milestones with their family.

Other people don't have any local family or have uninvolved family, so they miss out on that aspect of community. One option for those who wish they had a caring, involved family but don't is to create a family of choice, with friends who are like family. Friends who are like family can sometimes feel closer than siblings or blood relatives because they're the family you choose.

TIP

In order to create a family of choice, you have to make friends who are also looking for the same thing. Some people are already content with their friends and family and aren't looking for any more because they have those strong, nurturing connections already. People who are more likely to want the same things include those who have no local family or uninvolved family, are single, or are newcomers.

Many LGBTQIA+ individuals have created a family of choice, either because their family of origin didn't fully accept them or because they feel more comfortable with the family they choose. To do this, you need to work hard to nurture strong relationships with friends and invite them to get together and celebrate holidays and milestones with you.

Creating a family of friends

The benefits of creating friends who are like family are that you have people who deeply care about you and who support you, to be there for you and to comprise your community. When you create a family of friends, you have people:

>> To celebrate holidays and milestones with

>> Who will show up for you

>> Who you may have more in common with than family because you share similar values and interests

>> Who you can turn to for help

>> To vacation with

>> Who can be there for you in an emergency

EXAMPLE

Eloise doesn't have any local family, which has always bothered her. She and her husband always spent every holiday alone, because their family was too far away. Eloise wanted to improve her situation and start spending holidays with friends. She started by hosting a Friendsgiving for her acquaintances and friends who were alone on Thanksgiving. Over the years, the number of people attending her Friendsgiving grew until she had a full house every year. Eloise loved how having friends over on Thanksgiving made the holiday feel more special for her.

Exploring online surrogate family sites

If you're looking to create a family of choice other than by trying to develop closer relationships with friends or people you already know, another option is to explore surrogate family sites online. These sites are meant to connect random people who are looking for surrogate family members, especially surrogate grandparents, who can stand in for blood family members who are unable to or disinterested in being close.

One such site, Surrogate Grandparents-USA on Facebook (www.facebook.com/ groups/SurrogateGrandparentsNorthAmerica), connects people from all over the country looking for surrogate family members and allows people to make posts where they describe what kind of connections they're looking for. Some may be looking for grandparents for their children, whereas others are looking for a mother/daughter or cousin relationship. It's easy to join and connect with others on these kind of sites.

WARNING

Just make sure to get to know someone through messaging first before giving out your personal contact information, and never invite a stranger to your home. Always meet in a public place until you get to know them better.

Knowing When You've Built Community

Many people long for a stronger sense of community and try to take the steps needed to start building community. But how will you know when you've created a sense of community for yourself or your family? Here are several indicators to look for:

>> You run into people you know when you're out and about, and you have a nice chat. This makes your larger community feel like a smaller world.

>> If you want to go to a movie, go out to dinner, or attend an event, you have several people you could invite to accompany you.

>> At holiday time, if you don't have any plans and mention that you'll be solo to people, someone invites you to join their celebration.

>> When it's time to fill out an emergency contact form, you can easily think of several people to write down.

>> You have multiple people you can call if you're sick or in an emergency situation to come and help you, and you know they'll be happy to do so.

>> You have someone to call if you're running late and can't pick up your kids on time or to help with emergency childcare.

>> You have people to celebrate holidays and other milestones with, and if you want to celebrate your birthday, you have several people you could invite and know they'll come.

>> You're happy to come back from vacation because you have people you want to see and missed while you were gone.

VALUING INTERGENERATIONAL FRIENDSHIPS

Intergenerational friendships are great ways to build your social support network and enhance your sense of community. Making friends of different ages and stages can help you get to know new people who may have more time and space in their lives to make new friends and who may more strongly share your values of the importance of building community. Additionally, you may find that people older or younger than you can be more supportive than similar-aged peers. Intergenerational friendships can be a cherished part of your social support network.

Making an older or younger friend is the same process as making same-age friends, but you may need to explore different settings than you'd ordinarily frequent to find these friends. To do this, brainstorm some new groups to join or new venues to meet people of older or younger ages. For instance, consider joining a social group that has a wide variety of ages to make new friends of different ages and stages.

Here are several ideas of places to look for intergenerational friendships:

- **Your workplace:** One of the beneficial features of most workplaces is that you have coworkers of all ages. Meeting older or younger coworkers is a great way to get to know someone new whom you have things in common with. Start by stopping by a coworker's desk to chat. Then, if you feel like you have things in common and have a connection, consider inviting the friendly coworker down the hall to have lunch or coffee with you during the workday.

- **Your religious congregation:** Religious congregations appeal to people of all ages, and some offer groups or committees where you can get to know people better. You can meet with your religious leader to find out if there are any lonely older people at your congregation who might like to make a new friend.

- **A social or hobby group that attracts a variety of ages:** Joining a women's walking group, a brunch group, a book club, or a knitting group can be a great way to meet new people of all ages and stages. In a knitting group, for example, people of all ages gather to focus on the camaraderie of knitting. This can be a great way to casually dip your toe in the water to get to know an older or younger person.

- **A support group:** Support groups appeal to people of all ages who are struggling with a particular challenge. They can be great places to meet people of all ages.

4

Handling Friendship Foibles

Inevitably, every friendship hits a rough patch now and then. It's how you handle these tough spots that determines the longevity of your friendships. This part shows you how to communicate more effectively with your friends when disagreements arise, how to handle conflict appropriately, how to end a friendship with grace, how to cope with loneliness, and what to do when you can't make a friend no matter how hard you try.

Chapter **15**

Navigating Common Friendship Challenges

You've made a new friend and things are going well . . . until you hit a bump in the road. Friendship challenges are common, and all friends have their disagreements from time to time. Most of the time, a friendship can recover from these challenges, as long as you focus on effective communication and are willing to put in the effort to resolve your differences. Your friendship may even grow stronger after being tested by a friendship challenge.

If a friendship problem arises, don't panic! Instead, think through the situation calmly, raise the issue in a kind and respectful way, and work together on a compromise or resolution. There is usually an amicable way to solve most challenges if both parties are willing to be honest with each other, communicate effectively, and compromise.

In this chapter, I describe the most common friendship challenges and give you helpful pointers on how to resolve those concerns. Next, I give you specific tips on how to work through general friendship challenges. At the end of the chapter, I delve into how to communicate more effectively with your friends.

Navigating the Most Common Friendship Challenges

Friendships are supposed to be fun and enjoyable, but challenges can pop up from time to time. Friends become frustrated and disappointed with each other for many different reasons. If you want to hold onto the friendship, it's important to try to work through these issues. Sweeping problems under the rug and avoiding bringing them up can lead to smoldering resentment over time.

TIP

In a friendship, it's best to address concerns as they arise, diplomatically and respectfully. If you bring up something that's been bothering you about the friendship and your friend won't acknowledge that you have a valid concern or change their ways, you may decide to step back from the friendship or spend more time with other friends.

In the following sections, I cover the most common friendship challenges and offer strategies for working through them.

Dealing with mismatches in expectations

One common friendship challenge is when you and your friend have different expectations for the friendship. Perhaps one friend wants to meet up every week, while the other friend is content to get together a few times a year. Or one friend is happy to meet up occasionally for a casual beer, while the other friend wants to sign up for a weekly class together. When friends have different expectations, it can lead to resentment and disappointment.

Sometimes a mismatch in expectations develops because, unlike romantic partners, friends don't usually talk about what their friendship expectations are at the beginning of their friendship. Friends don't usually delve into specifically what they're looking for from the friendship and what things are deal-breakers for them. As the friendship continues, when their needs are not met or things turn out differently than they expect, little annoyances and resentments slowly build up over time. If the issue isn't dealt with, one friend may be upset and the other has no idea why. The friendship may dissolve with one person being left in the dark about what went wrong.

Friendship expectations aren't usually discovered until you've been friends for a while, so they can't be easily discussed when you first meet someone. You may eventually find out that you're not compatible with someone after you've invested a lot of time and energy into the friendship.

Here are some examples of common mismatches in expectations:

>> Desired frequency of meeting up

>> Desired frequency of keeping in touch through texts, emails, or phone calls

>> Expectations about the types of get-togethers you'll do

>> Expectations about the closeness of the friendship (for example, activity partners versus confidantes, or casual friends versus good friends)

>> Expectations of confidentiality

EXPLORE

As an exercise, think about any mismatches in expectations that have arisen in your past friendships. How did you handle them? Did you bring them up to your friend, and if so, how did that go? Was your friend receptive, or did they become defensive? Were any lasting changes made after you raised the issue? If you didn't bring it up, how did you handle your resentment and frustration?

TIP

At the beginning of a new friendship, it can be helpful to feel things out to see if you and your friend are compatible — asking your friend directly about their friendship expectations would be awkward. For example, if weekly get-togethers are important to you, you can ask some questions to gauge how busy your new friend is. If you learn that your new friend works full-time, has a family, and is taking care of their elderly parents, it's unrealistic to expect them to have time for weekly get-togethers. If you find out that your new friend can't meet your expectations for how often you want to get together, you can adjust your expectations, try to compromise, or decide to spend more time with other people who do meet your friendship needs.

If you realize that you and your friend have a mismatch in expectations, there are ways to work on the situation. First, decide if you want to raise the issue or if it's something minor enough that you can let it go. Choose your battles wisely — if you bring up too many issues, your friend may become annoyed and decide that the friendship isn't worth it. Most people want their friendships to feel light and fun.

If it's something you do want to work through, bring up the issue in a respectful way, discuss what you've noticed, and ask for your friend's thoughts on the matter. Make it a collaborative discussion. See if your friend is willing to compromise or work to resolve the situation. Be clear about what you'd prefer to see and why.

EXAMPLE

For example, you might say, "Hey, I noticed that we only seem to meet up a few times a year. I'd really like to see you more! I feel disconnected when we see each other so infrequently. Do you have room in your schedule to meet up more often?"

If your friend isn't interested in changing their ways, then you can decide to do one of the following:

>> Accept the situation as is and make the best of it.

>> Dial back the friendship with this person and spend more time with other friends who meet your needs better.

>> Decide to leave the friendship. (See Chapter 16 for more on this topic.)

Dealing with a bossy friend

Another difficult friendship challenge is dealing with a bossy friend. A bossy friend may have the attitude of "It's my way or the highway" and be the one to decide and plan all your get-togethers without considering your needs and preferences. If you're always doing what they want to do, when they want to do it, it's important to raise the issue and let them know what you're experiencing and why it bothers you. If they're unwilling to compromise and let you plan things too sometimes, that may end up being a friendship deal-breaker. Let them know what you've been noticing and what you would like to be different. Use *I* statements to express your feelings. *I* statements are a type of effective communication skill that puts the emphasis on what you're feeling (see the end of this chapter for more on *I* statements).

EXAMPLE

For example, you may say, "Hey, I noticed that the last five or six times we've met up, you've suggested the plans and we've done what *you* wanted to do. I've suggested some things, too, but we didn't end up doing them. I'm feeling kind of frustrated. How about I take a turn in planning our next get-together? I have some ideas for things that I think we'd both be interested in!"

Dealing with a competitive friend

Another difficult friendship challenge is having a competitive friend. This friend may keep tabs on you to see what you're up to and then try to downplay your accomplishments. They may ask a lot of nosey questions, not out of genuine interest, but to get information so they can one-up you or rain on your parade. This type of friend may show fake support for you and your dreams but then not show up for you (but expect you to show up for them). Or this friend may ignore your accomplishments altogether because they're jealous. They may also make passive-aggressive comments when they hear about your goals and accomplishments to try to bring you down. You may feel like they're never really rooting for you and don't have your best interests at heart. You may start to feel like you have a "frenemy," not a real friend.

If you notice you have a chronically competitive friend, the first step is to figure out if this characteristic is a deal-breaker for you. If it is, see Chapter 16 to explore whether you're going to end your friendship over it. If it's not a deal-breaker for you, you have a couple options:

>> **Keep the friendship but don't share the kind of things with them that they may become competitive about.** If you go this route, your friendship may fizzle over time.

>> **Raise the issue and see if your friend is willing to change their ways.** If you do raise the issue, be delicate, because they may deny their competitive nature.

EXAMPLE

For example, you might say, "I'm feeling hurt because you didn't acknowledge when I told you my art had just been accepted to an art gallery. This was a huge accomplishment for me and I was hoping that you'd be interested. Instead, you told me about the new car you just bought. It makes me feel like you don't care about something I worked really hard for. Next time I share something about my art, I would really appreciate it if you could be more supportive, because your friendship and support mean so much to me."

WARNING

One common friendship challenge that often results in jealousy is when two friends have differing financial situations. For example, one friend may earn a high income and the other friend may be struggling financially. Even if the better-off friend downplays their money and doesn't make it an issue in the friendship, the less well-off friend may still feel jealous.

What can help in this situation is for the better-off friend to make sure the outings and activities they suggest are doable for their friend. Suggest free or low-cost activities so your friend can fully participate. Avoid mentioning expensive items you've bought or talking about money. As long as the better-off friend is sensitive to their friend's needs, the friendship should work.

Handling the chronically late friend

Some people are punctual and others are chronically late. If you're a punctual person who has a chronically late friend, you may often find yourself stewing in frustration. Sitting at a restaurant for 45 minutes waiting for your friend to show up can be irritating. The chronically late friend usually means well, but their constant lateness can make you feel that they're rude and thoughtless and that they don't value your time. Also consider that they may have attention-deficit/hyperactivity disorder (ADHD), which may explain their tardiness.

If you have a tardy friend, decide how much this issue bothers you, which may be directly related to how late your friend tends to be. A friend who is occasionally 10 minutes late may be easier to deal with than a friend who always leaves you waiting for 30 minutes or more. If the tardiness is something that really gets on your nerves, consider bringing it up with your friend; otherwise, your resentment will fester. It's important to communicate what you've noticed and why it bothers you so that your friend has a chance to rectify the situation.

TIP

If your friend has ADHD, *time blindness* (when someone has a hard time determining how long something takes) may be the cause of their chronic lateness. Time blindness is a common symptom for those who have ADHD, but it can also occur on its own or with other conditions such as depression. Someone who has time blindness may assume they can get ready in 5 minutes when it actually takes them 30 minutes. One coping strategy if you have a friend who struggles with this issue is to suggest that the two of you meet up earlier than you need to (tell them your reservation is for 5:45 when it's actually for 6 p.m.), so if they're late it won't affect the start time of your plans as much.

Dealing with the flaky friend

Some people are flaky — they either don't respond to your invitations to get together, or they cancel at the last minute. Either way, you can't depend on them. When you're dealing with a flaky person, you never know if this friend will do what they say they'll do.

TIP

Decide how much flakiness bothers you. If it's a minor annoyance and you don't want to bring it up, you can spend more time with non-flaky friends who are more dependable. If it bothers you and you do want to bring it up, let your friend know what you've noticed and describe the behaviors that are bothering you. Ask them if there is anything getting in the way of their showing up or doing what they say they'll do. If they don't agree to work on this issue, you may want to reevaluate whether the friendship is meeting your needs.

Being betrayed by a friend

One of the most painful friendship challenges that you may need to navigate is being betrayed by a friend. There are different levels of betrayal, from minor betrayals to major betrayals that you can't recover from. A moderate betrayal could be that you told your friend something embarrassing, and they blabbed it to others. Or you may have told them a secret, and they used it against you. A severe betrayal may be that your friend got romantically involved with your partner behind your back, which is one of the most painful betrayals.

REMEMBER Regardless of how a friend betrayed you, it's shocking and it hurts.

When you're betrayed by a friend, it can help to talk things out with a trusted spouse/partner, family member, or therapist. When you've processed your feelings, decide how you want to handle the betrayal. You may be so angry and upset that you want to end the friendship, or you may decide that you can move forward, but you want to make sure that your friend knows how much their betrayal hurt you. If your friend acknowledges the betrayal and apologizes, the friendship may be able to be saved.

Dealing with lack of reciprocation and one-sided friendships

Lack of reciprocation is a common friendship challenge that can lead to resentment. Here's what it looks like: You may invite your friend over to your home multiple times, but your friend doesn't invite you to theirs. Or, you may invite your friend to get together many times, but your friend never invites you. Lack of reciprocation is emotionally painful and can lead to resentment.

TIP
Reciprocation doesn't have to involve "keeping score" — you don't have to keep detailed notes on whether your friend reciprocates every time. But if you get the general sense that you're the only one reaching out and making plans or you're putting in all the effort, it can feel like you're in a one-sided friendship.

Lack of reciprocation can also make you feel like the other person doesn't care about you or value you as much as you value them. In a friendship, both parties should be roughly equally enthusiastic about putting energy into the friendship. If you get a sense that your friend doesn't want to put in the same energy you're expending on the friendship, ask yourself why. Could it be a temporary lull in their enthusiasm (which could be explained by a busy period in their life), or has this lack of reciprocation been going on a long time? If they're not reaching out to you and inviting you to do things at least some of the time, it can signal that they're no longer interested in a friendship.

TIP
How do you know if you're in a one-sided friendship? Here are some of the signs:

>> You're putting way more energy into the friendship than your friend is.

>> You're the one always reaching out first.

>> You text, email, or call them, and they don't initiate communication with you.

>> They're not responsive when you reach out.

>> They invite others to do things, but not you.

>> You get the sense that you're not high on their priority list.

>> You're there for them, but they don't show up for you.

>> You do thoughtful gestures for them, but they're not reciprocated.

When you're always the initiator, you may become resentful and annoyed that your friend isn't putting as much energy into the friendship as you are. If you're always the initiator, here are a few ways to handle it:

>> **Pull back on the friendship and see if your friend steps up to initiate.** If they don't, that can be a sign that they're feeling lukewarm or disinterested in the friendship.

>> **Raise the issue about lack of reciprocation and see how your friend responds.** If they're willing to work on it, see how things go.

>> **Decide you're not interested in a one-sided friendship and end the friendship.**

>> **Decide you're okay with the way things are.** Continue being the initiator, and focus on the other strengths your friend brings to the friendship, like a great sense of humor or a fun personality. Decide that you're not going to let their lack of reciprocation bother you.

ONE-SIDED RELATIONSHIP PITFALLS

Do you find yourself frustrated and disappointed that you often end up in a one-sided relationship? Do you wonder why you're always the one texting, making plans, and inviting others, while friends and acquaintances don't ever reach out to you? There are several ways to interpret what's going on.

Some people find that they fall into the initiator role in every friendship they're in. They're natural initiators and leaders, who are good at thinking of ideas and making plans. Others have more of a passive, follower personality type — they're happy to accept invitations and go along with plans, but they rarely initiate or reach out to others.

There are benefits to being in the initiator role — you get to come up with interesting ideas and do what you want to do, and others are happy to go along with your ideas. However, the drawbacks of being in this role include feeling frustrated and resentful when you have to do all the work, and others don't reciprocate. You may feel taken advantage of or feel like you're not being valued by your friends. You may decide to put less energy into these friendships and only give back the energy that others put in, to decrease your resentment.

Handling a lack of responsiveness

Another common friendship challenge is a lack of responsiveness. Sometimes friends are unresponsive to your messages or invitations, or less responsive than you would like them to be. They may wait a long time before replying or not respond at all. It can be very hurtful to feel like your messages are being ignored.

Before getting too worked up about this situation, think about whether your friend has other major things going on in their life — maybe they're caring for a sick parent or child, they have a chronic illness, or they're swamped at work. Is this just an unusually busy time for them, and they're normally more responsive? Or has it been a pattern from the beginning?

Decide how much a lack of responsiveness bothers you and whether you want to raise the issue. If you do raise the issue, explain that responsiveness is very important to you and you'd appreciate if your friend could be more responsive in general. If they're not willing to, and this is a deal-breaker for you, you may need to reevaluate the friendship.

Being rejected

Being rejected and excluded by someone you thought was a friend is a painful feeling. For example, you may find out that your friend had a party and invited everyone in your friend group except for you. Or, your friend may plan get-togethers with others but not invite you, even doing so in front of you. Being rejected and excluded by a friend is extremely painful.

REMEMBER

Being rejected by a friend doesn't reflect on your worth as a person. Being rejected may make you feel insecure, but it doesn't mean you're unworthy of friendship or unlikable. It says more about your friend — that they're mean, inconsiderate, and exclusionary — than it does about you.

You can decide to raise the issue with your friend or pull back from the friendship and distance yourself for a while to see if things change. Or, you may decide that being rejected and excluded is a deal-breaker for your friendship (see Chapter 16 for more on how to end a friendship).

Growing apart

Another common friendship challenge is when you and your friend start to grow apart. At first, you may notice little things that distance you, like you find you don't have as much to talk about or you can't relate to them as well as you used to. You may feel like you have less and less in common, or they may become interested in things you have no interest in. Your friend may take on a new hobby or job and start making new friends and connections that they're drawn to more than you. Then your lives start to go in different directions and you communicate with and see each other less and less.

Sometimes friends grow apart when one friend starts to have great career success, while the other lags behind. Other times friends grow apart when one moves far away or starts dating someone new. Growing apart can cause a wedge in the friendship if you feel that you're no longer on the same wavelength.

If you sense that you and your friend are growing apart, you can raise the issue and describe what you're noticing and how it makes you feel, and see if your friend feels the same way. Or you can make peace with the fact that you and your friend are growing apart, and let the friendship fade naturally.

Working Through Friendship Challenges

Even the closest of friends has to work through friendship challenges from time to time. If you and your friend are experiencing conflict or arguing, or if things just seem off, it can feel painful and unsettling. Don't despair — you *can* work through most friendship disagreements in an amicable way, and you may find that the process of getting things out into the open results in your friendship growing even closer.

In the following sections, I walk you through some simple steps to take when resolving friendship disagreements.

Step 1: Identifying the issues and your feelings

When you feel frustrated and annoyed with something your friend said or did, first identify the issues. It's important to figure out what the specific issues are and how they're making you feel. For instance, you may be able to easily and quickly identify that it's really upsetting you that your friend hasn't been very responsive to your texts in the last few months.

Next determine how you're feeling about this issue. You may discover that this lack of responsiveness is causing you to feel frustrated and disappointed.

TIP

Sometimes it helps to talk out the situation with your spouse/partner, a family member, or a therapist so that you can start to identify the issues and process your feelings. Just saying things out loud sometimes helps you gain new perspectives and insight. Another option is to write down in a journal what's been bothering you about your relationship with your friend. Journaling your feelings can be an extremely effective way to process difficult emotions and clear the chaotic thoughts out of your head.

TIP

After you've identified the issues and how you feel about them, if it turns out there are several, choose one or two to raise at first. You don't want to overwhelm your friend with a barrage of problems — that may make them feel defensive, overwhelmed, or attacked. Choose the most important or pressing issues to bring up first, and if there are others, save the rest for later.

Step 2: Determining how much it bothers you

After you've identified the issues and your feelings, think about how much these issues are bothering you. This will help you decide if these issues are friendship deal-breakers.

How much the issue bothers you is related to several factors, including how close of friends you are, how often your friend is doing the behavior that's bothering you, and your value system. For example, if quality time is something you really value, and your friend only wants to meet up a few times a year, you may decide that this issue is extremely bothersome. That will help guide how you want to handle it.

EXPLORE

As a self-reflection activity, you can ask yourself, on a scale from 1 to 10, with 10 being extremely bothered, how would you rate how much you're bothered by this issue? How does this compare with how you felt about it a few months ago?

TIP

Try to keep a balanced perspective by taking stock of all the positives of your friendship. This will help put the issue in perspective and help you determine whether this one issue is eclipsing all the other positive aspects of your friendship.

Step 3: Deciding what to let slide

Some issues are worth bringing up, and others are probably best to let slide. To help you better evaluate the issue, ask yourself if it's a big problem or a little problem. Did your friend poach your partner — if so, that's a big problem. Is your friend occasionally late? Maybe that's worth not sweating.

Everyone has different thresholds for what they consider the "small stuff." Only you can decide what's worth bringing up and what you can sweep under the rug for now.

TIP

A good litmus test for determining what to bring up and what to let slide is to ask yourself if this situation is still going to bother you in a month, three months, or six months from now. If so, it's probably worth bringing up and dealing with. However, if you believe the issue will no longer bother you after a week (or another short period of time), you may decide that it's so minor that it may not be worth raising. Also, ask yourself whether this issue is really worth getting into a conflict about or worth the drama. If not, it may be best to let it go and focus on all the other positives about your relationship.

Step 4: Managing your anger

If you're feeling frustrated or angry about something your friend said or did, it's important to manage your anger effectively before bringing it up. Otherwise, if you're caught up in the heat of the moment, you may say or do something you'll regret later.

Here are the steps to managing your anger effectively:

1. **Notice when you're feeling angry.**

   What sensations do you notice in your body? Flushed cheeks, racing heart, an internal boiling feeling, sweating, and clenched fists are some clues that you're angry.

2. **Take a break.**

   When you notice that your anger is rising, it's time to take a break. The purpose of taking a break is to put some distance between your anger and your reaction before you impulsively react. You can take a break by counting to ten, taking a walk, getting some fresh air, or taking deep breaths. Then, when you're feeling less hot and bothered and you're thinking more clearly, you can figure out how to respond. Taking a break helps ensure that you don't act impulsively in the heat of the moment and do something like writing them a harsh email or unfriending them on social media. Instead, take a break from the situation to calm yourself and regroup, and then decide how you'll proceed after you're feeling calmer.

3. **Decide how to respond.**

   You may decide to directly address the issue with your friend, table it for now, or let it go.

EXPLORE

Practice these anger management strategies anytime you find yourself getting angry, so they become more automatic. Notice what it feels like to put some distance between noticing the anger sensations in your body and your response. Do you find that taking a break leads to a calmer feeling and better decision-making?

Step 5: Considering your friend's perspective

When a friendship challenge arises, it's important to consider your friend's perspective and put yourself in their shoes in order to try to feel what they're feeling. This is called *empathy.* To empathize with your friend, think about why your friend may be acting the way they are and what may be the underlying reasons. What are their reasons for feeling as they do? Try to have empathy for your friend's situation, which can help decrease your anger and resentment.

Step 6: Advocating for yourself

Confronting a friend about a problem is hard. Some people are conflict-averse and just thinking about confronting someone makes them uncomfortable. They may fear the other person getting upset or angry, they may be concerned that the confrontation will ruin the friendship, or they may worry about falling apart during the confrontation and not knowing what to do or say if the other person verbally attacks them. Sometimes people who are conflict-averse will try to minimize or ignore a problem in order to avoid conflict at all costs.

Instead of thinking about your upcoming conversation as confrontational, reframe it and see it as advocating for yourself. Advocating for yourself when needed is an important life skill. In order to build your self-advocacy skills, you may need to work on building your self-confidence. You can do this by:

>> **Practicing advocating for yourself in small ways:** You can advocate for yourself in small ways at a store or business, or with a family member. Then gradually build up to advocating for yourself with friends and acquaintances.

>> **Rehearsing what you'll say:** You can practice what you'll say before you actually talk to your friend and advocate for your needs. Make notes on the points you want to cover.

>> **Using positive self-talk:** Positive self-talk means giving yourself a little pep talk to psych yourself up for advocating for yourself. You might say to yourself, "I'm a good friend, and my needs in this friendship are important too."

Step 7: Asking for feedback

If there's a problem in your friendship — for example, your friend is acting distant or has gone radio silent, or their usual pattern of communication has experienced a drastic change — ask for feedback. This will help you know if there is something in your friend's life that's responsible for the change or if you're doing or saying something that's upsetting them. When you get feedback, you can start to problem-solve.

EXAMPLE

For example, you can say, "Hey, I haven't heard from you in two months since our last dinner get-together. Is everything okay? Please let me know if I said or did anything to upset you."

Step 8: Taking a break

If advocating for yourself doesn't go well, and your friend is not receptive, you and your friend may need to take a break from the friendship to give each other some space. If you both agree that's the next step, there's nothing wrong with taking a friendship break for a while. A breather from the friendship can help clear the air and help both of you gain new perspectives.

Communicating Effectively with Your Friends

Effective communication is always important in friendships, but it's especially crucial when you and your friend are in the midst of trying to work through a friendship challenge. Communicating effectively involves advocating for your needs and making sure that your friend understands how you're feeling. Communicating clearly and effectively helps everyone be on the same page and decreases misunderstandings.

TIP

Here are several tips for effective communication with your friends:

>> **Focus on clarity.** To communicate effectively, focus on being more clear, eliminating long and winding explanations or going off on tangents, and communicate your point succinctly. Communicating friendship problems in person or over the phone is better than texting or emailing because intonation and feeling can be communicated more clearly with vocal clues (as opposed to in writing, which can sometimes come across as harsher than you intended).

» **Be respectful.** Don't interrupt or talk over each other — that can come across as aggressive. Instead, give each person the opportunity to speak, so both of you feel fully heard. Wait until your friend is finished speaking to begin talking.

» **Be present.** When your friend is talking to you, put your phone away. Give them your full attention without looking all around the room. Make good eye contact to show that you're paying close attention. Listen intently to what they're saying and ask follow-up questions to clarify your understanding.

» **Practice being an active listener.** Listen calmly to your friend and hear them out without trying to jump into the conversation or fix anything and without getting defensive. Let them vent until they're finished. Encourage them to talk by nodding your head or saying, "Tell me more." When you hear someone out fully, you show that you respect their feelings.

» **Practice reflection.** Reflect your friend's words back to them to show you're listening and understanding. Using the tool of reflection shows that you're fully understanding what they're saying. A reflective statement could be something like: "It sounds like you're upset that I made plans with Ingrid and Molly and didn't invite you. Am I hearing that right?"

» **Use anger de-escalation strategies.** If your friend is raising their voice or yelling, don't join them. Keep your voice calm, low, and slow, and take deep breaths. This will usually get your friend to calm down, too.

» **Validate your friend's feelings.** Listen for the message behind the words. Validate their emotions so your friend feels heard. For example, if your friend is angry because you were late and left them sitting at the restaurant for an hour, validate their feelings: "It sounds like you're frustrated that I was running so late. That must have made it seem like my time is more important than yours. I'm so sorry, and I'll make sure not to let that happen again."

Using I statements

One of the most effective communication strategies that helps to clearly communicate your perspective is to use *I* statements, which were developed by Thomas Gordon in the 1960s.

I always recommend *I* statements to my clients who want to communicate more effectively because they place the focus on the speaker's thoughts and feelings versus placing blame on the other person (as is common with *you* statements). *I* statements are a way to avoid putting your friend on the defensive or accusing them of something, which lowers the emotional temperature in your communications. *I* statements communicate what *you're* feeling and experiencing, which reduces conflict and opens the door for further communication.

You can use *I* statements in a variety of contexts and with anyone (they're especially helpful to use with your spouse/partner). To use an *I* statement, just follow the following formula:

I feel X when you do Y/because of Y.

After your *I* statement, you can add a sentence about what you need or what you'd like to happen instead.

EXAMPLE

Table 15-1 lists some *you* statements and corresponding *I* statements. Notice how you feel when you're reading through the *you* statements versus the *I* statements.

TABLE 15-1 ### You Statements versus I Statements

You Statement	I Statement
You never respond to my texts. You don't care about me.	I feel hurt when you don't respond to my texts because it makes me feel like you don't have time for me. Please remember to respond to my texts next time.
You never invite me to do anything. I've invited you ten times in a row and you haven't reciprocated once. You don't care about our friendship.	I feel upset that I've invited you to meet up with me ten times and you haven't reciprocated. It makes me feel like you're too busy for me. I'd really appreciate it if you would plan our next get-together.
You're so rude! I can't believe you invited Mia and Perry to dinner right in front of me, without including me. You have no manners, and it made me feel terrible.	I felt upset when you invited Mia and Perry to dinner right in front of me and didn't include me. It made me feel invisible and uncared for.

When upset, most people blame the other person, which isn't helpful because it usually results in the other person getting defensive and/or shutting down. *You* statements put the other person immediately on the defensive because they feel blamed or verbally attacked. In response, they'll start defending themselves, which won't move the conversation in a helpful direction.

So, remember to use *I* statements. They'll greatly improve your communication with other people.

Avoiding the blame game

Part of effective communication is avoiding blaming your friend when you bring up a problem or issue. You can do this by being sensitive and respectful with your language and avoiding accusing them of anything. Instead, when you're pointing out a problem in your friendship, adopt a mindset of curiosity and talk about what you've noticed rather than assigning blame. Using *I* statements helps to avoid blame because it puts the focus on what *you're* thinking and feeling, not what the other person has said or done.

Deciding to make changes

After you've brought up the issue that's bothering you and you've talked about it, see if your friend is willing to make changes. Are they willing to compromise or is their attitude "it's my way or the highway"?

REMEMBER

Keep in mind that sometimes people are willing to change for a little while, but they aren't willing to make lasting changes. If this happens, you may have to make a decision about whether you want the friendship to continue (see Chapter 16 for knowing when it's the right time to end a friendship).

Chapter **16**

Ending Friendships the Right Way

T here's a poem called "A Reason, Season, or Lifetime," attributed to Brian A. Chalker, that I've always thought is a very wise and practical way to view the longevity of friendships. This poem has a particularly insightful line: "People come into your life for a reason, a season, or a lifetime." Reflecting on this important concept can help you to make the right decisions when a friendship isn't working out or you feel that you and a friend have drifted apart. It can also help you feel better when you wonder why a particular friendship isn't as long-lasting as you had originally hoped.

Some close friendships are lifelong, but other friendships last only a few months or years. It can be disheartening to realize that so many of our friendships are situational and that when we leave a job, our kids change schools, or we move away, our friendships aren't strong enough to survive these changes.

Some friendships will inevitably end, and it's often painful when they do. Some of these friendships fade away quietly as the situation that brought the two of you together changes, whereas other friendships end dramatically with a huge confrontation and hurt feelings. How a friendship ends depends on several factors:

» How long you've been friends

» How good friends you are

» The situations involved that are contributing to the decision to end the friendship

Ending friendships in a healthy manner is an important skill. This chapter first explores the most common reasons why friendships end. Next, it explains several different ways to end a friendship. Finally, it explains how to effectively cope with the painful feelings that often occur when your friendship has ended.

Exploring the Most Common Reasons Why Friendships End

Think about the friendships you've had in the last 20 to 30 years and how they ended. Did most of your friendships end gradually because you or your friend drifted apart, or did your friendships end with a dramatic argument and cutting of ties?

It's likely that most of your friendships ended with a quiet drifting apart, where the two of you realized you had grown apart for a while and lost interest in the friendship over time.

There are many different reasons why friendships end. Some friendships end because both parties decide the friendship has run its course. Other friendships end because one person unilaterally makes that decision and ghosts the other. Most friendships end because both people lose interest in the friendship and drift apart.

Sometimes friendships end for a very blatant reason, like your friend wronged or betrayed you. Other times friendships end over more subtle things, like you and your friend slowly stopped having things in common. Occasionally friendships end, and one friend has absolutely no idea why.

In the following sections, I detail the most common reasons why friendships end.

Outgrowing the friendship

Sometimes over time, two people outgrow their friendship and realize that they don't have as much in common as they used to. They may have started out as close friends, but over the years, they grew apart and the interests or values that used to connect them have changed. When they do get together, there may be lots of awkward silence as they struggle to figure out what to talk about. Ultimately, they realize they've drifted apart and they end up spending less and less time together.

EXAMPLE

For example, Jon and Riley were college roommates. They lived together for a while in their twenties, but then Jon got married, had three kids, and moved to a different state. Riley stayed in their college town, remained single, and still hung out with their old college buddies every weekend. Over time, Jon and Riley started growing apart, until they found they didn't have much in common anymore, other than having gone to the same college. Now they text each other on their birthdays, but they don't get together or talk on the phone anymore.

This situation is common with friendships, but realizing that you or your friend has outgrown the friendship can be painful. If it's your friend who has outgrown the friendship, it can feel like rejection, and it can make you feel insecure.

Here are several signs that you've outgrown your friendship or drifted apart:

>> You find you have less and less to talk about.

>> You used to have a lot in common, but you don't anymore.

>> You start to question why you were even friends in the first place.

>> Your differences start to get on your nerves.

>> You find yourself actively trying to put distance between you and your friend or avoiding them altogether.

>> You don't like your friend as much as you used to.

>> Your friend makes you feel bad about yourself in some way.

EXPLORE

If you and your friend have grown apart, take the time to figure out if the relationship should continue or if it's better to go your separate ways. Do some self-reflection about the things that you currently have in common and whether those are enough to sustain your friendship.

When two people outgrow a friendship, it often ends with a slow fade. If you decide that the friendship isn't worth saving, it can help to remind yourself about all the fun times the two of you shared and what your friendship meant to you. It's okay to give yourself permission to downgrade your friendship or end it altogether. It can also help to remind yourself of all the other friends you have whose friendships you haven't outgrown or about the ways that you can find new friendships that seem like a better fit. Finding new groups to join that are a good match for your current interests is a great way to form new friendships.

Moving away

Many friendships end when one friend moves away. Friendships can and do survive moves, but only when both parties put extra effort into compensating for the distance. If neither friend is willing to put in the extra time and energy and make the effort to stay in touch and visit, it's likely that the friends will grow apart or the friendship will end altogether.

TIP

Video calls are a great way to keep in touch when you live far from your friend. Schedule regular video calls to keep each other up to date on what's happening in your lives.

If your friend tells you that they're moving away, it can come as a shock, especially if it's sudden and unexpected. Your friend may have a sudden job transfer or have to move for a family emergency. Occasionally your friend may move away without even telling you, because they're embarrassed about the reason why they have to move away (for example, maybe a messy divorce is involved).

When you find out your friend is moving, you may feel angry and resentful toward your friend. You may feel frustrated that you put so much time and energy into the friendship and feel that it was all for nothing. You may also feel upset if you've made several good friends lately all of whom ended up moving away.

REMEMBER

A friend moving away is a loss that takes time to grieve.

Changing the environment

Many friendships are situational — you're friends with the other person because you're on the same softball team, you work at the same place, or your kids are in the same school. You don't have much in common other than the shared environment, and often you don't get together on your own. When that season of life ends, there's not enough there to keep the friendship going. The friendship usually fades out gradually without any drama, because neither friend wants to put in the effort, or one person does put in the effort to keep it going, but the other isn't interested.

EXAMPLE

For example, Taylor and Camryn are both moms of preschoolers. They're mom friends and often do playdates with the kids, but they've never gotten together on their own without the kids. After both kids start kindergarten at different schools and start making new friends, Taylor and Camryn don't see each other as much and their friendship fades. By the time their kids have finished kindergarten, they've only gotten together once for coffee and they barely talk anymore. Camryn thinks their friendship probably won't last long because all they had in common was that they had kids the same age at the same preschool.

Becoming one-sided

Some friendships end when one friend feels that the relationship has become one-sided. One friend may always be the one taking the initiative, making the plans, and putting in the work, while the other friend puts little to no energy into the friendship.

WARNING

When a friendship becomes one-sided, resentment can build. The friend who is putting in lots of energy feels neglected and resentful. Over time, the friendship can erode when the amount of energy being put into the friendship isn't equal.

TIP

In order for a friendship to flourish, both friends should be putting in roughly equal amounts of energy. If your friendship becomes one-sided, try to figure out why this is happening. Is your friend just too busy to initiate but contributes to the friendship in other ways, or do you think their overall interest in the friendship is waning? Also check out Chapter 15 for an in-depth discussion of one-sided friendships.

Having irreconcilable differences

Sometimes friendships end when two friends develop differences that can't be worked out, and those differences become a source of conflict in the friendship. Political differences, religious differences, and differences about heated topics like abortion or immigration are some examples of differences that often can't be worked through. Some friends can still make the friendship work if they agree to disagree or don't bring up the topic with each other, but other friends find they feel uncomfortable because of their differences or they end up in volatile arguments too often.

Experiencing major life changes

Some friendships take a long break (or sometimes end) when one friend is going through a stressful or all-consuming time in their life and needs to pull back on the friendship. This can occur when a friend is going through a health scare, has just lost their job, is pregnant, or just had a death in the family. The friend going through the tough time can turn inward and shut the other friend out. This can be confusing and upsetting for the other friend, who may not even have any idea what's happening.

TIP

If you notice this happening with a friend, try to start a conversation with them about it, mentioning what you've noticed. You could say something like, "I've noticed I haven't heard from you in a while. Is everything okay? I care about you and want to make sure you're doing okay."

Feeling unappreciated and unsupported

Sometimes friendships end when one friend feels chronically unappreciated and unsupported. You may have gone through either a positive or negative event in your life, and when your friend didn't show up for you or acknowledge the event in the way you expected, it can feel like a major letdown. Or you may feel like you're the one who is always putting in the effort and your friend doesn't reciprocate. Sometimes when there is unequal energy in the friendship it can cause the person who puts in more energy to feel chronically resentful and angry.

REMEMBER

If you find that you're constantly feeling unappreciated and unsupported by your friend, it may be time to move on from the friendship. Consider letting them know what you've been noticing and advocating for what you'd like to see be different. If they're not willing to acknowledge or change, then you can think about whether you want to keep the friendship.

Not liking how you feel around your friend

Some friendships end when you start not liking how you feel around your friend. You don't like who you are around them the way you once did. Maybe your friend brings out negative personality traits in you or makes you feel badly or insecure about yourself. They may try to tear you down instead of building you up. This situation can be upsetting, especially if the two of you used to be great friends.

If you've brought up your concerns to your friend and they haven't tried to change, think about if this is a friendship you really want to be in right now.

Starting a new relationship or having a child

A friendship can change dramatically or even end when your friend starts a new relationship or has a child. Your friend's priorities may change, and they may spend all their time and energy on their new baby or with the new partner, so your friendship becomes a lower priority. You may feel resentful and neglected by their sudden change in attention.

REMEMBER

It helps to be understanding and to give your friend grace while they navigate this exciting new period in their lives. In the meantime, you can choose to hang out with other friends who have more time and energy to invest in your friendship. But if your friend's lack of time and attention significantly bothers you or doesn't change when things eventually settle down for them, you may decide to pull back on the friendship.

If you find yourself in this situation, try to be patient and give it a little time first before considering having a discussion with your friend about it. The last thing a new parent needs is a lot of pressure from a friend. You could wait a few months for things to settle down for your friend and then have a gentle discussion with them about what you've noticed, how you're feeling, how much you've missed them, and how you hope they can make more time for the friendship. If they're unwilling to hear you out or unwilling to compromise, you may decide to put more energy into other friendships.

No longer enjoying their company

Some friendships end because one friend no longer enjoys being around the other friend. This can happen when you outgrow your friendships and drift apart, or when one friend takes on new personality traits or characteristics that the other friend doesn't like. For example, one friend gets a new job with a higher salary and starts constantly bragging about all their new and expensive purchases.

TIP

If you find that you're no longer enjoying your friend's company, that can be a sign that it's time to end the friendship or make new friends whose company you do enjoy.

Experiencing betrayal

Some friendships end over one friend betraying the other. Betrayal can occur if you trusted your friend with a secret that they then spread without your permission, or if a friend turns on you and demonstrates a lack of loyalty. Betrayal can also occur when your friend becomes romantically involved with someone you care about who is off-limits to them (like a spouse or partner).

REMEMBER

Whatever the case, being betrayed by a friend is devastating and heartbreaking. It can lead to the end of the friendship because some things are unforgiveable.

Having a conversation with the friend who betrayed you can help you understand their motivations, give them the opportunity to apologize, and allow you to advocate for yourself.

Knowing When It's Time to End a Friendship

When things haven't been going well in a friendship for a while, it's an important skill to know when it's time to end things or whether to give the friendship another chance. You have to decide how much this friendship means to you and whether it's worth fighting for. Some friendships are worth fighting for, whereas others are not.

Ending a relationship feels very final, and some people want to end a friendship only as a last resort. People end up keeping a friendship going that's past its expiration date for many reasons. One is that they're hesitant to end it when they've put so much time and effort into it already. If they decide to end the friendship, they may feel that all that effort they put in was a waste of time, which is a hard pill to swallow.

REMEMBER

Another reason is that they don't want to upset the other person or cause drama. Sometimes it's easier to let a bad friendship carry on because it's easier than making waves.

TIP

Here are some questions to ask yourself to explore whether it's time to end the friendship:

>> Have you outgrown the friendship to the point that the two of you have nothing in common anymore? If so, do you feel this is unlikely to change in the future?

>> When you spend time with your friend, do you like who you are with them? Do they make you feel bad or bring out negative emotions in you? Do you feel constantly annoyed or frustrated around your friend?

>> When you spend time with your friend, do you find that the two of you struggle to find things to talk about, but the conversation flowed more freely and naturally before?

>> Is your friendship one-sided, where you do all the reaching out and putting in all the energy and your friend doesn't reciprocate?

>> Do you feel that your friendship isn't positively enhancing your life anymore, but instead is draining your energy? Do you feel like you're just not getting anything positive from the friendship anymore?

>> Do you feel chronically unsupported by your friend? Have you tried to address this situation, but they still won't change?

>> Is your friend inflexible and rigid, insisting that you do things their way all the time? Does it always feel like it's their way or the highway? Are they unwilling to compromise?

>> Has your friend repeatedly violated your friendship deal-breakers, even when you've made them aware of them?

>> Does your friend repeatedly disrespect your boundaries?

>> Does your friend repeatedly break your trust?

>> Do you and your friend have irreconcilable differences that are unlikely to change in the future?

>> Has your friend done something so incredibly horrible that there's no coming back from it? Examples would be trying to seduce your spouse or divulging an important secret you told them to keep confidential.

Writing the letter you'll never send

Another important way to know whether it's the right time to end a friendship is to do some self-reflection involving writing a letter that you'll never send. This letter will help you explore and process your feelings about the friendship. In this letter, you can write about how you're feeling about your friend and all the hurts that have built up over time. This kind of therapeutic writing may help you process your feelings more effectively.

TIP

After you've written the letter, you can either tear it up or put it in a safe place, or read it to your spouse or therapist to help further process it. The benefit of writing this kind of letter is that it helps you process your feelings, gives you an outlet for your anger, and helps you feel calmer about the situation.

Exploring other considerations when thinking about ending a friendship

You've started to wonder whether it is the right time to end your problematic friendship, but you know that it's complicated and not a cut and dry situation.

EXPLORE

Here are several self-reflection questions that will help you further explore the pros and cons of keeping the friendship versus ending it:

>> **How long have you been unhappy in the friendship?** If it has been a short time, maybe it's worth figuring out if changes can be made. If you've been unhappy for a long time, you'll want to consider how receptive your friend is to making changes.

>> **How long have you known your friend?** If you've only known them a short time, you may decide that the friendship isn't worth saving if the issues are severe enough, or you may decide you still have lots of time to improve the situation. If you've only known them a short time, it's easier to let a friendship go because you haven't invested much. If you've known them a long time, you may have so much history with them that the friendship is worth fighting for.

>> **Are your needs being met in the friendship?** If your friend is falling short in one area, do they make up for it in other areas? For example, if your friend is always late and that bothers you, but they show up for you in many other thoughtful ways, that can balance out the punctuality issue.

>> **Have you previously tried to talk to your friend about your friendship issues?** If so, did they brush you off or agree to try to work on these issues? Are they willing to make changes? If your friend is dismissive of your concerns or isn't willing to compromise, you may not want to stay in the friendship.

>> **Has your friend broken any of your friendship deal-breakers?** Many people have friendship deal-breakers (for example, your friend is constantly asking you to borrow money or frequently complains about things). Do some self-reflection about what your friendship deal-breakers are and whether your friend has violated them. This can help you determine if it's time to end the friendship over serious concerns.

>> **If you end the friendship, do you have other friends to lean on?** If you have no other friends, you may want to think twice about ending the friendship until you've made at least one other friend.

Identifying How Divorce Impacts Friendships

Divorce negatively impacts friendships for many people and can make keeping the friends you made as a couple challenging. When a couple divorces, they often lose most of their couple friends and some of their individual friends, which can be traumatic. A couple's mutual friends often take sides, especially if infidelity is involved in the divorce.

Some divorcing people end up losing their entire friend group. Why do divorcing people lose so many friends? There are several reasons:

>> **People don't want to take sides.** Sometimes people are hesitant to take sides after their couple friends divorce, so they distance themselves from the

couple or from the person who caused the divorce (such as the unfaithful partner).

>> **People play the blame game.** A friend may start blaming the member of the couple who instigated the divorce and decide to end the friendship with that person, especially if they were friends with both spouses. A friend may also side with the victim of the divorce and estrange themselves from the divorce instigator.

>> **People disapprove of the divorce.** Another reason that a friend may end a friendship with the divorce instigator is if they disagree with the idea of divorce in general or don't approve of the reasons behind the divorce.

>> **People avoid awkwardness.** If a couple is good friends with a divorcing couple, sometimes they decide to end the friendship with the couple because being friends with just one of them can feel awkward. If they do remain friends with just one member of the divorcing couple and hang out with that person, then the recently divorced person can start to feel like they're a third wheel.

>> **The divorce instigator usually loses more friends.** A friend may feel like they're betraying the other spouse by being friends with the instigator of the divorce. This is especially true if there is infidelity, when friends may decide to end the friendship with the cheating partner.

REMEMBER

Losing friends can be traumatic for the divorcing couple. Plus, it's just one more negative thing that comes out of a divorce situation. Conversely, sometimes the divorcing couple themselves decides to end friendships because they fear their friends' judgment. They may want to start fresh as a new divorcee with all new friends.

Keeping your mutual friends after divorce

It can be tricky, but if you want to keep your mutual friends after your divorce, you'll usually need to downgrade their friendship from best friend or confidante to more casual friends. Many of your mutual friends will want to stay neutral, which can make it feel like you can't be yourself with them.

TIP

Instead, focus on the individual friends you have who have always been there for you and who will continue to support you after your divorce.

Finding new friends after divorce

After divorce, it can be helpful to make new friends and get a fresh start. After things have settled down, consider joining some groups to make new friends, like an activity group or another type of social group. (Turn to Chapter 5 for ideas of groups to join to make new friends.) There are also divorce support groups you can join, to find others navigating the same journey. Check out DivorceCare (www.divorcecare.org) to find helpful divorce recovery support groups in your area.

If you're moving out and into a new neighborhood, that also provides a new opportunity to make new friends. Start chatting with your new neighbors, and try to join any neighborhood events or activities. You can also get involved in a new gym or community center near your new residence.

Deciding to Downgrade instead of Ending a Friendship

When you realize that a friendship is not working anymore, or you don't feel as close to someone as you once did, you don't need to end it. Instead, you can downgrade the friendship level. For instance, if you have a best friend and the friendship is no longer working, downgrade them to a casual friend or acquaintance instead. This can be tricky to do in practice — it typically involves a slow fade.

What this means in practice is, instead of the friend being the first one you call when something exciting or sad happens, you call someone else instead. Instead of getting together weekly, you put some distance in between you and see them less and less. When they contact you, you're less responsive and less available over time. You can do this by not answering their messages right away and not accepting every invitation to get together.

The benefits of downgrading are that you preserve the friendship and avoid any dramatic confrontations that can be stressful. You just make yourself less responsive and less available over time until you no longer feel resentful about the amount of energy you're putting into the relationship compared to the amount your friend is putting in. Another benefit is that your relationship can pick back up where it left off at any time if both parties are committed to making the friendship work. It can also feel like less of a devastating loss if you know that the person is still in your life in some way.

EXAMPLE

For example, Cory and Beth were best friends for many years. In the last year, Beth started doing things Cory didn't like, and Cory tried to talk to Beth about it, but she was unwilling to change. Cory didn't want to completely end the friendship, because they had been best friends for so long. Instead, Cory decided to downgrade the friendship. First, she started slowly distancing herself from Beth. She started being less responsive to Beth's texts — instead of responding right away, she would wait a few hours, and then a day or more to respond. She also stopped being available to hang out all the time — instead of jumping at Beth's invitations, she started to say no more often. Eventually, Beth got the hint and pulled back from the friendship, too. Now they only talk a few times a year, which seems to be comfortable for both of them.

Here are several ways you can downgrade your friendship:

>> Stop confiding in your friend.

>> Become less responsive.

>> Hang out with them less.

>> Become more neutral toward them, which will replace the previous warm feelings.

>> Become less supportive, and don't go out of your way to show up for them.

>> Stop making thoughtful gestures toward them.

Exploring Different Ways to End a Friendship

Just as it's important to learn the social skills involved in making new friends, it's crucial to learn the skills needed to respectfully end a friendship. Breaking up with a friend isn't something most people like to think about, but you need to know how to do it in a kind, considerate way.

REMEMBER

Friendship-ending skills aren't typically taught in school, and many adults don't know how to properly end a friendship. They usually want to avoid drama, so they take the easy way out and ghost their friend instead, which can cause resentment and hurt feelings.

When you've decided to end a friendship, there are several ways to do it. The ideal way is to have an honest conversation with your friend. You can gently and tactfully bring up what went wrong and why you believe it's not fixable, and let your friend know how much they meant to you, but that it's best if you go your separate ways. If you can't bring yourself to do this, then the slow fade is another way that can also work.

Following are some of the typical ways that people end friendships.

Ghosting

Ghosting is a common way to end a relationship these days, but it's not a good way to do so. Ghosting involves suddenly disappearing with a complete cessation of all communication. Often the person doing the ghosting will also block their friend on social media, with no explanation and no discussion.

In a ghosting, what happens is that the relationship is humming along like usual, and then one day you just stop hearing from your friend altogether. They just stop communicating with you entirely. If you try to reach out to them, you get no response. The person who was ghosted is left feeling devastated and completely confused.

REMEMBER

Ghosting is disconcerting because it's an abrupt cutting of ties. If you're on the receiving end of a ghosting, you may wonder what you did wrong and why your friend valued the relationship so little that they would do this to you. You may feel shocked, upset, and angry at your friend that they would feel that the friendship was so disposable that they would just end all communication. You may wonder if the friendship ever meant anything to them in the first place.

Some people view ghosting as a cowardly way to end a friendship. Other people see a benefit in ghosting — it's a quick way to end a friendship and avoids a long, drawn-out slow fade or an explosive confrontation.

REMEMBER

The only legitimate reason to ghost someone is when your personal safety is at risk — if someone is threatening you or being abusive, walking away with no explanation makes sense. But otherwise, you owe it to your friend to either have an honest conversation or fade out slowly.

Doing the slow fade

The slow fade, also known as distancing, is how many friendships come to an end because it's seen as a humane way to end things. If you're the recipient of the slow fade, and your friend has decided to end your relationship, they'll become less and less responsive over time — taking longer to respond to texts, emails, and phone calls. Over time, they'll decrease the number of times they reach out to you, until they stop reaching out completely.

The communication will get fewer and farther between until you barely speak to your friend anymore. Your friend will also become less available to get together. For example, if you previously hung out weekly, now they'll likely be available once a month or less often. In addition, you may notice that your friend stops confiding in you and only talks about surface-level things. They'll also seem less interested in you and the things going on in your life.

Gradually, over time, the friend who wants to end the relationship puts more and more distance between the two of you. The communication fades out gradually until you're no longer in communication at all.

If you're the one doing the fading out, and your friend contacts you to ask why you've been so distant recently, you can choose to say something vague about how you've had some things come up that have taken all your time and attention lately and you need to step back from the friendship.

REMEMBER

The drawback of this approach is that the person who is being faded out can feel confused and wonder what they did wrong to deserve this kind of treatment. They may feel that the friendship was going well and have no idea why their friend is breaking up with them.

Some people prefer the slow fade-out over other methods because they think it's low-drama. It's more gentle than a stressful, dramatic confrontation or an abrupt ghosting, and it gives the friend plenty of time to process the situation and make a new friend to lean on.

It also means that the friend who is ending the friendship doesn't have to directly confront the person and tell them why they're ending the friendship, which can be stressful and awkward. The friend doing the slow fade hopes the other person will eventually get the message and accept the fade-out gracefully.

REMEMBER

Sometimes the recipient of the fade-out doesn't understand what's happening and tries valiantly to save the friendship by becoming more insistent that their friend return their calls, emails, and texts or asking to get together. If you're the one doing the fade-out and this happens, it's best to be more direct with your friend and let them know that things aren't working out.

TIP

If you're the recipient of the fade-out, it can help to process what's happening with your spouse/partner, a therapist, or another trusted friend to get a neutral opinion about whether the fade-out is actually occurring or whether you're misinterpreting things. If it is occurring, you can either choose to let the fade-out unfold naturally or gently confront your friend, say that you've noticed they've been distant lately, and see how they respond.

Having an upfront friend breakup discussion

Another option for ending a friendship is to have an actual friend breakup discussion, which can be a considerate, gentle discussion or a big, explosive blowup. Many people shy away from this option because it creates drama and involves an unpleasant and potentially explosive confrontation that they dread.

People also shy away from this approach because it involves being honest with your friend and telling them that you no longer want to be friends with them and why. Most people don't want to hurt other people's feelings or cause someone to cry, and having a discussion that you want to end a friendship will inevitably end with someone's feelings getting hurt.

There are ways to soften the blow, however, such as using *I* statements (in which you lead with how you've been feeling instead of accusing or blaming the other person), but there will inevitably be some hurt feelings and a potential argument with accusations on both sides. Here is an example of a gentle, considerate friend-ship breakup using an *I* statement. (For more information on *I* statements, turn to Chapter 15.)

EXAMPLE

Jamal, I've been feeling neglected as a friend over the past year since you've started dating Mike and you've gotten so busy. I know it's natural to spend all your free time with a new partner, but it feels like your priorities have changed and you don't have time for me anymore. I've felt hurt when I've invited you to meet up and you don't even respond to my texts. I know you're busy, and I value our friendship, but I think it's probably better if we go our separate ways. What I need in a friendship is someone who is more responsive. What are your thoughts?

EXAMPLE

Here is another example of an *I* statement:

For a while now, I've been feeling hurt and upset because I've been putting more effort into this friendship than you have. I tried to let you know in different ways that I've been resentful about always reaching out first and planning all our get-togethers, and I recently decided that this isn't working for me anymore. I think it's best if we end our friendship and go our separate ways.

Coping with a Friendship's End

It's normal to feel a range of emotions when a friendship ends, from distress and bitterness to sadness and anger. Let yourself feel all the emotions as they come up. On the one hand, you may be angry and resentful of your friend for unilaterally ending the friendship; on the other hand, you may feel a sense of relief if things have been going downhill for a while.

REMEMBER

Also, remember that throughout your life, you'll have many friends who come and go depending on the situations you're in, whether it's changing jobs, moving away, or moving into a new neighborhood. This is true for everyone, and it's just one of those things that you have to accept. It's usually only best friends who are there for most of your life, through thick and thin. Casual friends tend to come and go as the situations or environments that brought you together change.

WARNING

A friendship ending can be as heartbreaking as a romantic breakup, especially if you've been friends for a long time. It's important to process your feelings about the friendship ending, feel validated, and use coping strategies to get through this challenging time.

TIP

Sometimes it just takes time to feel better about the situation. As you get used to the friendship's end over time, the pain starts to feel less acute. At some point, not having the friendship as a part of your life starts to feel like your new normal. Time truly does heal.

The following sections fill you in on some of the best ways to cope when a friendship ends.

Navigating through grief and loss

Most people grieve when a loved one passes away, but many people also grieve the loss of a friendship. You can grieve any kind of loss, whether it's the loss of a friend, loss of a job, loss of a home, or loss of health.

Many people go through the grief process when a friendship ends, especially if the friendship's dissolution came out of the blue and they weren't expecting it or they didn't want the friendship to end. Everyone goes through the grief process differently, but they may proceed through Elisabeth Kübler-Ross's five stages of grief in any order: denial, anger, bargaining, depression, and acceptance. You may notice that you go through all these stages after a friendship ends, or only a few (or even just one).

TIP

Give yourself time to process all your feelings of grief, and talk with a trusted family member, other friend, or therapist about how you're feeling. It can also help to process your feelings by writing in a journal.

It's also normal to feel lonely after a loss. You may feel that you've lost not just a friend but also a confidante, and you may feel like you don't have anyone to share things with anymore. Think about other ways that you can find the close bond you once shared with new people. When you're ready, you can go out and make a new friendship.

Processing your feelings by journaling

Journaling is a therapeutic way to cope with the loss of a friendship. You can write about your thoughts and feelings paragraph style, or if writing isn't your thing, just jot down a list of notes about how you're feeling on paper or in the notes app on your phone.

Journaling offers many benefits, but one of the biggest ones is that it helps get all the swirling, chaotic thoughts out of your head and contained on paper (or electronically). Getting all the negative thoughts out can help you in the following ways:

>> It helps you clear your head.

>> It helps you process the friendship breakup more effectively.

>> It makes the chaotic thoughts feel not as overwhelming.

Some people who struggle with insomnia after a friend breakup find that journaling before bed can help them sleep through the night more easily, because they don't have as much on their minds during the night.

TIP

For an in-depth discussion of journaling, with many helpful exercises, check out *Journaling For Dummies*, by Amber Lea Starfire (published by Wiley).

Talking it out

Talking it out is especially helpful for people who process their feelings better by verbalizing them. Sharing your feelings with your spouse/partner, a family member, another trusted friend, or a therapist is helpful for those who like to talk about their feelings. Talking things out helps you feel seen and heard, validates your feelings, helps you consider new perspectives, and helps you sort everything out.

You can also gain new insights just by hearing yourself talk through things out loud. It's always amazing to me how many times my clients talk through a problem out loud and then have their own groundbreaking insights into their situations that they had never thought of before. Sometimes the simple act of saying something aloud clarifies it in a new and unexpected way.

REMEMBER

If you don't have anyone in your life you can talk things out with, processing your feelings with a therapist can be a good way to work through it all. You can find a therapist through your insurance website, a referral from your doctor, or through the *Psychology Today* website (head to www.psychologytoday.com, and click Find a Therapist).

Leaning on other friends

When one friendship ends, it can feel like there's a gaping hole in your life. It will take some time to get used to this void, but in the meantime, it helps to lean on other friends if you have them. When one relationship ends, it opens up new space in your life for someone else to take that place. If you do have other friends to lean on, turn to them.

If you don't have other friends to lean on, consider rekindling older friendships or nurturing ties with extended family. Or you can follow the steps in this book to work on making new friends. Joining groups to meet others who share your interests is one of the best ways to make new friendships.

Celebrating what was positive about the friendship

You may be tempted to focus on all the negative things about a friendship when it ends, especially if you're feeling bitter about it. But it's healthier in the long run to reframe your negative thoughts into more balanced, positive thoughts. How you think determines how you feel and behave, and you don't want to get mired in negative feelings about the relationship, which can keep you feeling stuck.

TIP

Instead of focusing on negativity, think about what the friendship meant to you. Celebrate and remember what was positive about the friendship and the fun times you shared with your friend. Thinking about how the friendship enriched your life can make it feel like it was time well spent.

EXAMPLE

It can be helpful to have several positive self-talk statements or positive affirmations that you say to yourself to feel better about the friendship. An example of positive self-talk regarding a friendship ending would be:

> Chantal was a great work friend when I was at my old job, but after I left, we both got busy and didn't keep in touch. I loved having her as such a great coworker, but it wasn't a super-close friendship that was going to last for many years, and that's okay. I'm making new friends already at my new job, which feel meaningful to me.

Coming up with a closure ritual

Sometimes it's helpful to have some kind of closure ritual to mark the ending of a friendship. A closure ritual can help bring a sense of peace and acceptance to your journey with this friend.

Here are some ideas of closure rituals that may be helpful for you:

>> Write a final journal entry about the friendship and what it meant to you.

>> Collect photos of the two of you and any mementos from the friendship and put them in a small box to open later when you're feeling nostalgic.

>> Write a letter to your friend that you'll never send, and read it to your spouse or therapist. Or write the letter you'll never send and tear it up if you're feeling angry.

>> Plant a seed in a garden and watch it bloom into a flower to honor your friendship.

REMEMBER

When your friendship ends, it's healthy to try to move on. Even if you're angry about the friendship ending, think of the old saying, "When one door closes, another opens." Think about the new doors that can now open because this friendship ended, providing you with opportunities for new friendships that you hadn't previously considered.

IN THIS CHAPTER

» Reflecting on past friendship successes and challenges

» Reconnecting with old friends

» Finding a friendship mentor

» Seeking guidance and feedback from professionals and peers

Chapter **17**

Identifying What to Do When Making Friends Seems Impossible

Sometimes despite all your best efforts, your friend-making journey doesn't go your way. You've tried absolutely everything you can think of to make a new friend, and you've put into practice many of the recommendations in this book, but nothing has worked. You may feel frustrated, lonely, or depressed. These feelings are normal, and you're not alone. You're in a tough spot, and it's natural to feel disappointed. Although this can feel like an incredibly disheartening situation, it's not time to throw in the towel quite yet.

This chapter helps guide you through what to do next when making friends just isn't happening. It takes you through the process of evaluating what's worked and what hasn't on your friend-making journey, helps you pinpoint what you're willing to work on and change, and shows you how to cope when things just aren't going your way.

REMEMBER

When things are tough, it's important to focus on the small wins to keep yourself moving forward!

Understanding Why Nothing Has Worked

There are two different "camps" when it comes to making new friends. One camp's perspective is "If it happens, it happens." These people don't put much effort into making a new friendship. They just wait to see if a friendship forms organically, and if it doesn't, they're okay with that.

The other camp puts in a lot of effort to make a new friend, because they're very motivated and they believe that friendships don't just happen organically. They've joined groups to meet new people, they've worked on their small-talk skills, and they've made the effort to reach out regularly, but they haven't gotten anything back. They try everything under the sun to make a new friend, and sometimes, despite their best efforts, they don't succeed.

TIP

The truth is, making new friends as an adult is universally challenging, and it's not necessarily anything personal at all. Some factors just work against you, like the fact that most adults are busy juggling work, family, and household management, and they don't have a lot of free time to make new friends.

This may mean that making new friendships isn't high on many adults' priority lists, and it has nothing to do with you specifically. The few adults who *are* open to new friendships can also be picky about who they decide to spend their limited free time with. If you don't check all their boxes (for example, if you don't work in tech and rock-climb on the weekends), they may decide not to put in the effort to get to know you.

Other friendship factors are out of your control. Maybe you happened to move to an area where most people already have full social circles and are closed off to new friendships. Or maybe the culture of your workplace, retirement community, or child's school makes it so that these places aren't conducive to making new friends. For example, the people at your job may be significantly older or younger than you are, which can sometimes make it more challenging to find friends. Or perhaps most people at your retirement community are married/partnered while you're single, which can make it harder to find like-minded pals.

Whatever the reason, take comfort in the fact that you're not the only one with these feelings. Many people these days are wondering why they feel so friendless and alone.

Reflecting on Past Friendship Successes and Challenges

Sometimes we repeat patterns in friendships, both good and bad. You may have a pattern of giving a friend the silent treatment or cutting ties at the first sign of a conflict, or you may be too needy with most friendships. Reflecting on your past friendship successes and challenges can help you become aware of any positive or negative patterns in your friendships — your previous experiences can help inform your current journey.

Even if you're having difficulty making new friends now, you may have some close friendships from previous eras in your life that you've kept. If you made friends successfully in the past, you can likely do so again now! Do some self-reflection about these friendships — what went well and what was challenging.

Thinking back on past friendships

Think back to friendships in your early days, even as far back as elementary school. What were your friendships like then? Did you have good friends in grade school? If so, it can be helpful to ponder the following self-reflection questions:

>> Were you happy with your grade-school friendships?

>> How did you make new friends back then?

>> What types of people did you gravitate to?

>> Did you have any difficulty making new friends in grade school, and if so, what did your parents do to help you?

Next, think back to high school and your college or young adult years, which is when many people make their most enduring friendships. Ask yourself the following self-reflection questions about your friendships from this time:

>> Did you have friends back then? If so, were you happy with those friendships?

>> What were your friends like? How did you meet them?

>> What was the social situation like for you in high school and/or college? Did you have good social experiences?

>> Do you stay in touch with any of your high school or college friends? If not, what has gotten in the way of keeping in touch? Would you still be friends with them today if you could?

REMEMBER

Thinking about old friends, what drew them to you, and what worked in your past friendships is helpful because it reminds you that you're capable of making and maintaining friendships, even if you're having trouble making friends right now. Thinking about past friendships may also give you some ideas as to what types of friendships may work for you now and how you can find them.

Reflecting on past friendship milestones

Some people are fortunate to get to participate in a variety of friendship milestones, like being in a friend's wedding party, being invited to bachelor and bachelorette parties, hosting baby showers for their friends, and hosting milestone birthday celebrations.

Other people don't get the chance to participate in these kinds of milestones, mainly because they don't have close friends during those particular life stages.

REMEMBER

If you never got a chance to participate in these kinds of friendship milestone events, it's normal to feel like you've missed out. It can be painful to realize that you had a tiny wedding because you didn't have anyone to invite or that you never got to have a baby shower like you wanted because you didn't have anyone to throw one for you. Acknowledging what you missed out on and grieving that loss can be helpful.

EXPLORE

Reflect on the friendship milestones that you wish you'd gotten the chance to participate in over the years. What friendship milestone do you feel most sad that you missed out on?

REMEMBER

If you're feeling down because you missed out on these milestone events, a good way to cope is to focus on being the kind of friend now that you wished you had had back then. This can involve making sure to show up for other people's milestone events and being there for your friends. Focus on the milestones still to come that you may be invited to, like a birthday party or retirement party.

Trying to reconnect with old friends

One of the best ways to make friends, especially if you're struggling with new friendships, is to reconnect with old friends. Reconnecting with old friends warms the heart because it's nice to get back in touch with people who "knew you back when."

Reconnecting with old friends is usually easier than making new friends. You already knew them once and liked them before, so theoretically it should be easy to rekindle that connection again, especially if they live in your area. The past experiences you once shared — whether it's a shared school history, neighborhood history, or workplace — can provide a good jumping-off point for renewing the friendship now.

In most cases, after you reconnect, it feels like no time has passed at all. Old friends know your history and you can reminisce about the good old times together. There's an easy, relaxed comfort with old friends that takes time to build with new friends. Old friends can be the truest friends because due to your shared history and deep roots, they may show up for you in ways that newer friends won't.

When reconnecting with old friends, it can be helpful to figure out why you lost touch. Reflect on what got in the way of keeping these friendships going over the years. Is losing touch with old friends a pattern for you? If so, you may want to strengthen your skills in maintaining friendships (see Chapter 13).

Where can you find old friends to reconnect with? Try the following:

>> **Search on social media.** For example, on Facebook, type the person's name into the search box and see if you can find them. If they have a common name, try adding their last known city to the search to narrow the results.

>> **Search online.** By typing their name into your favorite search engine, you may be able to find an old friend's work, personal website, or contact information. You may also find an article about their recent work or personal accomplishments and be able to reach out to them that way.

>> **Search LinkedIn.** LinkedIn is a career-networking website, but many people have profiles there. Type your friend's name into the search box, and see if you can track them down. Try adding their job or school or the city where they live if you're having trouble narrowing the search.

>> **Ask friends of friends.** If you're still in contact with some people from the past who knew your old friend, ask if they know your old friend's most recent contact info. They may be able to put you in touch with your old friend or know how you can reach them.

>> **Check your school's alumni database.** Many private schools, colleges and graduate schools have alumni databases. You can contact your school's alumni office or career center to find out the login information you'll need. If you do find an old friend this way, send them an email to reinitiate contact.

>> **Look through your old email contacts.** Especially if you've had your email account for many years, it's possible you still have an email address for your old friend.

>> **Attend reunions.** You can also reconnect by attending high school or college reunions, which many schools hold every five years. To find out if your school hosts reunions, contact their alumni office. Reunions are a wonderful way to feel a sense of community with your alma mater, reminisce about your school days, get a big dose of nostalgia, and reconnect with old classmates and friends. Reunions are especially helpful if you're lacking a close community in your current location because they can remind you that you *do* have a community that embraces you, even if it's from your past. If your school hosts reunions, you could also sign up to be on the reunion planning committee, which can put you back in touch with previous classmates and old friends.

Reconnecting with long-lost family members

If you're struggling to make friends, another way to regain a sense of community and reduce loneliness is to reconnect with long-lost family members. Maybe you have distant cousins in another state or country that you've lost touch with and who would love to rekindle a relationship with you.

Make a family tree to figure out if you have any relatives who may enjoy hearing from you and with whom you could connect. Ask your parents or other family members if they can find their contact information or follow the tips in the preceding section to try to find your long-lost family member.

When you have your long-lost family member's contact information, send an email or text message to start reconnecting with them. They'll more than likely be happy to hear from you, and you'll feel more connected getting back into regular contact with them.

Identifying Your Friendship-Making Strengths and Weaknesses

When you're struggling to make new friends, it can be helpful to do some self-reflection on your friendship-making strengths and weaknesses. Your friendship-making strengths allow you to make new friends easily, and your weaknesses make it harder for you to connect with others. When you can identify these strengths and weaknesses, you can focus your efforts more on your strengths and work to improve or resolve your weaknesses through self-reflection, feedback, reading, observation of others, and practice.

Your friendship-making strengths may include

>> Laughing easily

>> A friendly demeanor

>> A charismatic personality

>> Good conversation skills

>> The ability to support others

>> The ability to easily make people feel interesting and valued

>> Taking the initiative and reaching out to others

>> Warmth and the ability to make someone feel at ease

>> Strong follow-up skills and the ability to maintain friendships long-term

Your friendship-making weaknesses may include

>> Not remembering people's names easily

>> Struggling to reach out or initiate plans

>> The tendency to hold grudges

>> Being quiet around people, which can be mistaken for coldness or aloofness

>> Monopolizing conversations and not asking about the other person

>> Struggling to make small talk

>> Being critical or judgmental of others

EXPLORE

Do some self-reflection to determine what your friendship-making strengths and weaknesses are. To determine your strengths, think about compliments you've received or what other people seem to like about you. To determine your weaknesses, think about what may be getting in the way of making good friendships, or any negative feedback you've received.

After you determine what your strengths are, make sure to do more of those when making new friends. And after you determine your weaknesses, pinpoint what you're willing to work on. You can improve those weaknesses by acknowledging what they are and learning how to compensate for them. For example, if one of your friendship weaknesses is that you tend to forget people's names, you can work on special mnemonic devices to remember people's names more easily.

For example, Ashandra always gets a lot of compliments about how she shows up for others in friendships. She makes sure to be consistent about bringing her friends meals when they have surgery and attending her friends' special events. She knows her friends appreciate her efforts. She's aware, however, that she isn't a very good conversationalist, and she often struggles to figure out what to talk about with people. To improve, Ashandra works on her conversation skills by watching conversation videos online, reading articles about conversation skills, and making sure to have a list of five to ten conversation starters memorized that she can use when needed.

Doing a Deep Dive Into Your Friendship Challenges

If you're having difficulty making friends, there may be an identifiable reason why. Perhaps you're doing one or more things (possibly unconsciously) that are off-putting to others. If you can identify what's getting in the way of your making new friends, you can make changes if you want.

Read through the following list of off-putting behaviors to see if any of these may explain why you're having difficulties making new friends:

>> **Looking unapproachable:** Sometimes people who look unapproachable have a harder time making new friends. They may look angry or like they're deep in thought, and people hesitate to approach them, because they don't give off a welcoming vibe. If this sounds familiar, try to work on looking more approachable. Instead of reading a book or staring at your phone, sip your coffee and look around to catch someone's eye. Make sure to smile and look relaxed and friendly. It's more likely that someone will come up to you if you seem open to conversing and have a pleasant expression than if you seem preoccupied and look grumpy.

>> **Struggling with resting bitch face (RBF):** Similar to the challenges of looking unapproachable are the people who struggle with RBF, which is when your resting expression looks angry or upset, usually because the corners of your mouth turn down naturally or you just have more of a stern or blank expression. You may be feeling perfectly fine and think you have a neutral expression, but you may come across as grumpy or annoyed. There are several ways to compensate for RBF, including keeping a slight smile on your face, being expressive with your voice and hands, and using certain makeup and fashion styling tricks.

>> **Giving off needy vibes:** Someone who gives off needy vibes makes others uncomfortable because people don't want to feel like they're your only friend or that you're chasing after them too aggressively to become your friend. Needy vibes include calling or texting too often, initiating the next get-together too soon after the last one, and making it clear how badly you want this person to be your friend. Instead, it's better to give the other person some breathing room, unless you're already very good friends. To avoid giving off needy vibes, try to have multiple friends or activity partners so you don't overwhelm any one friend with too much attention.

>> **Emotionally dumping on friends:** Emotionally dumping on others is a big no-no in friendships — save that for your therapist. No one wants to be someone's emotional dumping ground, where someone unloads all their problems. Don't unload too much, too soon on new friends. Start by revealing a little about yourself, and then, over time, slowly unpeel the onion a little more, until you reach the level of emotional intimacy you'd like.

REMEMBER

Most people get uncomfortable when other people share their major problems because they don't know what to say. If you overwhelm someone with your problems too soon, they may decide that you're too high maintenance to be friends.

>> **Being overly negative:** Being overly negative is another trait that may be off-putting to potential new friends. People typically like being around upbeat, positive people who make them feel good. Someone who is often complaining and negative brings others down. If you find that you grumble a lot or if people call you a "complainer," consider finding other ways to cope with your negativity. See a therapist or journal your feelings as an alternative to sharing negative feelings with your friends. If you're feeling negative, find ways to create an action plan to change the things that you're not happy with.

>> **Being too braggy:** Bragging is another off-putting characteristic that may be getting in the way of making new friends. No one likes a braggart — when you're boasting about your accomplishments, money, or travels, you may make other people feel insecure. If you tend to brag, consider toning it down while you're with a potential friend. Learn to be secure in your own accomplishments and successes so you don't feel the need to brag to others in order to feel good about yourself.

>> **Having poor personal hygiene:** Having poor personal hygiene is another factor that makes it harder to make new friends. Take a close look at your personal hygiene. Do you shower regularly, brush your teeth daily, have fresh breath, wear deodorant, have clean nails, wear clean clothes, and wear clothes that fit well and don't have rips or tears? If so, you're probably doing well with personal hygiene that won't offend others. If you feel like some aspect of your personal hygiene is lacking, consider working on the issue in the name of friendship.

>> **Invading people's personal space:** Some people invade others' personal space, which can cause friendship problems. When someone invades your personal space, it can make you feel uncomfortable. Make sure you're not standing too close to someone, doing unwanted touching, hugging when it's unwanted, or getting too affectionate with a new friend before your friendship has had time to blossom.

>> **Not reaching out:** Some people don't take the time to reach out to others or expect others to always do the reaching out. They sit back and wait for others to contact them instead of reaching out first. When you want to make new friends, you have to be proactive and not wait for someone to contact you first. If you find yourself falling into this pattern, change things up and reach out to another person first for a change. See what it's like to put yourself out there. If you worry about rejection, as many people do, remind yourself that rejection is just a normal part of making new friendships, and that everyone gets rejected from time to time. If you do get rejected, use positive self-talk to remind yourself that it's just one person rejecting you, and not everyone rejecting you, and that you can move forward and reach out to someone else who will be more receptive.

Finding a Friendship Mentor

When you're struggling with friendships and you feel like making friends has been an insurmountable challenge, having a friendship mentor can be helpful. A friendship mentor can be a real person you know who has a bustling social life, or they can be a character in a book or movie. Your mentor can also be a self-help book about friendships, such as this one. Finding a friendship mentor can be a helpful way to figure out how to improve your ability to make friends and what you should be doing more of.

TIP

Study what your friendship mentor does to make friends. Do they initiate a lot of get-togethers and keep reaching out to people? Do they have a certain charisma that draws people to them? Study what they do and don't do and figure out what you can emulate.

REMEMBER

If your mentor is a fictional character, you can ask yourself all those same questions, but keep in mind that those characters may not be the most realistic, depending on the character you choose. It's easy to look at TV shows and movies that portray close friendships and wish your social life were more like that. Remember that everyone's circumstances are different, and make sure that the ways you'd like to improve socially are realistic for you and your situation.

If your friendship mentor is a book, decide what tips and recommendations you want to put into practice. Then consider trying out one new tip per week or month to see if any of the tips or recommendations help to improve your situation.

Coping with Frustration, Sadness, and Loneliness

When making friends seems impossible, it's natural to feel a lot of negative emotions, including frustration, sadness, and loneliness. Putting yourself out there and getting rejected over and over is a bad feeling. It's important to remember that many adults struggle with making new friends and you aren't alone.

While you're waiting to make a friend, there are many ways you can cope with the loneliness in the meantime. Focusing on personal development is one of the best ways to make use of the solo evenings and weekends when you wish you had social plans. Take an online or in-person class, make a personal reading list, participate in webinars or learn a new skill or language. These are all great ways to invest in yourself while you're continuing to try to make new friends. Also, check out Chapter 21, which provides ten inspiring strategies for having a vibrant social life, even when you don't have any friends yet.

Here are some other ways to cope with these difficult feelings:

>> **Go to places where you can be around people, like a bookstore, shopping mall, coffee shop, or park.** Just being around people in a lively setting can make you feel better even if you're not directly talking to anyone.

>> **Focus on small connections.** Making friendly small talk with cashiers, baristas, servers, and receptionists can brighten your day and theirs! Plus, you never know when a small connection will turn into something bigger.

>> **Have structure to your day.** Making sure your day has structure can go a long way toward helping you cope with these challenging feelings. If you find you have too much free time that leaves you feeling restless and at loose ends, add in a daily walk, exercise, reading, errands, chores, and yard work (or some combination of those) to your day.

>> **Adopt a pet.** Pets provide unconditional love and an outlet for your nurturing energy. If you can't adopt a pet, consider other ways to volunteer with animals. Being around a furry friend and petting them releases oxytocin, the feel-good hormone — which is something you may be lacking if you don't have good friendships.

>> **Sign up for an online class or webinar.** Learning something new and interacting with other students can help you feel better. Plus, you may make a new connection through the class or webinar.

>> **Focus on setting your own goals and working toward them.** Focusing on your own personal development is a great way to spend your free time and can take your mind off feeling lonely. You can set personal goals and work toward them one-by-one, which will help you feel productive and potentially facilitate you meeting new people. For example, if learning Italian is one of your personal development goals, taking an in-person Italian class will put you in contact with others who share the same interest, and you may make a new friend.

>> **Attend community events, sporting events, and school reunions.** Find activities where you can be around other people in a lively setting, where everyone is cheering for the same team, working toward a common goal, or celebrating a common milestone. That feeling of being a part of something greater can significantly boost your mood and outlook.

Calling in the Professionals

When making friends just isn't working out the way you had planned, it can feel frustrating and depressing. You may want to do something beyond keeping the feelings bottled up inside or venting to your spouse or a family member. Consider working with a therapist, finding a support group, or finding a therapy group to help you process your feelings and learn new coping strategies.

Working with a therapist

Consider working with a therapist when you need a safe, nonjudgmental place to vent and process your feelings. A therapist can help you feel validated and understood, and also help you figure out why you're struggling to make friends. They may give you a different perspective than you had considered before or help see your situation from a new angle. Their feedback can help you identify ways you may be pushing people away and what you can do to improve the situation.

You can find a therapist through a recommendation from your doctor, a friend, or a family member, or by going on the *Psychology Today* website and using their Find a Therapist database — head to www.psychologytoday.com, and click Find a Therapist. Enter your city or zip code, and search. From there, you can filter on whether you want a male, female, or nonbinary therapist; whether you want in-person or online therapy; your insurance; the issues you'd like to work on; and more. Many therapists offer early morning, evening, or weekend hours to accommodate your schedule.

Many therapists have long waiting lists these days, so call or email as many as you can.

Finding a support group

Another option to process your feelings and seek feedback is to find a support group for people struggling with loneliness, social skills challenges, or depression. You can find support groups by asking your therapist for recommendations, doing an internet search, or going to the *Psychology Today* website (www.psychologytoday.com), clicking Get Help, and clicking Find a Support Group. Anyone can join a support group, and there are usually no intake interviews. You also usually can attend as many sessions as you'd like with a support group.

Support groups are either run by peer volunteers (people with lived experience in a particular area) or by therapists, and they offer a chance to give and get support from group members who are going through the same things as you are. Many people find it helpful to share their feelings and challenges in a support group setting, because it's a great way to feel heard by others going through similar difficulties.

Looking for group therapy

Another option is to look for group therapy, which can help you process your feelings and gain new skills in a more formal, structured group setting. A therapy group is different from a support group because group therapy is a form of psychotherapy led by a mental health provider who uses a specific *modality* (an approach to treatment, like cognitive behavioral therapy) to help group members work through particular problems, like social anxiety, anger management, or chronic illness. Group therapy is more structured, meaning the therapist leads each group session in a specific way and may have specific questions that the group ponders and discusses. Group therapy can either be open or closed. Open group therapy means that participants can join at any time, whereas closed group therapy means that participants can join the group only at the beginning.

Group therapy usually requires an intake interview by the therapist to learn more about you and to make sure the group is the right fit.

Group therapy can be found through recommendations from your therapist or through the *Psychology Today* website (www.psychologytoday.com), clicking Get Help, and clicking Find a Support Group (group therapy is included with the support groups).

Chapter **18**

Coping with Loneliness

I f you've struggled to make friends for a while with little to no success, you may be feeling lonely. Loneliness is when you yearn to be with others, but you're not able to have the relationships you want or can't form close connections. You feel lonely when your needs for connection are not met. Loneliness can even occur when you're around lots of people but aren't connecting with them in a meaningful way. You could be at a crowded party but still feel quite lonely if you're not able to go beyond superficial connections. As a result of feeling lonely, you may feel empty, disconnected, or like there's no one who "gets" you. Lonely people can also feel chronically dissatisfied or unhappy.

Take heart: Loneliness is incredibly common. In fact, a 2018 survey by Cigna found that most U.S. adults are lonely. If you're struggling with loneliness, you have plenty of company, and there is a lot you can do to cope while you ride out the situation and wait to make new friends.

In this chapter, I discuss the differences between loneliness and solitude, help you understand the implications of loneliness on quality of life, and help you cope more effectively when feelings of loneliness do crop up.

Distinguishing Between Loneliness and Solitude

Being alone doesn't always equal loneliness. In fact, many people enjoy spending time alone and don't feel a hint of loneliness. That's because there is actually a difference between loneliness and solitude.

Loneliness is when you crave companionship but aren't getting what you need right now. You want to connect with others, but you aren't able to connect in the meaningful way you want because you don't have friends, your friends are too busy, or your relationships are not satisfying to you.

You don't have to be alone to be lonely — you can be lonely surrounded by people, if you feel that you aren't connecting with any of them. You can have lots of acquaintances, go out every night of the week, and still feel lonely, if your connections feel superficial. You can also feel lonely within your family, within your marriage, or within a group of friends if they're not giving you the time and satisfying connection that you need.

EXAMPLE

For example, Juana is a young adult who lives in a multigenerational household with her mother, grandmother, and siblings, but despite being surrounded by family all the time, she still often feels lonely. Juana feels that her family doesn't understand her, that they don't really know her, and she is not close with her siblings. Juana wishes she could make a friend or two who she could authentically connect with. Juana decides to join a social group for twentysomethings and eventually meets several friends she connects with. Juana starts to feel less lonely over time.

Solitude, on the other hand, is when you're alone but you're feeling content being alone. You're enjoying your own company and being your own friend. When you're enjoying your solitude, you may be taking a walk in the woods by yourself and enjoying the tranquility. Or you may be at a restaurant with a good book eating solo and feel completely content being alone.

TIP

Solitude can be especially refreshing for people who have demanding jobs and want some quality "alone time" or busy parents who are taking care of their young children and need a break. Sometimes just spending a few hours by yourself doing something you like to do can be very nourishing and restorative.

REMEMBER

When you're enjoying your solitude, you don't feel lonely and you don't pine for the company of others. It's possible to work on cultivating more of an appreciation of solitude. Try to find more moments of solitude in your day where you're doing something enjoyable and are content being alone. Some ideas include reading, going to a museum, gardening, or going to a movie.

EXPLORE

Do some self-reflection about the differences between loneliness and solitude for you. Think of several times in the past when you've felt lonely, and several times in the past when you've been content in your solitude. When you were content to be in solitude, what were you doing? Is there a way to add in more moments of solitude to your week?

Differentiating Between Chronic Loneliness and Transient Loneliness

There are several types of loneliness, but two that are especially important are chronic loneliness and transient loneliness. *Chronic loneliness* is when you feel lonely most of the time, which can be for months or years on end. This can happen to anyone, but it's especially common in older adults who have lost their spouse/partner or friends. Chronic loneliness is also common in recent divorcees, empty nesters, and people whose spouses travel frequently for work. Chronic loneliness is also prevalent in people who have struggled for years to make friends and build a community but haven't had any luck yet.

Transient loneliness, on the other hand, is shorter term and often more situationally dependent. It can be the result of moving to a new area and leaving close friends behind, or starting a new job and not knowing anyone for a while. Transient loneliness usually dissipates, when you start making friends and building community (but can also come back later), but chronic loneliness can become an entrenched, serious, long-term problem.

EXAMPLE

For example, Mike just retired, and left behind a job and coworkers he'd been with for the past 40 years. He had to retire suddenly due to a health condition and didn't have a plan in place for what he would do with his new free time. Mike started to quickly feel very lonely. His wife encouraged him to volunteer or find a hobby, but he felt restless and didn't quite know what to do with himself. He went months without talking to anyone but his wife, and mainly stayed home and kept to himself. Mike started experiencing chronic loneliness.

TIP

How lonely do you feel? Sometimes it's hard to tell. It turns out that there is actually a way to objectively measure loneliness. The UCLA Loneliness Scale, created by Daniel Russell, is a 20-item questionnaire and measures a person's level of loneliness. You can find the scale online to take on your own. If you find that your loneliness scores are high and you feel that it's negatively impacting your life, there are things you can do to manage and reduce your loneliness. At the end of this chapter, you'll find a variety of strategies you can use to cope with your loneliness.

REMEMBER

Loneliness is not just an uncomfortable feeling; people who are chronically lonely can face a variety of health and mental health implications, including increased cancer, stroke, and heart disease risks, as well as an increased risk of depression and anxiety. So, if you're noticing you're lonely often, it's a good idea to make it a priority to work on coping more effectively.

Understanding Why You're Feeling Lonely

Now that you know you're experiencing loneliness, you may be wondering why you're feeling this way. You may be asking yourself, "How did I become so lonely? Why does everyone else seem to have deep and meaningful connections except me?"

Knowing why you're feeling lonely can help you gain new insight into your past experiences and how they're affecting you today. Read on to learn about the most common reasons why you're feeling so lonely.

Having fewer connections

Some people feel lonely because they objectively have fewer friends and connections, so they feel like they're all alone in the world. This may describe the person who lives far from family, has few or no friends, and works from home. This person is lonely due to their situation working from home (and not seeing coworkers in person) and living far from family, but they also may not have put in the work required to build a social support network. If this individual puts a little more energy into joining groups, making small talk with people, taking the initiative, and inviting people to do things, chances are, they'll be able to make a friend or two, and they'll probably feel less lonely.

Having difficulty making friends

Another reason why you may be feeling lonely is because you've tried really hard to make friends and nothing has worked out yet. This can be a very lonely feeling because you've put a lot of time and effort into making new friends, but for various reasons you've been unsuccessful. This can make you feel inadequate or that no one cares about you. If this describes your experience, check out Chapter 17, which will help give you some additional ideas about what to do next when making friends has been an uphill climb.

You're socially isolated

Some people feel lonely because they're socially isolated. This means that they don't come into contact with other people often. Maybe they work from home and rarely see anyone other than on a video call, maybe they're single and wish they had a spouse or partner, or maybe they're homebound due to physical illness, older age, or disability. Being socially isolated often leads to loneliness.

TIP

If you're socially isolated and you want to improve the situation, start small. Work on finding an online community to belong to and making an online friend or two. From there, you can join an online or in-person class, get to know your neighbors better, or join a group. With baby steps, you can improve your isolation and get into contact with more people.

You feel like you don't fit in

You may feel lonely because you feel different from others, like you don't fit in. You may have tried to make friends and join groups in the past, but you've always felt like the odd one out, the one who is always on the sidelines or on the outside looking in. If you feel different and that you don't belong, it can lead to persistent feelings of loneliness.

If you feel lonely because you don't fit in or don't belong, try different things to find your "people." Peruse different groups in your area and try out a few to see if they're the right fit. Go to places where you feel a sense of belonging, whether that's feeling the camaraderie of other fans at a professional sports game or being a regular at your local coffee shop. You can also try joining a religious congregation, volunteer with a nonprofit that interests you, or become involved in your neighborhood, community, or child's school. Having a sense of belonging can help greatly with feelings of loneliness.

REMEMBER

Loneliness can be a self-fulfilling prophecy. When you feel lonely, you may distance yourself and act cold or aloof with others, because you're feeling so low. As a result of being cold and aloof, others may distance themselves from you, and then it becomes a recurring pattern. What can help break the cycle is faking it 'til you make it, and acting upbeat and positive in social interactions, even if you're not feeling it.

EXPLORE

Think back to the last time you felt a sense of belonging. Where were you, who were you with, and what were you doing? How can you re-create that kind of belonging experience more often?

You experienced childhood emotional neglect

Some people experience loneliness because their emotional needs weren't met in childhood by their parents and, as a result, they suffered from a condition known as *emotional neglect*. If parents ignore their children, invalidate them, are not emotionally responsive, or don't connect with them, even if it's unintentional, emotional neglect can result.

REMEMBER

People who experienced this situation in childhood can experience loneliness as adults. Loneliness that stems from childhood emotional neglect can feel like a cavernous void that can never be filled, no matter how many friends you have. As a result, a person can feel chronically dissatisfied with their relationships and all alone in the world.

EXPLORE

If you're someone who feels chronically lonely, think about the roots of that loneliness. When did you first notice feeling lonely and where do you think that feeling came from? Do you feel different from others or feel like you've never belonged? Feelings of lack of belonging can lead to loneliness and can stay with a person for many years.

For an in-depth discussion of the reasons why you're feeling lonely, check out the thought-provoking book, *Loneliness For Dummies* by Andrea Wigfield (published by Wiley).

Understanding Why Society Is Lonelier Than Ever

Modern life is a very lonely time for many people. In fact, the U.S. surgeon general has declared that there is currently a "loneliness epidemic" in the United States that is causing significant emotional distress as many people feel isolated and alone. A huge 2018 survey by Cigna found that 46 percent of Americans feel alone some or all the time. That's a significant number of people who are feeling lonely.

The reasons for modern-day loneliness are many, and some have to do with our preferences to stay home and go online when we're feeling bored or lonely instead of meeting with people face-to-face. We can get most of our needs met without having to leave the house or interact with anyone, so many people do just that. However, there is a huge cost: pervasive feelings of loneliness.

With people always on their electronic devices and preferring to text their friends instead of call, or post vacation updates on social media instead of sharing about their trip over lunch, it's no wonder why we're all mired in loneliness. It's easier to learn about other people's lives on our social media feeds instead of picking up the phone and scheduling a coffee date with them to catch up. These days many high school kids prefer to text their friends or play video games with them online instead of calling or getting together in person.

Club and organization membership is decreased from decades ago, partly because people can join interest groups online, and more and more people prefer to take online classes and webinars instead of going to their local community center for an in-person class.

The pandemic didn't help this situation — in fact, it made it even easier to stay at home, isolated from friends and a support network, with the increase in work-from-home jobs, videoconferencing, online classes, and virtual groups.

REMEMBER

The implications for society from all this keeping to ourselves are vast. Our quality of life and well-being are negatively impacted. However, you can make a different choice for yourself and make a dent in this pervasive epidemic of loneliness that is blanketing society. A good first step is to try to limit your time online and spend more time trying to make meaningful in-person connections.

Exploring the Implications of Loneliness

Loneliness is difficult to deal with emotionally, but it has also been shown to negatively affect people's quality of life and well-being. Read on to learn more about the health risks and social implications of loneliness.

Identifying the health risks

People who are lonely have been shown to have more health and mental health issues in general, including a higher risk of: anxiety, social anxiety, and depression, as well as a higher risk of cancer, cardiac issues, and stroke. Many research studies have looked at the health implications of loneliness and found some alarming results. For example, lonely people have a 29 percent increased risk of heart disease and a 32 percent increased risk of stroke, according to a 2016 study in the journal *Heart*. A 2023 advisory from the U.S. surgeon general said that chronic loneliness has been shown to have the same negative effects on health as smoking 15 cigarettes per day. That means that loneliness is just as bad for your health as being a heavy smoker. Let that sink in for a minute.

Loneliness is bad for your physical health, but it's detrimental to your mental health as well. Multiple studies have found out just how damaging loneliness is to mental health. A 2022 study about loneliness during the COVID-19 pandemic, published in *Scientific Reports*, found that extremely lonely people were 14 times more likely to have major depressive disorder and 11 times more likely to have generalized anxiety disorder than those who were minimally lonely.

When you're lonely and you can't get your needs met through connections with others, you may turn to substance use to fill the void. This isn't a healthy coping mechanism, but lonely people sometimes do it.

REMEMBER

There is some good news about aging and loneliness: The older you are, the less likely you are to feel lonely. According to a 2018 survey by Cigna, adults age 72 or older are *less* likely to feel lonely than younger adults. The report found that adults ages 18 to 22 are actually the loneliest of all the age groups. Does this finding surprise you? It sure surprised me!

Understanding the social implications

When you're lonely, social interactions are often few and far between. This can lead to the following social implications:

>> **Oversharing:** When you don't get to socialize much, and you finally do find someone to talk to, it can lead to oversharing. You may say too much, too soon, because you have so much to say after keeping it all bottled in so long. That's why it can be very helpful for lonely people to work with a therapist, so they have a weekly outlet to vent their problems.

>> **Talking excessively about themselves:** Similar to oversharing, when lonely people do get to talk to someone, they can tend to talk excessively about themselves, sharing minute details about their experiences that aren't that important to others.

>> **Rusty social skills:** When you've been lonely for so long, your social skills can atrophy, similar to the way your muscles get weaker if you lay in bed for several days. Conversation skills can get so rusty that you don't remember that conversation should be about give-and-take.

If you're lonely and worried about the negative consequences for quality of life and well-being, don't despair. There are things that can help. Read on to find out about the best coping strategies for loneliness.

Exploring Coping Strategies for Loneliness

If you're feeling lonely, you're not alone. Many people struggle with loneliness. You can cope with the loneliness in a variety of ways while you try out other suggestions in this book for making new friends and expanding your support network. Consider trying several of these coping strategies:

>> **Assemble your dream team.** If you're feeling lonely and you're unable to make friends right now, consider assembling your dream team of professionals instead. Your *dream team* is a group of service providers who give you individualized attention and help you feel your best. This group may include any of the following:

- Personal trainer

- Life coach

- Makeup artist

- Therapist

- Nutritionist

- Massage therapist

- Physical therapist

- Esthetician

Having a dream team member who you regularly see and interact with and who makes you feel cared for can help decrease loneliness. And working toward your health and wellness goals with your dream team will help you feel more productive, too.

>> **Find supportive people to meet up with.** Even though you're having difficulty making new friends, you can still find a group of supportive people to hang out with now. You can find them by:

- Joining a new social or hobby group through Meetup (www.meetup.com)

- Starting your own social or hobby group

- Joining your child's school's parent–teacher association (PTA)

- Volunteering in your spare time

- Joining a walking club, support group, or board-game group

The key is to find a group that meets often (weekly is best but every other week is good, too). You'll get to know people when you start getting involved and attending recurring meetings, even if you don't become actual friends with them. (Turn to Chapter 5 for more information on joining groups.)

Being around a supportive group of people, even if they aren't actual friends, will help you feel less lonely.

>> **Attend reunions.** Attending reunions for your high school or college can help you feel less lonely. Reunions are festive environments where everyone is happy to be back at the school and catching up with their classmates. Being around people who knew you "back when" is often very nourishing. Plus, immersing yourself in the nostalgia can help you feel better (as long as you had a good experience at the school — if you didn't, then skip this one). Catching up with old friends who you've lost touch with can help decrease your loneliness, and you can also make new connections at reunions. To further get to know your old classmates, consider volunteering to help plan your next reunion.

>> **Lean on family more often.** If you're feeling lonely, consider leaning more on family. Are there any cousins, aunts, or uncles who you can get to know better or deepen your current relationship with? It's not the same as having friends, especially if family isn't local to you, but it can provide a safe space to connect and share your feelings and experiences.

>> **Create a daily a routine.** When you're lonely, creating a daily routine can help you manage your loneliness more effectively. When you're lonely, you may feel restless or antsy and not know what to do with yourself. This is especially true if you have large amounts of free time. Creating a daily routine with a lot of structure can help with this problem. Ideas for creating a daily routine include adding in blocks of time for exercise or a walk, chores or errands, socialization, work or volunteer activities, reading, and creative pursuits.

>> **Get out of your comfort zone.** When you're lonely, it's easy to get in a rut and stay in your comfort zone. You may find you don't leave the house as much, don't go out as much, and settle into a stagnant routine. The way to cope with this is to try to get out of your comfort zone more often. Try new things, and if an opportunity comes along that sounds appealing, take it. Say yes to more opportunities.

>> **Focus on personal development.** Investing in yourself is a good way to combat loneliness. Personal development can take many forms, including signing up for online classes or webinars, creating a personal reading list, learning a new skill or hobby, or improving your exercise or health routines. Taking an online class or in-person class can put you in contact with others who share your interests, and a friendship may form. Working on personal short-term and long-term goals can give you a sense of purpose and help you feel like you're moving forward. If you struggle with lonely nights and week-ends, focusing on personal development can help fill that time.

>> **Go on solo dates.** When you wish you were spending time with a friend, but you're alone instead, consider taking yourself out on solo dates so that you still feel like you're getting out and about. Make a list of the activities and events you wouldn't mind doing solo, like browsing at a bookstore, seeing a movie, or going to a museum. Then create a plan for making these solo dates happen! You'll feel better being able to go out and do some of the things you want, even if you have no one to do them with.

>> **Get a pet.** Getting a pet is a proven way to decrease loneliness. Caring for a pet can be a good outlet for your nurturing energy, and pets provide unconditional love. Taking a dog for a walk gets you out of the house and exercising, provides structure to your day, and is an instant conversation starter — many people love to stop and say hi to cute dogs. It can also help you meet more people in your neighborhood, because walking a dog gives you an excuse to be outside. It's also gratifying to come home to a furry friend who's so excited to see you — a pet's love and exuberance can really lift your mood. If you can't get a pet, consider volunteering with animals at an animal shelter or rescue group.

>> **Go on message boards or discussion forums.** Message boards or discussion forums, like Reddit (`www.reddit.com`) or City-Data.com (`www.city-data.com`), can be great ways to post questions and get responses, which can help you feel less alone. When you create an account, you also may be able to message other members and strike up online conversations.

>> **Make an online friend.** When you can't make a real-life friend, an online friend can be the next best thing. You can make online friends on social media and by joining online groups that focus on your interests (like Facebook groups), Reddit groups (known as *subreddits*), and group chats like Discord (`https://discord.com`). Online friends can be great for helping you feel less lonely, and you can even decide to eventually do video calls or phone calls with your online friends.

>> **Volunteer for a cause you're passionate about.** When you're lonely, giving back, getting involved, and focusing on others can take your mind off your troubles. Finding a volunteer gig can be the perfect way to spend time doing something meaningful, give back, be around new people, and spend your time in a structured way. There are many ways to find volunteer positions, including doing an internet search in your area. Also check out VolunteerMatch (`www.volunteermatch.org`), a national database of volunteer opportunities.

>> **Spend time in third places.** One way to cope with loneliness is to spend time in what sociologist Ray Oldenburg called *third places* — places like coffee shops, restaurants, community centers, and anywhere else where you can become a regular and people start to recognize you and eventually know your name. Remember the show *Cheers*, where the characters were regulars at the Cheers bar? Maybe you can find a coffee shop or other spot that can become

your own Cheers. It's a great way to build a sense of community because you'll gain a hangout space and start seeing the same people. See Chapter 14 for more on third places.

Coping with an Empty Social Calendar

When you're feeling lonely, it can be hard to look at your calendar and not see any social plans. You may realize that you have no social plans all summer or during the holiday season and feel sad that people aren't thinking of you and reaching out. You may feel overlooked and forgotten. You also may feel resentful, realizing that the only way you'll have social plans is if you're the one reaching out and making the plans. If you do all the initiating in your friendships, you may feel frustrated and perplexed about why you always seem to end up in one-sided friendships (head to Chapter 15 for more on this subject).

TIP

If a lack of social plans is getting you down and causing you to feel more lonely, filling your calendar with your own plans can help. To make your own plans, look through community events and decide which ones to attend, join some social groups and attend their events, or reach out and invite an acquaintance to meet up with you.

Building Resilience

When you're feeling lonely, improving your resilience can help you pick yourself back up when things get tough. *Resilience* means the ability to bounce back from challenging situations. It's important because being more resilient helps you keep moving forward in life, instead of staying stuck and dwelling on past setbacks and failures. Resilience is an important character trait to cultivate, because it helps you adapt well to difficult situations. How can you improve your resilience?

EXPLORE

If you had to describe your resilience right now, how would you rate it? Are you able to bounce back easily (high resilience), or do you tend to be easily stymied by negative situations and experiences (low resilience)?

You can build your resilience in the following ways:

>> **Improving your coping skills:** The more coping strategies you have in your toolbox, the more easily you're able to bounce back. You may already have

several helpful coping strategies you use often to bounce back from challenges, such as journaling your feelings, focusing on positive thinking, talking to a supportive friend, or doing deep breathing when you're feeling stressed or anxious. You can learn additional effective coping strategies by reading self-help books or workbooks, reading online articles, or working with a therapist. Trial and error will help you improve your coping skills. If one coping strategy like journaling your feelings isn't working for you, try another strategy like reframing your negative thoughts into more positive ones, to see if that helps you feel better.

» **Remembering past challenges:** You can also build your resilience by remembering times in the past when you felt lonely and how you got through it. What strategies did you use in the past to work through tough times? Maybe these same strategies can also work for you now.

» **Having an action plan:** You can build your resilience by having an action plan and thinking through all the possible paths you can take when faced with a challenge. When you feel prepared, you can take action more effectively.

Engaging in positive self-talk

A big part of building resilience involves changing your inner monologue and making sure what you say to yourself is positive and uplifting. Our thoughts influence how we feel and behave, so make sure that your thoughts are positive and helpful. Unrealistic, unhelpful, and negative thoughts will only keep you stuck.

You can start working on reframing your negative thoughts in a more positive way. Adopting a growth mindset can really help with this, which means focusing on potential growth and the ability to improve rather than setbacks in a given situation. Here's an example of growth-mindset positive self-talk: "I'm feeling lonely because I haven't made friends *yet*." Adding on that *yet* is vitally important because it shows you that there is still potential to make new friends and that you shouldn't give up hope.

REMEMBER

Make sure to say your positive self-talk statements to yourself regularly until they become part of your internal monologue.

Celebrating small wins

Any time you have a small win, celebrate it. This keeps you motivated and moving forward. That may mean celebrating if you make small talk with the grocery store cashier in line and felt good about it or if you introduced yourself to someone new at a friend's party and had a good conversation. Celebrating small wins can keep you moving in a positive, forward direction.

Improving your self-esteem

Improving your self-esteem is an important strategy that can help you cope with loneliness more easily. To improve your self-esteem, make sure you're using positive self-talk statements often — you want to talk to yourself in a kind and respectful way.

TIP

Starting small and working up to bigger things is a key strategy to help improve your self-esteem. Practice making small talk or inviting an acquaintance out for coffee. Gradually work up to bigger actions when you feel ready. Accumulating small wins will gradually help you improve your self-esteem, which will allow you to go out and take the actions that will improve your loneliness.

5

The Part of Tens

This part explains the most common reasons why you're having difficulty making new friends. It also includes a fun collection of the top ten friends you really need, from the older and wiser friend to the connector friend. It ends with a comprehensive list of how you can have an active social life when you don't have any friends yet.

Chapter **19**

Ten Reasons Why You're Having Trouble Making Friends

I f you're reading this book, it's safe to say that you're having some trouble making new friends. You may have spent a lot of time pondering why that is, perhaps posting in online discussion forums to try to get others' perspectives, reading articles or blog posts, talking about it with your partner or close family members, or even seeing a therapist to try to figure it out. Sometimes people can identify right away why they're having difficulty forming close connections, and other times they feel completely in the dark. It can be stressful not knowing why you're struggling with friendships.

Based on my experience as a mental health therapist, here are the top ten reasons why it may be challenging for you to make new friends. Acknowledging which of these reasons resonates with you the most is the first step to making a change. When you can identify why you're having trouble making new friends, you can take proactive steps to work on the problem.

You Won't Put in the Time

Some people complain about not having any friends, but when you ask them what they've done to try to make friends, they give you a blank stare. New friendships are a lot of work, and if you're not willing to put in the time, it's going to be a lot harder, if not impossible, to make new friends. You've got to make the effort and focus on the long game.

If you've been hesitant to put in the time, think about why that is. Do you feel that your schedule is too crazy-busy to have enough time left over to devote to new friendships? Have you avoided making the time because it feels too overwhelming or like too much work? Are you so tired from a long workweek that you just don't have the energy to devote to new friendships? Have you been rejected so often that it now feels pointless to keep on trying? Doing some self-reflection on why you haven't made the time is the first step to figuring out whether now is the right time for you to pursue new friendships.

According to a 2018 study by Professor Jeffrey Hall in the *Journal of Social and Personal Relationships*, it takes between 40 and 60 hours to turn an acquaintance into a casual friend, and it takes over 200 hours of togetherness before you can make a best friend. That's a lot of hours, and not everyone has that kind of time, especially busy working adults with families. A coffee date here and there just won't cut it — at that rate, it would take *years* to make a casual friend. Instead, try to make the time for regular get-togethers to build up those hours.

TIP

If you're not willing to put in the time, that's okay, but you may need to accept just having acquaintances or not making close friends until you're in a quieter stage of life — after your kids are grown or when you've retired. You can also find other ways to build meaningful interpersonal connections that may not require as much of a time commitment in the meantime, such as through volunteer work.

You're Not Prioritizing Friendships

You want to make friends, and you're willing to put in the time, but there never seems to be *enough* time. You have a to-do list a mile long, and meeting an acquaintance for coffee is at the bottom of that list, after your dentist appointment and mowing the lawn. If you never manage to get around to nurturing your friendships, then you're not prioritizing them the way you should be. Friendships are like a garden, and they need to be tended if they're going to blossom. If you want to make friends, you need to treat it like a priority. That means regularly reaching out, initiating plans, and making the time in your calendar to get together with friends. It also means showing up for your friends in their time of need and showing that you care.

First, be honest with yourself about whether making friends is a priority right now. If it is, you need to think about how you can make friendships more of a priority so that you can give them the time they need.

TIP

One strategy is to block weekly or monthly time in your calendar for socializing, like every Friday afternoon from noon to 2 p.m. Or make it a goal to attend one social group per week or organize one event per month until you make a friend. Try to treat your socializing time as protected time, the same way you'd block time out for an important appointment.

You can also set a reminder to reach out to certain acquaintances once or twice a month to check in and see how their week is going, in order to build those relationships.

You Want One Friend to Be Your Everything

You may remember your best friend from childhood fondly. As a young person, it's relatively easy to make a best friend, because you encounter so many new people at school over the years and have so much time to spend with them. You may have done everything with your best friend, and they were your go-to person.

Many adults also want to have a best friend, but it's much harder to make a *new* best friend when you're older (not counting best friends you've made in previous life stages that you've kept throughout adulthood). Not only do adults tend to be around fewer people (especially if they work from home or are retired), but because they have less free time, they're pickier about who they spend time with. According to Jeffrey Hall's research study, it takes more than 200 hours of time spent with someone to make a best friend. For most busy working adults, racking up 200 hours with a new person can take many years. The idea of making a new best friend quickly as an adult may be an unrealistic expectation.

TIP

Instead, a healthier and more practical approach may be to have different friends for different areas of your life, while you're working on making a best friend. In other words, focus on making activity partners. You may have a running buddy, a book club friend, and a golf friend. Or you may have a coworker friend, a neighborhood walking friend, or a friend from church. Because making a new best friend who is your everything is much harder as an adult, you may need to readjust and lower your expectations. Also, if you're turning to one person to hang out all the time and to fulfill all your emotional needs, that's tremendous pressure on a new friendship and may not be something that a busy working adult has the time and space for in their life. Better to start smaller with a running buddy or book club friend, and then slowly, over time, see if you can grow the friendship into a best friendship.

You're Not Interested in Others

In order to make new friends, you need to be genuinely interested in other people. You need to listen intently, ask questions to show interest, listen more than you talk, and follow up on people's responses. If you're not that interested in other people, it's going to be very hard to make a new friend.

Some people aren't really that interested in getting to know others for a variety of reasons. They may not have the mental energy, they may be content on their own, they may prefer a one-sided friendship, or they may be too wrapped up in their own problems.

TIP

If this sounds like you, and you don't have the emotional bandwidth right now to be interested in others, but you still want to be social, you may do better with an activity partner or socializing in large groups where there's less need to deeply get to know someone one-on-one. Focus on joining activity groups through Meetup (www.meetup.com), going to classes at a local community center, or enjoying the programming at a senior center.

You're a Little Too Needy

Needy people have a harder time making friends because being needy is a major turnoff for most people. Needy people try too hard and give off a vibe of desperation, which drives potential friends away. When someone senses that you're too needy, they may get scared off. Ways that you may be inadvertently demonstrating neediness include texting too frequently, inviting someone to do something too often, relying on one person for all your social and emotional needs, or not taking no for an answer if they decline to meet up.

TIP

Instead, give people some breathing room. One way to do this is to have friends for different areas of your life so that you're not too reliant on just one person. Additionally, let people miss you a little bit by not requesting another meetup right after you just saw them. Remember the adage "Absence makes the heart grow fonder." Give it a few weeks before you ask the person to meet up again.

Also, don't expect instant response times. Give people grace, recognizing that most adults have a lot on their plate. Remember that you're just one person in someone else's life, and accept that they have other obligations to attend to, which may get in the way of spending time with you as much as you'd like.

You're Doing Something Off-Putting

Another reason why you may not be making friends is that you're doing something off-putting. Sometimes you have an idea about what you're doing that is driving people away. But other times, you have no idea. If you have a sense that you may be doing something off-putting, you can do some self-reflection about what it may be or seek honest feedback from a close friend, your spouse or partner, a close family member, or a therapist about anything you're doing that makes it harder to connect with others.

WARNING

Off-putting things that may be keeping people away include the following:

>> Looking unapproachable

>> Having a grumpy or sullen expression (see the nearby sidebar)

>> Not making eye contact

>> Using closed-off body language (for example, having your arms crossed in front of you, being hunched over instead of having an open torso, or being immersed in your phone so you look too busy to chat)

>> Having poor hygiene or body odor

>> Talking over people

>> Bragging or trying to one-up people

>> Always expecting the other person to reach out

>> Interrupting people

>> Talking mostly about yourself

>> Telling long-winded stories that make people's eyes glaze over

>> Having poor social skills

>> Expecting others to always do what you want to do

TURN THAT FROWN UPSIDE DOWN: TACKLING RBF

TIP

One off-putting characteristic that some people have that gets in the way of making friends is so-called *resting bitch face* (RBF). Resting bitch face is when your natural resting expression is grumpy looking, mad, or sullen, and it can happen with men and women alike. It usually occurs when the corners of your mouth are naturally downturned, which can also happen during the aging process. RBF can be off-putting to others because you come across as cold, aloof, and unapproachable.

The good news is, there are ways to compensate for RBF, including practicing having a neutral look or slight smile, having an expressive voice, and making sure to have expressive facial expressions. Focus on smiling more often than you normally would to compensate for your RBF. Face yoga can also be helpful in retraining certain muscles in the face.

The next time you have an unsuccessful social encounter, refer back to this list to see if any of these issues could've been the reason why your friendship didn't take off.

You're Not Willing to Reach Out

In a friendship, someone has to make the first move and reach out. If you're always waiting for the other person to reach out first, the friendship may not take off, and it's going to be harder for you to make friends. Ideally, there's eventually reciprocity in a friendship, but at first someone needs to get the ball rolling. That person may as well be you.

Sometimes people have the attitude that they want the other person to show interest in them, and they feel desperate or awkward making the first move because they don't want to communicate their level of interest. It can feel like a big risk to put yourself out there, but sometimes that's what you need to do in order to make a friend.

TIP

In order to build up the self-confidence to make the first move, start small. Invite an acquaintance out for coffee, ask for someone's phone number at a networking event, or invite someone in your exercise class out for smoothies afterward.

Remember the rule of three: If you've reached out three times and the other person hasn't taken you up on your offer to meet up (or hasn't suggested an alternative date), they're probably not interested in a friendship. After reaching out three times, consider moving on.

It's Your Way or the Highway

Some people are flexible, go-with-the-flow types — they're accommodating, open to suggestions, and willing to do activities that others suggest. Other people are more inflexible and set in their ways. These rigid types can find it harder to keep friendships, because they want you to always do things their way. If you always want the other person to do the activities *you* want to do or go along with *your* ideas, you may find it harder to keep friends. Friends can get turned off if your attitude is "It's my way or the highway." *Remember:* Friendships require compromise and give-and-take.

People who have a lot of friends are usually more easygoing, adaptable, and willing to compromise. In a friendship, sometimes you do the things you want to do, and other times you do the things your friend wants to do.

If you find that rigidity is getting in the way of keeping friendships, work on your compromising skills. If you suggest the activity this time, then next time invite your friend to choose. Or work on choosing an activity that works for both of you.

You Have Too Many Friendship Deal-Breakers

Another reason why you're having difficulty making friends is because you have too many friendship deal-breakers. Busy adults tend to be choosy about friendships, because they don't have much free time to spend with friends. As a result, only someone who checks off *all* of your boxes makes it into your friendship circle. But that can be limiting. For example, if you're a parent of young kids, you may only want to make friends with other parents of young kids and discount a friendship with someone who doesn't have kids.

The danger of being too picky is that you may be missing out on a wonderful friendship. Consider reflecting on your friendship deal-breakers to see if any of them may be too rigid. Maybe a friendship with someone who has different life circumstances than you could be a refreshing change. The next time you meet someone you're unsure of, consider giving them a chance. When you get to know them, you may discover that you're more compatible than you originally thought.

You've Gotten Used to Rejection

Being rejected is traumatic for everyone. Some people who have a tough time making friends have experienced many social rejections and feel hesitant to put themselves out there for fear of being hurt yet again. All these rejections add up and cause significant emotional pain, so they keep people at a distance to avoid being hurt repeatedly.

The problem with this mindset is that it becomes a self-fulfilling prophecy. You go into an interaction expecting to be rejected, because that's what always happens, and you act distant in an attempt to protect yourself from getting hurt again. The other person senses this detachment and decides that you're not the type of friend they're looking for and you get rejected. It can be a vicious cycle that results in your feeling perpetually sad and lonely.

TIP

One strategy that helps break this cycle is "faking it 'til you make it." Act friendly and warm with a new friend, even when you're anxious about being rejected. Assume people will like you when you go into a social situation. In a 2018 study in *Psychological Science*, researchers found that people underestimate how much they're liked by their conversation partners after they talk with someone. So, the next time you go into a social situation, assume the other person likes you, because they probably do. You'll act more warmly to them as a result, and a friendship is more likely to blossom.

Chapter **20**

The Ten Types of Friends You Really Need

You may have heard that it's ideal to have a variety of friends to suit different parts of your life. At the top of the list, most people long to have a best friend — the one person in whom they have complete trust, who's always there for them, and with whom they do everything. However, having other types of friends diversifies your friend group and helps prevent overreliance on any one particular person. Ideally, your set of friends should have different interests and strengths so that you can spend time with them in different ways and for different reasons.

Motivational speaker and author Jim Rohn says, "You are the average of the five people you spend the most time with." This concept promotes the idea that our friends influence us in both positive and negative ways, so it's best if a friend group has a variety of people who are interesting, positive, motivational, and inspiring. On the other hand, if you surround yourself with people whose traits you find negative, it may lead to your adopting these negative characteristics as well.

When you imagine your "dream team" of friends, what types of friends do you want to be on it? Read on to learn more about ten types of friends that you really need, as well as how to find and nurture these friendships.

The Activity Partner

When you think about making new friends, the holy grail for most people is a best friend who can be your go-to person for everything. But having a few activity partners you meet up with from time to time is also helpful and healthy, and it may be a better starting point if you're trying to make all new friends.

An activity partner is a casual friend you can contact when you'd like to meet up with someone for an activity like an exercise class, a walk, a craft event, or a book signing. You can meet up with an activity partner for one specific type of activity (an exercise buddy) or you can have a friend who likes to meet up with you for multiple activities (your fitness-focused friend might like to meet up for a Pilates class, a Zumba class, and rock climbing).

REMEMBER

An activity partner can be best categorized as a casual friend — someone who you're happy spending time with periodically but not someone you'd confide your deepest and darkest secrets to.

TIP

How do you find an activity partner? There are several ways:

» **Scour your current friend list.** Look for friends you already have who you have some things in common with. Do you have a friend who loves to walk? If so, invite them to meet up with you for a regular morning walk at a park. Do you have a literary friend? They may be the perfect person to call when you want to go to an author event or literary presentation.

» **Take a class.** When you're in the class, get to know a few people to see if they might like to meet up outside the class for related activities. If you're in a French language class, chat up someone who seems approachable and invite them to get crepes afterward with you. If you're in a painting class, invite someone to meet up for an art gallery opening on the weekend.

» **Start your own activity group.** If you love a particular activity but can't find anyone to do it with you, start your own group. Then you'll create a bevy of activity partners who will be eager to get together for the activities you plan. Love rock climbing but don't know anyone else who does? Start a rock-climbing activity group and meet up monthly at local rock-climbing gyms.

The Connector Friend

A connector is a very valuable friend to have because they know everyone and thrive on connecting people together. A connector loves to throw parties and introduce their friends to other friends and help them network. They also enjoy being on social committees and planning events that bring people together. A connector is outgoing, inclusive, and a social butterfly. They help you get out of your comfort zone to meet new people and help you broaden your social horizons.

TIP

If you're drawn to connector types, you can find them on social committees, in parent–teacher associations (PTAs), in outreach or community engagement positions at nonprofits, as well at networking groups and events. Look for the person who seems to know everyone or is in charge of a committee and introduce yourself.

EXAMPLE

Yvonne loves to go to networking events to meet new people. She's a business owner who joins many women-in-business events. Yvonne finds it very gratifying to introduce her friends to other friends they don't know and see them form their own bonds and connections. She also loves to be helpful and help her friends network together. People love Yvonne's generous spirit and her ability to include everyone.

The Older and Wiser Friend

An older and wiser friend is a wonderful type of friend to have. They give you a different perspective than friends your own age because of their wisdom and years of experience. The older and wiser friend can take on the role of a mentor, given their varied life experiences, or be a helpful sounding board. It's also nice to socialize with someone who is in a completely different life stage and has different priorities.

TIP

Having friends of all ages and stages is a nice way to diversify your friend group. Another benefit of having friends in different life stages than you is that they may have more time and energy to invest in a friendship. This is especially helpful if you've tried to make friends but everyone seems too busy. Someone who's retired may have more time to devote to forming new friendships.

EXAMPLE

Suki wanted to make an older friend because she got along better with older people than she did with her peers. She also believed that it was beneficial to have friends of varying ages. To make an older friend, she joined a local nonprofit to become a friendly visitor, where she was matched with a lonely older woman who was looking for more companionship. Suki visited her older friend every week and took her out to lunch and grocery shopping. Suki loved the bond they shared and enjoyed hearing her perspectives on motherhood and being a grandmother.

TIP

You can find older and wiser friends in the following ways:

>> **Volunteer.** You can volunteer with any nonprofit and seek out older friends (many people of retirement age have the free time to volunteer). Or volunteer at an older adult-focused organization, like a retirement community, senior ride service, or senior center; then befriend some of the older workers or residents/participants.

>> **Join groups.** Join social groups that are more likely to have a diversity of ages, such as pickleball groups, knitting groups, wine clubs, or hiking groups. There you may meet an older and wiser friend.

>> **Look online.** In the Surrogate Grandparents-USA Facebook group (www. facebook.com/groups/SurrogateGrandparentsNorthAmerica), people of all ages are looking to be or find surrogate grandparents and are also looking for intergenerational friendships.

>> **Ask friends to spread the word.** Let your friends know that you'd like to make an older friend and see if there's anyone who has a lonely neighbor or coworker who could use an extra friend.

>> **Befriend your elderly neighbors.** Do helpful things for them like shoveling their snow or bringing in their heavy packages.

>> **Consider your congregation.** Ask around in your religious congregation to see if there are any older adults who may be looking to make new friends. You can let your rabbi, pastor, or imam know that you're looking to make an older friend and ask if they can match you with someone. Your congregation may also have a committee or group that focuses on older adults or an opportunity to volunteer with older adults.

The Parent Friend

If you're a parent, especially of a younger child, having a parent friend in the same life stage to share the parenting journey with is invaluable. Parent friends can provide camaraderie, offer support, be a source of information about kids' classes and camps, help you navigate challenging developmental stages and situations, and just be a supportive presence when you're feeling stressed out. It's also fun in the early childhood years to make parent friends that you can arrange playdates with, so while the kids are playing, the parents can chat and commiserate.

TIP

Parent friends can sometimes be the easiest types of friends to make because parents are usually very open to making new friends, especially in the early childhood years. You can find parent friends in the following ways:

>> **Volunteer at your kid's school.** Become the room parent or serve on the PTA. You're bound to meet some new people while volunteering.

>> **Take a parent/child class.** You can meet new friends while doing a parent/child music or gymnastics class and chatting with other parents there. Or, while your child is doing a drop-off class, you can chat with other parents on the sidelines and get to know them.

>> **Talk to other parents at the bus stop.** The bus stop is a great place to meet other families in your neighborhood where the kids all go to the same school. Neighborhood parents can be a great resource for local parenting information.

>> **Join a parenting social group.** Joining a social group through Meetup (www.meetup.com) or another type of parenting social or playdate group (perhaps through a community center or religious congregation) is a great way to make new parent friends.

The Same-Life-Stage Friend

The same-life-stage friend is a friend who's at the exact same life stage as you are, which is helpful because you'll have a lot in common and a lot to talk about. If you're a parent, this can be a parent friend with a child the same age. If you've just started a new business, this can be a fellow small business newbie friend. If you're newly retired, it's great to have friends who are also newly retired. If you're a DINK (dual income, no kids), it's helpful to have other DINK friends. You get the idea.

These same-life-stage friends really get you and understand what you're going through, because they're dealing with similar challenges. The drawback to this type of friendship is that they can be more situational friendships where your friendship doesn't last when you no longer have the major thing in common that binds you together.

TIP

You can find these same-life-stage friends anywhere that people in your same life stage gather. Here are some ideas of where to find these friends:

>> Senior centers
>> Support groups for particular conditions

>> New parents groups

>> Social groups (like through Meetup) based on a specific demographic, like DINKS, thirtysomethings, or retirees

The All-Around BFF

This is the type of friendship people seem to want the most, but the one not everyone is able to make. The best friend forever (BFF) is usually not a brand-new friend, but instead someone you've known for a long time and who knows you inside and out. The BFF is your all-around confidante and go-to person who you can tell anything. They are super supportive, will always be there for you, are loyal, and will be brutally honest, in a kind and loving way.

The BFF is so coveted because they're a friend for life. They're usually in your wedding party, the one to throw the baby shower for you, and the person you call first if something big, exciting, important, or devastating happens to you. If you need them for something important at 2 a.m., they'll be there.

How do you find a BFF? Most adults who have a BFF made them in high school, college, or as a twentysomething, and the friendship has lasted the test of time. However, if you don't already have a BFF and want to make one, it's easier to turn a casual friend into a BFF than it is to start from scratch with somebody new. Think about who in your current roster of friends has the most potential. Then make the effort to nurture that friendship and spend more time with them.

REMEMBER

A 2018 study by Professor Jeffrey Hall, published in the *Journal of Social and Personal Relationships*, found that it takes around 200 hours before you can make a best friend. Make sure you're willing and able to put in the time to rack up those 200 hours with your new bestie.

The Group-Setting Friend

This is the friend you only see in a larger group setting, instead of individually. You may see this person while you're out with your friend group, or you may see them at hobby/interest group meetings, like a car enthusiasts group. Seeing them only in a group setting can be perfectly fine if you don't have enough in common to spend time with them one-on-one but you enjoy their company in a group setting where you can connect with them in smaller doses.

This type of friend can introduce you to new ideas, activities, and people and share a general camaraderie with you. They may have specific traits you really admire, like a good sense of humor or a fun and adventurous vibe, but overall you don't consider them to have close-friend potential. This friend may get you to do really fun things you otherwise wouldn't try, like karaoke or taking a belly dancing class.

TIP

You can find this type of friend by joining hobby/social interest groups (like a book club or a sports league) where you can regularly hang out in a large group together.

The Go-Getter Friend

The go-getter friend is someone who is all about personal development. They're always working on their own goals and dreams and inspire you to achieve your own. They have an impressive sense of ambition and are always up to something new and interesting. Whenever you talk to this friend, you're amazed by the exciting things they're doing, whether it's starting their own podcast, raising guide dogs, or traveling around the world. This friend motivates and inspires you to reach for your goals, and they're super supportive as well. Spending time with your go-getter friend helps you to become your best self.

REMEMBER

The go-getter friend likes to be around others who are similarly ambitious, so make sure to share about your own personal development goals with them. Then the two of you can motivate each other and be each other's accountability partners.

TIP

You can find a go-getter friend by joining career or business networking groups, discussion-based groups (like a book club), joining college alumni groups, joining hobby/interest groups, and getting to know work colleagues.

The Amateur Therapist Friend

This type of friend is your confidante and the person you go to when you need support and a listening ear. Any time you have a problem or challenge or you're just feeling low, you can go to them and know you'll feel seen, heard, and uplifted. You can tell this friend anything and know you'll be met with love, understanding, and empathy. This friend listens attentively, asks insightful follow-up questions, and validates your feelings without trying to fix your situation (unless you ask for advice). They also won't judge, so feel free to speak your mind. You can lean on them for support and know they'll be there for you. They also have amazing insights that help you look at your challenges in a whole new way.

Talking with the amateur therapist friend feels like you're really connecting with someone who gets you. And you can offer them the same type of support, too.

To find this kind of friend, consider if there is anyone you already know who is a caring, empathetic listener and who you've been able to open up to in the past. If not, good ways to find this kind of friend include participating in groups or activities that attract kind, caring types who have big hearts. Ideas include volunteering, especially in caring-focused roles, joining a Meetup group or other social group that focuses on social action or advocacy for a cause you're passionate about, or reconnecting with an old friend who you had a great rapport with in the past.

TIP

Test the waters by being vulnerable in small, gradual ways (see Chapter 10 for more on how to be vulnerable). Reveal a small challenge you're facing and see how that goes. If the person responds in an empathetic way, then gradually, over time, you can continue to confide in them a little more.

WARNING

Remember to avoid emotionally dumping on your friends. There's a fine line between sharing and emotional dumping. You don't want to overwhelm or drain your friend by venting a torrent of problems and complaints, especially when you're first getting to know someone. Instead, be mindful and considerate of their compassionate nature when deciding what to share with them, and make sure the timing is right.

The Blast-from-the-Past Friend

This oldie-but-goodie friend is an old friend from childhood, high school, or college who has known you a long time. You may have grown up with them or spent your formative years together so the two of you have a lot of history, and they know everything about you.

The beauty of the blast-from-the-past friend is that they knew you "way back when." It's a reassuring feeling to have a lifelong friend who knows all your old history (both the good times and the bad), can reminisce with you, and shares your nostalgia. This type of friend usually supports you unconditionally and can be refreshingly honest with you. These types of friendships can feel very comforting, like a cozy old sweatshirt, especially if you haven't made any new friends in a long time.

Your blast-from-the-past friend can be from grade school, high school, college, summer camps, high school jobs or internships, or the neighborhood you grew up in. Think about if there's anyone from your past who you'd like to reconnect with now.

TIP

How can you reconnect with this type of friend if you've lost touch? Consider searching on social media, doing an internet search to find their employment or personal website and contacting them by email, going to a high school or college school reunion, or asking your other friends from that time period if they have any contact information or know where they are now.

Chapter **21**

Ten Ways to Have a Vibrant Social Life When You Don't Have Friends Yet

Are you yearning to have a busy social life, but you don't have any friends yet? When the weekend rolls around, some people feel depressed that they're sitting home alone binge-watching TV shows while it seems like everyone else has exciting plans.

Wanting to do things but not having anyone to do them with can feel lonely and isolating. Maybe you're working on making new friends, but it just hasn't happened. Or maybe you've recently moved to a new city, and you don't know anyone yet. Or perhaps you're homebound for various reasons and your in-person social options are limited. Regardless of the reasons, having an empty social calendar can feel depressing.

If this describes your situation, don't despair! You can actually have a vibrant social life (and have social plans every day of the week, if you'd like), without having any friends.

REMEMBER

Many of the recommendations in this chapter involve joining groups or planning events, but if you're not able or ready to do that, just getting out of the house and being *around* people can help you feel less isolated and lift your mood. Going to your local bookstore, browsing books, and sitting in the café with a drink; going to a local park and enjoying nature; or hanging out at the local mall and people-watching can help you feel like you have something social to do. Take it one step further, and talk with strangers at the mall or make small talk with someone at the park or bookstore to help yourself feel less lonely.

TIP

One way you can have instant social plans is to invite an acquaintance to do something. Think of people who are already in your orbit, even if the only thing you know about them is their name. Are there any neighbors or coworkers you'd like to get to know better? What about a Facebook friend who you don't really know but are connected to in some way? Or a local alum from your high school or college who lives in your area?

You can even cold-contact people in your career field (to have an informational interview) and invite them for coffee in order to network and expand your professional circle. Even if you barely know someone, you can still extend an invitation for something casual, like coffee or a walk — you've got to start somewhere, right? Most likely, they'll be grateful for the invitation and take you up on it.

Joining Groups and Attending Events

You can easily fill your social calendar to the brim by joining groups through Meetup (www.meetup.com) or Facebook groups (www.facebook.com) and attending events. Look for groups that interest you and that offer a lot of events. You can join a brunch club, knitting group, pickleball group, or walking group — the options are endless. You could fill your whole week with social events by joining a few active groups and RSVPing to the events.

If you join a group that looks promising, but there aren't any events that you're interested in, *you* can be the one to plan an event, even if you don't know anyone in the group. Planning a simple event like a coffee gathering or walk doesn't take much effort, and the payoff could be huge in terms of meeting new people and making a friend. All you need to do is come up with an idea for an event, find a venue, plan the event, and show up with a sign. Think of an event that the group members would be interested in, and propose it to the organizer (or plan it yourself if the group allows that). With online event-planning tools in the group, you can have your event listed in a few minutes.

TIP

If you feel disappointed that you never have dinner plans and don't want to go to restaurants alone, there are plenty of food-focused social groups out there to join. You can join dinner clubs, brunch groups, happy-hour gatherings, or any other kind of food-related groups. The nice thing about joining a dinner or brunch group is that you can fill your weekends with these events and feel like you've had a very social weekend.

TIP

Another type of group you can join is a support group. There are in-person and online support groups for most conditions, from stroke support groups to breast cancer support groups to caregiver support groups. At the support group, you can get and give support, meet new people, and make new connections. And having a regular group to go to weekly or monthly can help you feel like you have something socially meaningful to do.

Attending Community Events

You can also fill your social calendar by attending events in your community. In any given week, your area probably has dozens of events you can attend (especially in the summer or around holidays), such as festivals and fairs, walks/runs for specific causes or health conditions, author readings, music events, events for seniors, and family-friendly events. You can find these events on Eventbrite (www. eventbrite.com), which is an online event-listing site where you can learn about events near you and buy tickets; through your local town or county web page; and through email blasts from businesses or nonprofits you're connected with. Local libraries also offers lots of free events, including book readings, art events, book clubs, and language classes.

You could fill nearly every waking hour going to community events. Browsing through all relevant event-listing sites and making a monthly spreadsheet of events that you'd like to attend can be helpful.

REMEMBER

When you're at an event, make small talk with fellow attendees. You never know when or where you'll strike up a friendship!

Creating Meaningful Experiences by Volunteering

Volunteering is a great way to fill your time with a meaningful activity that also allows you to socialize and meet new people. You can volunteer at a wide variety of nonprofits and organizations, including animal shelters, retirement communities, food pantries, and domestic violence shelters, among many others. After you've been accepted as a volunteer, you choose your shifts or when you'd like to volunteer, which can be as often as you'd like. You can schedule volunteer shifts anytime you want to fill your free time, even on weekends if the organization is open.

TIP

The best way to find volunteer opportunities is through VolunteerMatch (www.volunteermatch.org), Idealist (www.idealist.org), or your local town or county's volunteering website. Look through the volunteer opportunities until you find one that seems like a good match. You can do one-time or ongoing volunteer opportunities. You can make meaningful interpersonal connections with others by volunteering as a Big Brother/Big Sister, tutoring kids, volunteering with the elderly, walking dogs at an animal shelter, serving food at a homeless shelter, or cuddling babies at the hospital.

Becoming Involved in Your Religious Congregation

Getting involved in a religious congregation can provide a meaningful way to connect with your faith, build community, and meet new people. Attend services, join groups or committees, volunteer with the congregation, and participate in events. You can get as involved as you'd like, and you can get to know others better while participating in a congregational social group, serving on a committee, or volunteering at an event.

To find a religious congregation, you can do an online search to find the congregations closest to you that match your faith background; ask neighbors or coworkers for recommendations; or just stop by, attend services, and see if it's a good fit. Then you can learn about events, groups, and committees the congregation offers by listening for announcements during services, meeting with the religious leader to let them know you'd like to get more involved, talking with other congregants about groups that match your interests, looking at the congregation's website to find upcoming events, or reading the congregation's newsletter.

Joining a Senior Center

Senior centers are fantastic places for older adults (typically 50+) to get out of the house, meet new people, build community, and have a full day brimming with intellectually stimulating classes and activities. Senior centers can be found in nearly every community and offer interesting and meaningful programming, including exercise classes, speaker series, book clubs, arts and crafts, computer labs, lunch, and monthly trips. They often post their schedules online, or you can visit your local senior center, take a tour, and get a programming flyer to look over.

Senior centers are enriching and vibrant places to go where you can spend the whole day in a meaningful way. Plus, there are plenty of opportunities to socialize and make new friends at a senior center.

To find your local senior center, do an internet search, ask neighbors, or call your local Area Agency on Aging.

Having a Weekly Social Commitment

Having a standing weekly social commitment is a great way to add structure to your week and get regular social plans on your calendar. Knowing you'll see the same people each week at a set time and having somewhere specific to go can lift your mood when you're feeling lonely.

Taking an adult education class, joining a weekly knitting group, signing up for a weekly exercise class, or committing to going to the gym at a specific day and time each week are all ways to create a weekly commitment. Having that weekly commitment also provides accountability, which can be helpful for many people who struggle with procrastination.

Taking a class or joining a weekly group adds some structure to your day and allows you to socialize with other adults interested in the same topic or activity. Then, when you've gotten to know people in the class, and found one or two who you'd like to get to know better, you can suggest an outing, like getting coffee after the class. This is how you start to grow friendships — by getting to know someone outside of the setting you met them in.

Online classes are also great choices that may fit more easily into your schedule or be a good option if it's difficult to leave your home. Some popular online class providers include Coursera (www.coursera.org), Skillshare (www.skillshare.com), The Great Courses (www.thegreatcourses.com), and Udemy (www.udemy.com).

Starting Your Own Business

Another way to make meaningful interpersonal connections when you don't have friends yet is to start your own business. Starting a business is a major undertaking that should not be taken lightly, and there should be many solid reasons why starting a business makes career and financial sense for you, whether it's a weekend side hustle or a full-fledged, full-time business. That said, creating or selling a product or service that you're passionate about and nurturing connections with your customers can help you feel more socially fulfilled. Customers aren't friends, but getting positive feedback from them can still be very meaningful and can boost your self-confidence. And depending on the type of business you start, you can create your own events or be a vendor at different events, fairs, and festivals, which can provide a social outlet as you greet customers and explain about your products or services. You can also build new connections and expand your professional circle by networking with other business owners.

TIP

Starting a business requires a lot of hard work and potentially a big financial investment, depending on the business. You can find out more by doing online research or going to your local Small Business Development Center (www.sba.gov) — or check out *Starting a Business All-in-One For Dummies*, 3rd Edition (published by Wiley). There are also online classes you can take to learn how to start a business, and you can join relevant Facebook groups on the topic of your business to learn about the field, ask questions, and connect with others in the same industry.

Dating Yourself to Create a Fulfilling Social Life

If you don't have friends but you still want to go out and do exciting things, the easiest solution is to date yourself. *Dating yourself* means taking yourself on dates to do all the things you want to do. You can go to your favorite restaurant with a book and enjoy a nice meal, pack a picnic and have lunch at the park, or check out a new museum, for example.

You may wish you were doing these activities with someone else, but if you reframe the experience as getting to do whatever you want to do while enjoying your own company, it can help you feel more at peace with the idea. When deciding what to do on your solo dates, think of activities that are best done alone. Example of activities that you don't need another person to fully enjoy could include going to a bookstore and browsing for however long you want, going shopping, or going to a spa. Adding in some novelty can make dating yourself downright awesome — go somewhere you've never been before, try a new restaurant, do a day trip to an interesting place. You'll have exciting plans on your calendar, and you may even meet someone new while you're on your solo date.

Making an Online Friend

Making an online friend is often easier than making a real-life friend, and it's a great way to build a social life when making friends in real life isn't working or is slow going. Making an online friend who you can chat with and check in with and who supports you can help build your support system. Even if you never meet in person, many people consider online friends some of their closest friends. You can always do phone calls or video chats with your online friends to take the relationship offline.

You can make online friends in different social or networking groups, through social media, in gaming groups, via virtual communities, or in discussion forums.

REMEMBER

People online are often more open to new friendships, which makes it easier to build new connections this way. If you have social anxiety or are shy, you may have an easier time making an online friend because you may be more comfortable getting to know someone online versus face-to-face. It's also easier to make an online friend because, in a typical week, you probably visit several online groups or discussion forums (that can have tens of thousands of members) that put you into contact with more people than you encounter in a typical week doing your regular activities. Take a chance and send a message to someone online who seems interesting — you never know where one message will take you!

Being a Friendly Caller or Friendly Visitor

Another way to make a meaningful interpersonal connection when you don't have friends yet is to become a friendly caller or friendly visitor through a local seniors' organization. There are lots of lonely older adults who have no friends or family and wish they did. You can be a friendly caller or friendly visitor and set aside time each week to connect with a lonely senior. You can visit your senior friend at their home or retirement community or take them out for lunch or shopping. It feels great to help someone out with their grocery shopping or drive them to a doctor's appointment as a volunteer driver.

TIP

To find organizations in your community that can connect you with an older adult, search online for older adult nonprofits, contact your local Area Agency on Aging, or look on VolunteerMatch for volunteer opportunities with older adults.

Index

A

acceptance prophecy, 105–106, 180

acquaintances, turning into friends. *See also* deeper connections

  building courage and self-confidence, 187–188

  determining if there's friend potential, 174–177

  inviting to do something, 332

  noticing the shift, 181–182

  online friends, 188–189

  overview, 173

  recognizing acquaintances, 174

  signs of success, 188

  strategies for

    acting like they're already your friend, 180

    asking for favors, 179

    being good listener, 181

    being there when they need help, 181

    being vulnerable and authentic, 180–181

    creative ideas for friend dates, 179

    inviting them out, 177–178

    inviting them to your home, 180

    overview, 177

    showing that you're into them, 178–179

  taking things slowly, 186–187

  troubleshooting challenges, 176–177, 182–186

action plan, building resilience by having, 309

active listening, 117–118, 151, 259

activity partners, 12, 42–43, 57, 315–316, 322

ads, friend, 79

adult learning. *See* classes

adult sports leagues, 81

adulthood, making friends in. *See* assessing friendship needs; deeper connections; friendship-making; ideal friend, manifesting; places, to find new friends

advice, asking for during small talk, 118

advocacy groups, finding friends at, 79

advocating for yourself, 257

affirmations, positive

  friendship, 63–64

  to increase positivity and happiness, 139

  for overcoming shyness, 127

  related to making others feel good, 149

aging, and loneliness, 304. *See also* older adults

alone

  approaching people who are, 93

  being, versus loneliness, 298–299

alumni database, finding old friends in, 287

alumni groups, 81–82

amateur therapist friends, 327–328

ambiverts, 45

anger, managing, 256–257

anger de-escalation strategies, 259

anxiety. *See* social anxiety disorder

apathy, as challenge of making friends, 12–13

appearance

  approachability, increasing through, 142–143

  role in first impression, 101–102

appreciation

  feeling lack of, 268

  role in making friend feel valued, 215

  showing to make people feel liked, 153–154

approachability

  combating off-putting behaviors, 290

  demeanor of, 92–93

  importance of, 136–138

  making people feel liked

    being happy to see people, 151

    being responsive, 150

    checking in on people, 149

    connecting on social media, 150

    giving compliments, 153

    initiating plans, 152

    making people feel good, 148–149

bragging, 145, 291

brain, reaction to rejection, 202–203

branching out from regular routine, 70

break, taking from friendship, 258

breakup discussion, upfront, 277–278. *See also* ending friendships

breathing exercises, 128, 132–133, 195

bus stop, finding friends at, 233, 325

business, starting, 336

C

caring, increasing approachability by, 146–147

casual friends. *See* acquaintances, turning into friends; activity partners

casual get-togethers, 199–200

CBT (cognitive behavioral therapy), 131

celebrating small wins, 309

challenge, 30-day friendship, 61–62

challenges in friendships

  common

    betrayal, 250–251

    bossy friends, 248

    chronically late friends, 249–250

    competitive friends, 248–249

    flaky friends, 250

    growing apart, 253–254

    lack of responsiveness, 253

    mismatches in expectations, 246–248

    one-sided friendships, 251–252

    rejection, 253

  communicating effectively, 258–261

  overview, 245–246

  working through

    overview, 254

    Step 1: identifying issues and feelings, 254–255

    Step 2: determining how much it bothers you, 255

    Step 3: deciding what to let slide, 255–256

    Step 4: managing anger, 256–257

    Step 5: considering friend's perspective, 257

    Step 6: advocating for yourself, 257

    Step 7: asking for feedback, 258

    Step 8: taking a break, 258

challenges of making friends

  common nature of problem, 15–18

  lack of success

    coping with negative emotions related to, 293–294

    friendship mentor, finding, 292–293

    off-putting behaviors, identifying, 290–292

    overview, 283

    professional help for, 294–295

    as reason for loneliness, 300

    reflecting on past friendships, 285–288

    strengths and weaknesses, identifying, 288–290

    understanding reasons for, 284

  overview, 7–8

  people having harder time making friends

    LGBTQIA+ adults, 27–29

    men, 24–26

    neurodivergent people, 34–36

    older adults, 30–33

    overview, 23

    parents of older kids, 29–30

  reasons for trouble with friend-making

    apathy, 12–13

    fewer opportunities to make friends, 14

    friendship deal-breakers, too many, 319–320

    lack of interest in others, 316

    lack of time, 10

    moving away and starting over, 11

    neediness, 316–317

    not prioritizing friendships, 314–315

    off-putting behaviors, 317–318

    other priorities, 11

    overview, 8–10, 313

    rejection, being used to, 320

    rigidity, 11–12, 319

    rusty social skills, 14–15

    smaller social circles due to pandemic, 15

    social anxiety, 13

    time needed, not putting in, 314

    trust issues, 13

    unwillingness to reach out, 318–319

    wanting one friend to be everything, 315–316

helpfulness
  role in making friend feel valued, 215
  role in turning acquaintances into friends, 181
high school years, friendships from, 285
hobbies, asking about during small talk, 117
hobby/interest groups. *See also* groups
  developing social skills in, 15
  finding activity partners at, 43
  intergenerational friendships in, 242
  for men, 26
  for neurodivergent people, 35, 36
  overview, 12
  starting, 236–237
home, inviting people to, 180, 197, 239
homebound older adults, 31
honesty, 216
hosting events to find friends, 84–86
hugging, 140
humility, 145
humor, sense of, 53, 102, 143, 144
hygiene, 142–143, 291

I

I statements, 224, 248, 259–260, 278
icebreakers, 85
icons, explained, 3
ideal friend, manifesting
  friendship vision board, 62–63
  learning from past relationships, 55–56
  multiple friendship baskets, 56–57
  overall friendship-making strategy, 60–62
  overview, 51
  positive friendship affirmations, 63–64
  qualities important in, 52–55
  setting friendship goals, 57–60
ideal number of friends, determining, 40–42
ideal social life, self-reflection about, 47–48
improvisation (improv), 144
inclusive friend, being, 103,218
initiating get-togethers, 211, 219
initiating plans, to make people feel liked, 152

in-person time, importance to friendships, 17. *See also* get-togethers
Instagram, 79
intense experiences, role in deep friendships, 162
intensity
  friend-making challenges related to, 183
  tempering when befriending people, 186–187
intentionality, in search for ideal friend
  friendship vision board, 62–63
  goals, setting, 57–60
  overall friendship-making strategy, 60–62
  real estate agent, thinking like, 54
intentions, clarifying for gender-diverse friendships, 98–99
interest in others
  lack of, as reason for difficulty making friends, 316
  showing, as quality of good friend, 213–214
  showing to make people feel liked, 150–151
interests. *See also* groups; hobby/interest groups
  asking about during small talk, 117
  connecting with people due to mutual, 105
  evaluating importance in ideal friendship, 53
  looking for groups meshing with, 72–73
  starting social group based on, 84
intergenerational friendships, 242, 323–324
internet. *See also* social media
  online groups, 79–80, 307
  reconnecting with old friends on, 287
  role in epidemic of loneliness, 302–303
  using to build community, 238
interrogations, avoiding in small talk, 113
intimidating people, as challenge to friend-making, 184
introversion, 44–46, 207
invitations. *See also* get-togethers
  being willing to compromise, 200
  to build community, 239
  coping with rejection, 201–203
  dealing with no response, 201
  extending to acquaintances, 177–178, 180, 332
  keeping things casual, 199–200
  reciprocity, handling lack of, 204

qualities *(continued)*
    respect for friend's time, 217
    showing interest, 213–214
    showing up for friends, 215–216
    supportive, being, 210–211
    thoughtfulness, 217
    important in ideal friend, 52–55
quantity of friends needed, 40–42
queer people, friend-making challenges for, 27–29
questions
    asking to show interest in others, 151
    in deep conversations, 170–171
    not asking too many, 187
    during small talk, 116–117
quiet people, friend-making challenges for, 183–184

R

random persons, trying to befriend, 185
RBF (resting bitch face), 142, 290, 318
reaching out to people. *See also* good friend, being
    asking for contact information, 194–197
    being willing to compromise, 200
    coping with rejection, 201–203
    dealing with no response, 201
    failure to reach out as off-putting, 292
    following up, 203–204
    keeping things casual, 199–200
    not being willing to, 318–319
    overview, 193
    as part of being good friend, 219–220
    role in making friend feel valued, 214
    scheduling another get-together, 201
    successful get-togethers, 200
    taking initiative, 198–199
    timing of, 199
    "we should get together sometime" phrase, 197–198
reading, in preparation for deep conversations, 169
real estate agent, thinking like, 54

reciprocity
    handling lack of, 204, 220–221, 251–252, 267
    of liking, 148
recommendations, asking for during small talk, 118
reconnecting with old friends, 14, 286–288, 329
reflective listening, 181, 259
regular events to host at home, 239
regular meetings, looking for groups with, 73
regularly seeing same people, 236
rejection
    being used to, and difficulty making friends, 320
    coping with, 201, 253
    handling fear of, 185–186
    preparing for, 12
    risking, 88–89, 152, 188
relevant friendship goals, 59
religious congregations
    building community in, 234–235
    finding friends in, 78–79
    finding older and wiser friends in, 324
    intergenerational friendships in, 242
    involvement in, 334
Remember icon, explained, 3
remembering
    details, increasing charisma by, 103
    names, 118, 151
remote work, 21
reserved people, friend-making challenges for, 183–184
resilience, building, 308–310
respect
    in communication, importance of, 259
    for friend's time, as quality of good friend, 217
responsiveness
    evaluating importance in ideal friendship, 52
    lack of, handling, 253
    making other people feel liked through, 150
    role in making friend feel valued, 214
resting bitch face (RBF), 142, 290, 318
retirement, 21, 30–33

reunions, 288, 294, 306
Reysen Likability Scale, 144
rigidity, and difficulty making friends, 11–12, 319
role models, friendship, 208–209
romantic interest
in gender-diverse friendships, 98, 99, 100
in queer friendships, 27, 28
romantic relationships
prioritizing, as challenge to making friends, 11
starting new, friendships ending due to, 268–269
routine
branching out from regular, 70
daily, dealing with loneliness with, 306
rural areas, looking for groups in, 72
rusty social skills
as challenge of making friends, 14–15
loneliness as leading to, 304

S

sadness, coping with, 293–294
same-life-stage friends, 325–326
saying no respectfully, 225–226
scheduling another get-together, 201
school reunions, 288, 294, 306
The Second City, 144
seeing same people regularly, building community by, 236
selectively befriending people, 185
self-confidence, building, 36, 128, 187–188, 257
self-disclosure, role in deep friendships, 163–164
self-esteem, improving, 106, 310
self-talk, positive. *See* positive self-talk
senior centers, 33, 77, 335
sense of humor, 53, 102, 143, 144
sensitive subjects, downplaying, 216
serious people, friend-making challenges for, 183–184
sessions, committing to group for three, 74
sharing, role in deep friendships, 163–164
short-term friendship goals, 58

showing interest
to make people feel liked, 150–151, 178–179
as quality of good friend, 213–214
showing up for friends, 152–153, 163, 215–216
shyness
defined, 123
overcoming, 127–128
overview, 123–125
as result of both nature and nurture, 126
versus social anxiety disorder, 123, 125
symptoms of, 126–127
when people feel shy, 125–126
side by side activities, male preference for, 24–25
similarities
approaching people based on, 91
evaluating preference for in friends, 55
increasing charisma by looking for, 103
situational friendships, 266
slow fade, ending friendships through, 276–277
slowly befriending people, 186–187
small talk
conversation starters, 115–117
improving at, 120–121
making in new groups, 75
mastering art of, 115–118
moving to deeper conversations from, 168–171
overview, 109–111
practicing, 187
psyching yourself up for, 112–114
reasons to engage in, 111–112
when approaching new people, 95
wrapping up, 119–120
small things, finding joy in, 139
small towns, looking for groups in, 72
small vulnerabilities, sharing, 166–167, 180–181
small wins, celebrating, 309
smaller social circles due to pandemic, 15
SMART friendship goals, 59
smiles, 141

V

validating feelings of friends, 259

valued, making friend feel, 214–215

vision board, friendship, 62–63

visualization exercises, 132

volunteering

  building community through, 238

  dealing with loneliness through, 307

  finding older and wiser friends through, 324

  finding parent friends through, 325

  before having friends, 334

  meeting like-minded friends through, 82–83

  by neurodivergent people, 36

  as older adult, 33

vulnerability

  increasing approachability by showing, 147

  role in deep friendships, 165–167

  role in turning acquaintances into
    friends, 180–181

W

warmth, 52, 139–141

Warning icon, explained, 3

"we should get together sometime" phrase,
  responding to, 197–198

weaknesses, friendship-making, 288–290

weekly social commitment, having, 335

well-being

  importance of friendship for, 38

  while waiting to make friends, 49

where to find new friends. *See* places, to find
  new friends

widowhood, 21

work

  asking about during small talk, 117

  building community at, 233–234

  difficulty of making friends at, 9

  finding male friends at, 26

  from home, as friend-making turning point, 21

  importance of friendliness at, 137

  intergenerational friendships at, 242

  prioritizing, as challenge to friend-making, 11

  and social isolation, 18

  work friends, 57

wrapping up small talk, 119–120

Y

yes, saying more often, 13

you statements, 224, 260

young adult years

  loneliness in, 304

  reflecting on friendships from, 285

  social interaction in, 9

younger friends, making, 242

About the Author

Rebecca Greene, MSW, LMSW, is a mental health therapist in group practice and a self-help author. She works with all ages, but focuses primarily on adults and older adults who struggle with anxiety, depression, loneliness, friendship issues, social anxiety, attention-deficit/hyperactivity disorder (ADHD), and aging transitions. She helps people develop healthier and more meaningful friendships and overcome friendship challenges.

Becoming a therapist was a second career for Rebecca, who started out with a law degree (and also wrote *Law School For Dummies*). After realizing that the adversarial legal field wasn't the right fit, Rebecca decided to pursue a more nurturing career that combined her love of psychology and understanding of human nature with her ability to empathize and connect with others on a deep level. She received her Master of Social Work degree from The Catholic University of America in Washington, DC, and has worked as a therapist since 2012. Rebecca has worked in several different practice settings, including nonprofits, a care management company, and group practice.

Rebecca is also a prolific author who has written four nonfiction books on self-help, parenting, and education topics, and six books for children on social-emotional learning topics. Several of her books have won multiple awards, including *My Perfect Cupcake,* which was inspired by her son's journey with multiple food allergies. Rebecca's newest children's book is about intergenerational friendships. She writes and speaks frequently on the topics of friendship, social skills, and mental health.

When she's not in the therapy office or at her desk writing, Rebecca's main hobby is connecting with others. She enjoys meeting new people and bringing them together to facilitate meaningful connections in the spirit of fun and friendship. Rebecca has started 15 social groups in the last 20 years, including a women's walking group, a new moms' group, and a weekend brunch club. If there's a social committee, Rebecca is usually on it. She enjoys planning events (especially holiday events) for a variety of local groups.

In her spare time, she enjoys creative pursuits, reading nonfiction books, spending time in nature and at the beach, and volunteering in the community. Rebecca lives in the Washington, DC, metropolitan area with her husband, school-aged son, and two rambunctious Cornish rex cats.

Dedication

To my wonderful family — my son, Alex, and my husband, Brian — who always inspire me to become the best version of myself.

Author's Acknowledgments

I would like to say a big thank-you to everyone who helped this book come together. Creating a book is a team effort, and I would like to acknowledge the entire Wiley publishing team who worked tirelessly to ensure this book came together successfully.

First, I would like to say a special thank-you to my amazing and talented editor, Elizabeth Kuball, for all her expert guidance and top-notch project management skills throughout the entire writing and editing process. I would also like to thank Alicia Sparrow, whose enthusiasm for the book's topic helped this project gain momentum and get a fantastic start. I would additionally like to thank Tim Gallan, who helped with initial coaching and guidance as the project took shape. A very special thank-you to Nicole McNelis, LPC, who tirelessly read the entire manuscript and gave valuable and insightful feedback.

A hearty thank-you to all the incredible friends I have made in the last 15 years who have been so special and meaningful to me, especially as a new mother. And to all the people I interviewed for this book, thank you for sharing your personal friendship experiences with me.

Finally, a very special thank-you to my readers for acknowledging that you would like to improve your friendship-making skills and for choosing this book to help guide you. I hope this book inspires you to put yourself out there and make wonderful new friends, and helps you succeed on your meaningful friendship journey. I believe in you — you can do this!

Publisher's Acknowledgments

Associate Acquisitions Editor: Alicia Sparrow

Editor: Elizabeth Kuball

Peer Reviewer:
Nicole McNelis, M.Ed., NCC, LPC, PMH-C

Production Editor: Tamilmani Varadharaj

Cover Image: © 10'000 Hours/Getty Images

Special Help: Jennifer Yee

Leverage the power

Dummies is the global leader in the reference category and one of the most trusted and highly regarded brands in the world. No longer just focused on books, customers now have access to the dummies content they need in the format they want. Together we'll craft a solution that engages your customers, stands out from the competition, and helps you meet your goals.

Advertising & Sponsorships

Connect with an engaged audience on a powerful multimedia site, and position your message alongside expert how-to content. Dummies.com is a one-stop shop for free, online information and know-how curated by a team of experts.

- Targeted ads
- Video
- Email Marketing
- Microsites
- Sweepstakes sponsorship

20 MILLION PAGE VIEWS EVERY SINGLE MONTH

15 MILLION UNIQUE VISITORS PER MONTH

43% OF ALL VISITORS ACCESS THE SITE VIA THEIR MOBILE DEVICES

700,000 NEWSLETTER SUBSCRIPTIONS TO THE INBOXES OF *300,000* UNIQUE INDIVIDUALS EVERY WEEK

# of dummies

Custom Publishing

Reach a global audience in any language by creating a solution that will differentiate you from competitors, amplify your message, and encourage customers to make a buying decision.

- Apps
- Books
- eBooks
- Video
- Audio
- Webinars

Brand Licensing & Content

Leverage the strength of the world's most popular reference brand to reach new audiences and channels of distribution.

For more information, visit **dummies.com/biz**

PERSONAL ENRICHMENT

Staying Sharp

9781119187790
USA $26.00
CAN $31.99
UK £19.99

Facebook

9781119179030
USA $21.99
CAN $25.99
UK £16.99

Guitar

9781119293354
USA $24.99
CAN $29.99
UK £17.99

Investing

9781119293347
USA $22.99
CAN $27.99
UK £16.99

Beekeeping

9781119310068
USA $22.99
CAN $27.99
UK £16.99

Digital Photography

9781119235606
USA $24.99
CAN $29.99
UK £17.99

Meditation

9781119251163
USA $24.99
CAN $29.99
UK £17.99

Pregnancy

9781119235491
USA $26.99
CAN $31.99
UK £19.99

Samsung Galaxy S7

9781119279952
USA $24.99
CAN $29.99
UK £17.99

iPhone

9781119283133
USA $24.99
CAN $29.99
UK £17.99

Crocheting

9781119287117
USA $24.99
CAN $29.99
UK £16.99

Nutrition

9781119130246
USA $22.99
CAN $27.99
UK £16.99

PROFESSIONAL DEVELOPMENT

Windows 10

9781119311041
USA $24.99
CAN $29.99
UK £17.99

AutoCAD

9781119255796
USA $39.99
CAN $47.99
UK £27.99

Excel 2016

9781119293439
USA $26.99
CAN $31.99
UK £19.99

QuickBooks 2017

9781119281467
USA $26.99
CAN $31.99
UK £19.99

macOS Sierra

9781119280651
USA $29.99
CAN $35.99
UK £21.99

LinkedIn

9781119251132
USA $24.99
CAN $29.99
UK £17.99

Windows 10

9781119310563
USA $34.00
CAN $41.99
UK £24.99

SharePoint 2016

9781119181705
USA $29.99
CAN $35.99
UK £21.99

Fundamental Analysis

9781119263593
USA $26.99
CAN $31.99
UK £19.99

Networking

9781119257769
USA $29.99
CAN $35.99
UK £21.99

Office 2016

9781119293477
USA $26.99
CAN $31.99
UK £19.99

Office 365

9781119265313
USA $24.99
CAN $29.99
UK £17.99

Salesforce.com

9781119239314
USA $29.99
CAN $35.99
UK £21.99

Coding

9781119293323
USA $29.99
CAN $35.99
UK £21.99

Learning Made Easy

ACADEMIC

Algebra I dummies

Mary Jane Sterling

9781119293576
USA $19.99
CAN $23.99
UK £15.99

Basic Math & Pre-Algebra dummies

Mark Zegarelli

9781119293637
USA $19.99
CAN $23.99
UK £15.99

Calculus dummies

Mark Ryan

9781119293491
USA $19.99
CAN $23.99
UK £15.99

Chemistry dummies

John T. Moore, EdD

9781119293460
USA $19.99
CAN $23.99
UK £15.99

Physics I dummies

Steven Holzner, PhD

9781119293590
USA $19.99
CAN $23.99
UK £15.99

1,001 Practice Questions
SAT dummies

Ron Woldoff

9781119215844
USA $26.99
CAN $31.99
UK £19.99

Organic Chemistry I dummies

Arthur Winter

9781119293378
USA $22.99
CAN $27.99
UK £16.99

Statistics dummies

Deborah J. Rumsey, PhD

9781119293521
USA $19.99
CAN $23.99
UK £15.99

2016/2017
ASVAB dummies

Rod Powers

9781119239178
USA $18.99
CAN $22.99
UK £14.99

Includes Online Practice Tests
1,001 Practice Questions
Praxis Core dummies

Carla Kirkland
Chan Cleveland

9781119263883
USA $26.99
CAN $31.99
UK £19.99

Available Everywhere Books Are Sold

Small books for big imaginations

9781119177173
USA $9.99
CAN $9.99
UK £8.99

9781119177272
USA $9.99
CAN $9.99
UK £8.99

9781119177241
USA $9.99
CAN $9.99
UK £8.99

9781119177210
USA $9.99
CAN $9.99
UK £8.99

9781119262657
USA $9.99
CAN $9.99
UK £6.99

9781119291336
USA $9.99
CAN $9.99
UK £6.99

9781119233527
USA $9.99
CAN $9.99
UK £6.99

9781119291220
USA $9.99
CAN $9.99
UK £6.99

9781119177302
USA $9.99
CAN $9.99
UK £8.99

Unleash Their Creativity

dummies.com

dummies
A Wiley Brand